PUBLISHER'S PREFACE

The information contained herein are current as received through March 2012.

THE PUBLISHER

March 2012

California Northern District

Bankruptcy

COURT AND CHAMBERS PRACTICE MANUAL

BANKRUPTCY COURT
Selected General Orders
Court Guidelines
Procedures and Practices of the Oakland, San Francisco, San Jose, and Santa Rosa Divisions

INDIVIDUAL JUDGES
Procedures and Practices
Case Management Orders and Forms
Chambers and Biographical Information

Mid-2012 Edition

Compiled by Practicing Attorneys
Meliora Law

Printed and bound in the United States of America.
ISBN: 978-0-9838302-4-5

Meliora Law LLC
19250 Stevens Creek Boulevard, Suite 100
Cupertino, CA 94015
www.melioralaw.com

TABLE OF CONTENTS

San Francisco Division

San Jose Division

PART I

Bankruptcy Court

Selected General Orders

Court Guidelines

I. General Orders

A. General Order No. 26 – Amended Order Regarding Deposit and Investment of Registry Funds

**IN THE UNITED STATES BANKRUPTCY COURT
FOR THE NORTHERN DISTRICT OF CALIFORNIA**

**GENERAL ORDER NO. 26
AMENDED ORDER REGARDING
DEPOSIT AND INVESTMENT OF REGISTRY FUNDS**

The Court, having determined that it is necessary to amend local procedures to reflect the transition of accountability and administration of the Court Registry Investment System ("CRIS") from the United States District Court for the Southern District of Texas to the Administrative Office of the United States Courts pursuant to this Order, as well as ensure the continued uniformity in the deposit and investment of funds in the Court's Registry,

IT IS ORDERED that the following shall govern the transfer, receipt, deposit and investment of registry funds:

I. Transfer of Funds.

All funds existing in the Court Registry which are on deposit and invested in CRIS administered by the United States District Court for the Southern District of Texas shall be transferred to the custody and control of CRIS administered by the Administrative Office of the United States Courts, and be subject to the investment and fee deduction provisions of Paragraphs III and IV of this Order. Each deposit transferred will relate back to its original date of deposit in CRIS administered by the United States District Court for the Southern District of Texas.

II. Receipt of Funds

A. No money shall be sent to the Court or its officers for deposit in the Court's registry without a court order signed by the presiding judge in the case or proceeding.

B. Unless provided for elsewhere in this Order, all monies ordered to be paid to the Court or received by its officers in any case pending or adjudicated shall be deposited with the Treasurer of the United States in the name and to the credit of this Court pursuant to 28 U.S.C. § 2041 through depositories designated by the Treasury to accept such deposit on its behalf.

C. The party making the deposit or transferring funds to the Court's registry shall serve the order permitting the deposit or transfer on the Clerk of Court.

III. Investment of Registry Funds

A. Where, by order of the Court, funds on deposit with the Court are to be placed in some form of interest-bearing account, CRIS, administered by the Administrative Office of the United States Courts, shall be the only investment mechanism authorized.

B. Money from each case deposited in CRIS shall be "pooled" together with those on deposit with Treasury to the credit of other courts in CRIS and used to purchase Government Account Series securities through the Bureau of Public Debt, which will be held at Treasury, in an account in the name and to the credit of the Director of Administrative Office of the United States Courts, hereby designated as custodian for CRIS.

C. An account for each case will be established in CRIS titled in the name of the case giving rise to the investment in the fund. Income generated from fund investments will be distributed to each case based on the ratio each account's principal and earnings has to the aggregate principal and income total in the fund. Reports showing the interest earned and the principal amounts contributed in each case will be prepared and distributed to each court participating in CRIS and made available to litigants and/or their counsel.

IV. Deductions of Fees

A. The custodian is authorized and directed by this Order to deduct the registry fee for maintaining accounts in CRIS and the investment services fee for the management of investments. The proper registry fee is to be determined on the basis of the rates published by the Director of the Administrative Office of United States Courts as approved by the Judicial Conference. The investment services fee is assessed from interest earning according to the Court's Miscellaneous Fee Schedule.

B. If registry fees were assessed against the case under the old 45-day requirement prior to deposit in CRIS, no additional registry fee will be assessed.

V. Transition From Former Investment Procedure

This Order shall become effective May 19, 2011, and supercedes and abrogates all prior orders of this Court regarding the deposit and investment of registry funds.

IT IS SO ORDERED.

DATE: May 13, 2011

ALAN JAROSLOVSKY
Chief Judge
United States Bankruptcy Court

B. General Order No. 24 – Deposits into the Registry of the Courts

**IN THE UNITED STATES BANKRUPTCY COURT
FOR THE NORTHERN DISTRICT OF CALIFORNIA**

**GENERAL ORDER NO. 24
DEPOSITS INTO THE REGISTRY OF THE COURTS
AND ABROGATION OF GENERAL ORDER NO. 14**

I. RECEIPT OF FUNDS

A. No money shall be sent to the court or its officer for deposit into the court's registry without a court order by the presiding judge in the case.

B. Unless provided for elsewhere in this order, all money ordered to be paid into the court or received by its officers in any case pending or adjudicated shall be deposited with the Treasurer of the United States in the name and to the credit of this court pursuant to 28 U.S.C. 2041 through depositaries designated by the Treasury to accept such deposit on its behalf.

C. The party making the deposit or transferring funds to the court's registry shall serve the order permitting the deposit or transfer on the clerk of court.

II. INVESTMENT OF REGISTRY FUNDS

A. Where by stipulation of the parties and approval of the court, funds on deposit with the court are to be placed in some form of interest-bearing account, the Court Registry Investment System (CRIS) administered through the United States District Court for the Southern District of Texas, shall be the only investment mechanism authorized.

B. Under CRIS, monies deposited in each case under paragraph I.B., above, will be pooled together with those on deposit with Treasury to the credit of other courts in CRIS and used to purchase Treasury Securities, which will be held at the Federal Reserve Bank of Dallas in a safekeeping account in the name and to the credit of the Clerk, United States District Court for the Southern District of Texas, hereby designated custodian for CRIS.

C. An account for each case will be established in CRIS titled in the name of the case giving rise to the investment in the system. Earnings received from fund investments will be distributed to each case based on the ratio each account's principal and earnings has to the aggregate principal and income total in the fund each week. Weekly reports showing the interest earned and the principal amounts contributed in each case will be prepared and distributed to each court participating in CRIS and made available to litigants and/or their counsels.

III. REGISTRY INVESTMENT FEE

A. The custodian is authorized and directed by this order to deduct, for maintaining accounts in the fund, the registry fee. The proper registry fee is to be determined on the basis of the rates published by the Director of the Administrative Office as approved by the Judicial Conference.

B. If the registry fee was assessed against a case deposit subject to the old 45-day requirement prior to the deposit in CRIS, no additional registry fee on that deposit will be assessed.

IV. TRANSITION FROM FORMER INVESTMENT PROCEDURE

A. The clerk of court is further directed to develop a systematic method of redemption of all existing investments and their transfer to CRIS. New deposits into CRIS shall not occur until the severance of the relationship with the court's prior registry depositary and the clerk determines that CRIS is able to begin accepting new accounts.

B. Parties not wishing to maintain investment instruments in CRIS may transfer them to the litigants or their designees on proper motion and approval of the court.

V. ABROGATION OF GENERAL ORDER NO. 14

General Order No. 14 is hereby superseded and abrogated by this general order.

IT IS SO ORDERED.

DATED: June 13, 2009

____
RANDALL J. NEWSOME
Chief Judge
United States Bankruptcy Court

C. General Order No. 22 (Amended) – Adoption of Interim Bankruptcy Rule 1007-I

**IN THE UNITED STATES BANKRUPTCY COURT
FOR THE NORTHERN DISTRICT OF CALIFORNIA**

**AMENDED GENERAL ORDER NO. 22
ADOPTION OF INTERIM BANKRUPTCY RULE 1007-I**

Whereas, on October 20, 2008 the National Guard and Reservists Debt Relief Act (the Act) was enacted into law; and

Whereas, the provisions of the Act became effective on December 19, 2008; and

Whereas, the Advisory Committee on Bankruptcy Rules has prepared revised Interim Rule 1007-I designed to implement the substantive and procedural changes mandated by the Act; and

Whereas, the Committee on Rules of Practice and Procedures of the United States Judicial Conference and the Judicial Conference of the United States have approved this revised Interim Rule and recommended the adoption of the revised Interim Rule to provide uniform procedures for implementing the Act; and

Whereas, the general effective date of the Act has not provided sufficient time to promulgate rules after appropriate public notice and an opportunity for comment;

NOW THEREFORE, pursuant to 28 U.S.C. section 2071, Rule 83 of the Federal Rules of Civil Procedure, and Rule 9029 of the Federal Rules of Bankruptcy Procedure, the attached revised Interim Rule is adopted, effective December 1, 2009.

DATED: October 6, 2009

RANDALL J. NEWSOME
Chief Judge
United States Bankruptcy Court

Interim Rule 1007-I. Lists, Schedules, Statements, and Other Documents; Time Limits; Expiration of Temporary Means Testing Exclusion

* * * * *

(b) SCHEDULES, STATEMENTS, AND OTHER DOCUMENTS REQUIRED.

* * * * *

(4) Unless either: (A) § 707(b)(2)(D)(i) applies, or (B) § 707(b)(2)(D)(ii) applies and the exclusion from means testing granted therein extends beyond the period specified by Rule 1017(e), an individual debtor in a chapter 7 case shall file a statement of current monthly income prepared as prescribed by the appropriate Official Form, and, if the current monthly income exceeds the median family income for the applicable state and household size, the information, including calculations, required by § 707(b), prepared as prescribed by the appropriate Official Form.

* * * * *

(c) TIME LIMITS. In a voluntary case, the schedules, statements, and other documents required by subdivision (b)(1), (4), (5), and (6) shall be filed with the petition or within 14 days thereafter, except as otherwise provided in subdivisions (d), (e), (f), (h), and (n) of this rule. In an involuntary case, the list in subdivision (a)(2), and the schedules, statements, and other documents required by subdivision (b)(1) shall be filed by the debtor within 14 days of the entry of the order for relief. In a voluntary case, the documents required by paragraphs (A), (C), and (D) of subdivision (b)(3) shall be filed with the petition. Unless the court orders otherwise, a debtor who has filed a statement under subdivision (b)(3)(B), shall file the documents required by subdivision (b)(3)(A) within 14 days of the order for relief. In a chapter 7 case, the debtor shall file the statement required by subdivision (b)(7) within 45 days after the first date set for the meeting of creditors under § 341 of the Code, and in a chapter 11 or 13 case no later than the date when the last payment was made by the debtor as required by the plan or the filing of a motion for a discharge under § 1141(d)(5)(B) or § 1328(b) of the Code. The court may, at any time and in its discretion, enlarge the time to file the statement required by subdivision (b)(7). The debtor shall file the statement required by subdivision (b)(8) no earlier than the date of the last payment made under the plan or the date of the filing of a motion for a discharge under §§ 1141(d)(5)(B), 1228(b), or 1328(b) of the Code. Lists, schedules, statements, and other documents filed prior to the conversion of a case to another chapter shall be deemed filed in the converted case unless the court directs otherwise. Except as provided in § 1116(3), any extension of time to file schedules, statements, and other documents required under this rule may be granted only on motion for cause shown and on notice to the United States trustee, any committee elected under § 705 or appointed under § 1102 of the Code, trustee, examiner, or other party as the court may direct. Notice of an extension shall be given to the United States trustee and to any committee, trustee, or other party as the court may direct.

* * * * *

(n) TIME LIMITS FOR, AND NOTICE TO, DEBTORS TEMPORARILY EXCLUDED FROM MEANS TESTING.

(1) An individual debtor who is temporarily excluded from means testing

pursuant to § 707(b)(2)(D)(ii) of the Code shall file any statement and calculations required by subdivision (b)(4) no later than 14 days after the expiration of the temporary exclusion if the expiration occurs within the time specified by Rule 1017(e) for filing a motion pursuant to § 707(b)(2).

(2) If the temporary exclusion from means testing under § 707(b)(2)(D)(ii) terminates due to the circumstances specified in subdivision (n)(1), and if the debtor has not previously filed a statement and calculations required by subdivision (b)(4), the clerk shall promptly notify the debtor that the required statement and calculations must be filed within the time specified in subdivision (n)(1).

D. General Order No. 15 – Committee of Lawyer Representatives of the Court

GENERAL ORDER NO. 15
THE COMMITTEE OF LAWYER REPRESENTATIVES OF THE UNITED STATES BANKRUPTCY COURT FOR THE NORTHERN DISTRICT OF CALIFORNIA

The Judges of this District having determined to form a Committee of Lawyer Representatives of the United States Bankruptcy Court for the Northern District of California, and good cause appearing,

IT IS HEREBY ORDERED as follows:

1. The Committee shall be formed effective as of May 1, 1988 and be known as the Committee of Lawyer Representatives of the United States Bankruptcy Court for the Northern District of California ("the Committee");

2. The purpose of the Committee is to provide a forum for attorneys to discuss with the Judges of the Court the manner in which the business of the Court is being conducted;

3. The Committee shall be composed of nine attorneys, one private panel trustee, one chapter 13 trustee, and the United States Trustee. The criteria for selection of the nine lawyer members of the Committee shall be:

(i) a lawyer admitted to practice in the District Court and actively involved in bankruptcy practice;

(ii) a lawyer interested in the purposes and work of the Court;

(iii) a lawyer willing and able to contribute actively to the purposes and work of the Court;

(iv) a lawyer willing to assist in implementing Court programs with the local Bar; and

(v) a lawyer, who, together with others selected, will constitute a fair cross-section of practitioners before the Bankruptcy Courts of the District.;

4. Committee members shall be appointed by the Judges of the Court. The Committee shall solicit from the Bar applications for membership on the Committee to be submitted no later than November 1st. The Committee shall then recommend to the Judges of the Court three candidates for each of the three vacancies. The Judges shall directly solicit applications and select the private trustee and chapter 13 trustee members of the Committee. In the event of a vacancy created for any other reason other than expiration of a term, the Judges of the Court shall appoint a successor Committee member to serve out the balance of the term;

5. The initial members of the Committee will be appointed for terms of two, three and four years. Commencing in 1990, Committee members will be appointed to staggered terms of three years. Terms will commence on January 1st.

6. The Clerk of Court or the Clerk's designee shall serve on the Committee on

an *ex officio* basis.

7. A chair shall be selected annually by the Committee, with such selection to coincide with the appointment of new Committee members.

8. The Committee shall solicit questions, comments, criticisms and suggestions from the members of the Bar of the Northern District of California on the manner in which the business of the Court is being conducted, with the purpose of compiling, organizing and presenting topics of interest to the Judges of the Court.

9. The Committee shall meet with the Judges of the Court and the Clerk of the Court approximately twice each calendar year. The Committee shall provide to all Judges a proposed agenda for its meetings with the Court at least two weeks prior to such scheduled meetings, for the purpose of obtaining questions, comments or suggestions regarding the agenda.

10. The Committee, or subcommittee of the Committee, shall meet as often as the Committee or such subcommittees shall determine to be appropriate.

DATED: December 5, 1995

THOMAS E. CARLSON
Chief Judge
United States Bankruptcy Court

E. *General Order No. 13 (Amended) – Order Concerning Creditor List*

**IN THE UNITED STATES BANKRUPTCY COURT
FOR THE NORTHERN DISTRICT OF CALIFORNIA**

**AMENDED GENERAL ORDER NO. 13
ORDER CONCERNING CREDITOR LIST**

This General Order sets forth amended requirements regarding the list of creditors to be provided with bankruptcy petitions pursuant to FRBP 1007(a). The amended requirements shall become effective on February 1, 1996.

(1) Unless the debtor appears *in propria persona*, the debtor, or some other person as the court may direct, shall provide the clerk with a PC computer-readable diskette containing a file with a list of the name and address of each creditor ("diskette") and a scannable creditor list containing the same list of names and addresses ("scannable creditor list").

(2) In cases in which the debtor appears in propria persona with fifty more entities that hold either claims or interests, the debtor, or some other person as the court may direct, shall provide the clerk with a diskette and a scannable creditor list.

(3) In cases where the diskette is not required, the debtor, or some other person as the court may direct, shall provide the clerk with a scannable creditor list.

(4) The diskette and scannable creditor list shall be prepared in accordance with instructions and specifications as required by the clerk and shall be provided at the time the petition is filed. Failure to provide the diskette or the scannable creditor list in a timely manner may subject the case to dismissal.

DATED: December 5, 1995

THOMAS E. CARLSON
Chief Judge
United States Bankruptcy Court

1. Instructions and Requirements for Diskettes

Instructions and Requirements for Diskettes (Pursuant to Amended General Order No. 13)

All bankruptcy petitions submitted by an attorney for filing must be accompanied by a creditor diskette. For all cases submitted *in propria persona* with fifty (50) or more entities that hold either claims or interests, a diskette is required. For filing purposes, a scannable creditor list is also required. It is the responsibility of the filing party that the diskette of creditor names and addresses contains the same creditor names and addresses as on the scannable creditor matrix. Creditor matrix diskette can be created using any popular word processing software (*e.g.*, WordPerfect, Word) or bankruptcy software (*e.g.*, Matthew Bender). **Please adhere to the following requirements in preparing diskettes:**

Diskette format, file format and name and diskette label:

- The diskette must be 3.5" and formatted in MS-DOS or PC-DOS format.
- The creditor matrix file must be in ASCII (DOS text) format and must be named FILE.TXT. For instructions on how to save a document in ASCII format, refer to the software user manual.
- Place a label on the diskette with the debtor name, case number (if known), law firm name and contact person or debtor name if without an attorney, and phone number.

Format of creditor names and addresses:

- The text of the ASCII file must conform, as applicable, to the requirements of the scannable creditor matrix. Do not include matrix cover page or signature page, if any.
- Creditor names should be first name <space> last name.
- Creditor names and address should be in upper and lower case, not all upper case.
- Type creditor names and addresses in a single column.
- Have no more than five lines for each creditor name and address. Maximum of 40 characters per line.
- Put 3 blank lines between each creditor. See sample sheet attached.
- Do not include any Personal Data Document Identifiers. (e.g., DO NOT Include: Social Security numbers, Account numbers, Name of minor children, or dates of birth.).
- The last line of each name and address block must include the city, state, and ZIP code. Use a comma between city and state. Use the two-letter abbreviations without periods or other punctuation for state names (See the list at the right.) Nine digit ZIP codes should be typed with a hyphen separating the fifth and sixth digits.
- Do not include names and addresses of the debtor(s) or the United States Trustee.
- Do not use these symbols * " + & % # . Do not use the lower case "l" in place of the numeric "1." Do not use the upper or lower case letter "o" in

place of the numeric "0."

James Albert
123 Main Street
San Francisco, CA 94104

Anderson Company
4567 Maple Drive
Downers Grove, IL 60515

Bank of Sea Court
1610 Visa Avenue
San Mateo, CA 94020

Ann Barbara Brown
Ivers, Brown and Wong, Accountants
7890 Peachtree Industrial Blvd.
Atlanta, GA 30322

Coral Designs, Inc.
Attn: Amy Aubergine
Suite 1255
1010 Windsor Drive
Hartford, CT 06003

Barry Cressida
56 Broadway
Hicksville, NY 11802

Dupont Systems
678 A Street
San Mateo, CA 94111

2. *Instructions and Requirements for Scannable Creditor Matrix*

Instructions and Requirements for Scannable Creditor Matrix (Pursuant to Amended General Order No. 13)

All bankruptcy petitions submitted for filing must be accompanied by a creditor matrix cover sheet and a properly prepared creditor matrix. A scannable creditor list is required for all cases even when a diskette is required. It is the responsibility of the filing party that the list of creditor names and addresses contains the same creditor names and addresses as on the diskette. **In order for the matrix to be scanned, it must adhere to the following requirements:**

Paper and typeface quality:

- Use blank, unlined, standard white 8½ X 11 inch bond paper. The copy should be clean without smudges, smears or stray marks.
- Print must be letter quality. Dot matrix print is not acceptable. Use only one of the following typefaces: Courier 10 pitch, Prestige Elite or Letter Gothic.

Page format:

- The pages should be numbered on the back of each page, not on the front.
- All type must be at least one and one-half inches 1½" from any edge of the paper.

Format of creditor names and addresses:

- Creditor names should be first name <space> last name.
- Creditor names and address should be in upper and lower case, not all upper case.
- Make sure that the list is left justified in a single column. Do not use a 3 column format contained in some commercial bankruptcy forms packages. Do not place more than 8 name and address sets per page. *See* sample sheet attached.
- Have no more than five lines for each creditor name and address. Maximum of 40 characters per line.
- Put 3 blank lines between each creditor.
- Do not include any Personal Data Document Identifiers. (*e.g.*, DO NOT Include: Social Security numbers, Account numbers, Name of minor children, or dates of birth.)
- The last line of each name and address must include the city, state, and ZIP code. Use a comma between city and state. Use the two-letter abbreviations without periods or other punctuation for state names (*See* the list below). Nine digit ZIP codes should be typed with a hyphen separating the fifth and sixth digits.
    - AK, AL, AR, AZ, CA, CO, CT, DC, DE, FL, GA, HI, IA, ID, IL, IN, KS, KY, LA, MA, MD, ME, MI, MN, MO, MS, MT, NC, ND, NE, NH, NJ, NM, NV, NY, OH, OK, OR, PA, RI, SC, SD, TN, TX, UT, VA, VT, WA, WI, WV, WY
- Do not include the names and addresses of the debtor(s) or the United States Trustee.
- Do not use these symbols * " + & % #. Do not use the lower case "l" in place of the numeric "1." Do not use the upper or lower case letter "o" in place of the numeric "0."

II. Guidelines

A. Bankruptcy Petition Preparer Guidelines

BANKRUPTCY PETITION PREPARER GUIDELINES

The following are guidelines concerning the conduct and compensation of bankruptcy petition preparers (as defined in section 110 of the Bankruptcy Code (11 U.S.C. § 110)) who are not attorneys and who assist debtors in filing voluntary bankruptcy petitions (under Chapter 7, 11, 12 or 13), or in preparing any papers filed in connection with such cases in this court. These guidelines are issued pursuant to B.L.R. 9029-1.

1. The maximum allowable charge for a bankruptcy petition preparer's services is **$150**, including any and all expenses such as photocopying, messenger or courier charges, postage, telephone, etc. This fee does not include the filing fee that must be paid to the clerk of the bankruptcy court; the debtor(s) is to make that payment directly to the court.

2. If any money has been paid or any property transferred by the debtor to the bankruptcy petition preparer within one year of the filing of the bankruptcy petition, the court's filing fees may not be paid in installments.

3. The bankruptcy petition preparer is not an attorney and is not authorized to practice law. Specifically, the bankruptcy petition preparer ***may not*** instruct or advise the debtor(s):

i. Whether to file a bankruptcy petition

ii. Under which chapter of the Bankruptcy Code to file the voluntary petition;

iii. How to respond to the bankruptcy forms required in connection with the filing of the bankruptcy case;

iv. What exemptions should be claimed;

v. Whether any particular debts are dischargeable or nondischargeable;

vi. The effect of a bankruptcy filing upon a foreclosure and whether the debtor(s) may keep a home.

vii. Whether the debtor(s) may avoid or eliminate any liens or recover any assets in connection with the bankruptcy case;

viii. Whether the debtor(s) may redeem property;

ix. Whether the debtor(s) may or should reaffirm any debts;

x. Whether the debtor(s) is entitled to a discharge under the Bankruptcy Code, and what defenses the debtor may have to an objection to discharge; and

xi. Concerning the tax consequences of any aspect of the bankruptcy case.

4. The bankruptcy petition preparer may type forms and file documents.

5. Upon application of the debtor(s), a creditor or any party-in-interest, including the United States Trustee, or on the court's own motion, fees of a bankruptcy petition preparer may be reduced below the amount allowed by these Guidelines. All fees may be forfeited where the bankruptcy petition preparer has acted incompetently or illegally, or has failed to comply with these Guidelines. In addition to liability for criminal penalties, all fees are subject to forfeiture, in any case where the bankruptcy petition preparer has violated any provision of Bankruptcy Code § 110.

6. Before preparing a bankruptcy petition, schedules and statements (or the first of any other paper if the bankruptcy petition preparer has not prepared the petition), and before accepting any money from the debtor(s), the bankruptcy petition preparer must allow the debtor(s) to read and sign a **Notice To Debtors About Bankruptcy Petition Preparers** (in the form accompanying these Guidelines) and provide a copy thereof and a copy of these Guidelines to the debtor(s). The ***original*** of the Notice must be filed with the court along with the petition or the first paper prepared by the Bankruptcy Petition Preparer.

7. The court encourages debtors, trustees and others who believe a bankruptcy petition preparer has violated section 110 of the Bankruptcy Code (11 U.S.C. § 110) to advise the United States Trustee of the violation.

B. Guidelines for Cash Collateral and Financing Motions and Stipulations

GUIDELINES FOR CASH COLLATERAL & FINANCING MOTIONS & STIPULATIONS

(Effective 1/1/2006)

A. Introduction

The following Guidelines for Cash Collateral And Financing Motions And Stipulations ("Guidelines") are promulgated pursuant to B.L.R. 9029-1 and apply to uncontested motions or stipulations for the use of cash collateral (see Bankruptcy Code § 363(c)(2) and (3) and Fed. R. Bankr. P. 4001(b) and (d)) and to uncontested motions or stipulations for obtaining credit (see Bankruptcy Code § 364(c) and Fed. R. Bankr. P. 4001(c) and (d)).

B. Introductory Statement

Any motion or stipulation presented to the court for approval must include a completed Cash Collateral - Post Petition Financing Introductory Statement ("Introductory Statement"), which shall not exceed three pages and shall be signed and certified by the Certifying Professional as provided herein.

The Introductory Statement for cash collateral motions and stipulations must summarize all material provisions of the motion or stipulation, including:

- the name of each entity with an interest in the cash collateral;
- the purposes for the use of the cash collateral;
- the terms, including duration, of the use of the cash collateral; and
- any liens, cash payments, or other adequate protection (including any protections afforded by Bankruptcy Code § 364) that will be provided to each entity with an interest in the cash collateral or, if no additional adequate protection is proposed, an explanation of why each entity's interest is adequately protected.

Motions or stipulations for authority to obtain credit under Bankruptcy Code § 364, shall be accompanied by:

- a copy of the credit agreement;
- a proposed form of order; and
- the Introductory Statement, which must summarize all material provisions of the proposed credit agreement, including the amount of "new" money to be advanced, interest rate, maturity, events of default, liens, borrowing limits, and borrowing conditions.

C. Required Disclosures

If the motion, stipulation, proposed credit agreement or proposed order (either for use of cash collateral or for financing) includes any of the following provisions, the motion or stipulation shall describe the nature and extent of each provision, explain the reasons for each provision, and identify the specific location of the provisions in the proposed form of order, agreement, stipulation or other document:

1. The granting of priority or a lien on property of the estate pursuant to Bankruptcy Code §§ 364(c) or (d);

2. The providing of adequate protection or priority with respect to a claim that arose before the commencement of the case, including the granting of a lien on property of the estate to secure the claim, or the use of property of the estate or credit obtained under Bankruptcy Code § 364 to make cash payments on account of the claim;

3. A determination with respect to the validity, perfection, priority, or amount of a claim that arose before the commencement of the case, or of any lien securing such claim;

4. A waiver or modification of the provisions of the Bankruptcy Code or applicable rules relating to the automatic stay;

5. A waiver or modification of any entity's authority to file a plan, to seek an extension of time in which the debtor has the exclusive right to file a plan, or the right to request the use of cash collateral under Bankruptcy Code § 363(c), or to request authority to obtain credit under Bankruptcy Code § 364;

6. A waiver or modification of the applicability of non-bankruptcy law relating to the perfection of a lien on property of the estate, or on the foreclosure or other enforcement of the lien;

7. A release, waiver, or limitation on any claim or other cause of action belonging to the estate or the trustee, including any modification of the statute of limitations or other deadline to commence an action;

8. Indemnification of any entity;

9. A release, waiver, or limitation of any right under Bankruptcy Code § 506(c); or

10. The granting of a lien on any claim or cause of action arising under Bankruptcy Code §§ 544, 545, 547, 548, 549, 553(b), 723(a), or 724(a).

11. Provisions for "carve-outs" for professionals' fees and expenses.

D. Application of Rule 9024

The court may grant appropriate relief under Fed. R. Bankr. P. 9024 if it determines that the Introductory Statement did not adequately disclose a material element of the motion, stipulation or agreement.

E. The court will not ordinarily approve the following:

1. Cross-collateralization clauses, i.e., clauses that secure prepetition debt by postpetition assets in which the secured party would not otherwise have a security interest by virtue of its prepetition security agreement or applicable law. See Bankruptcy Code § 552. Also, "roll-ups," i.e., such as provisions deeming pre-petition debt to be post-petition debt or using post-petition loans from a pre-petition secured creditor to pay part or all of that secured creditor's pre-petition debt, other than as provided in Bankruptcy Code § 552(b), which deals with security interests in proceeds and profits. (*See* ¶¶ C. 1, 2)

2. Provisions or findings of fact that bind the estate or all parties in interest with respect to the validity, perfection or amount of the pre-petition secured party's lien or debt. (*See* ¶ C. 3)

3. Provisions or findings of fact that bind the estate or all parties in interest with

respect to the relative priorities of the secured party's lien and liens held by persons who are not party to the stipulation (This would include, for example, an order approving a stipulation providing that the secured party's lien is a "first priority" lien.). (*See* ¶ C. 3)

4. Waivers of, or grants of lien on, rights under Bankruptcy Code § 506(c), unless the waiver or grant is effective only during the period in which the debtor is authorized to use cash collateral or borrow funds. (Otherwise a future trustee might be faced with a duty to care for and preserve collateral in the trustee's possession and no financial means for discharging that duty.)(*See* ¶¶ C. 9, 10)

5. Provisions that operate, as a practical matter, to divest the debtor in possession or trustee of any discretion in the formulation of a plan or administration of the estate or limit access to the court to seek any relief under other applicable provisions of law. (*See* ¶ C. 5)

6. Releases of, or limitations on, liability for the creditor's alleged prepetition torts or breaches of contract. (*See* ¶ C. 7)

7. Waivers of, or liens on any of the estate's rights arising under Bankruptcy Code §§ 544, 545, 547, 548, 549, 553, 723(a), or 724(a), or the proceeds of any such rights. (*See* ¶ C. 10)

8. Automatic relief from the automatic stay upon default, conversion to Chapter 7, or appointment of a trustee. (*See* ¶ C. 4)

9. Waivers and modifications of the procedural requirements for foreclosure mandated under applicable non-bankruptcy law. (*See* ¶ C. 6)

10. Waivers or limitations, effective on default or expiration, of the debtor in possession's or trustee's right to move for a court order pursuant to Bankruptcy Code § 363(c)(2)(B) authorizing the use of cash collateral in the absence of the secured party's consent. (*See* ¶ C. 5)

11. Findings of fact on matters extraneous to the approval process. (For example, in connection with an application to borrow on a secured basis, a finding that the debtor cannot obtain unsecured credit would be acceptable if supported by competent evidence, whereas a "finding" that the lender acted in good faith in declaring the prepetition loan in default would not be acceptable.)

12. Provisions providing unreasonable treatment with respect to fees or professionals retained by a creditors' committee compared to any carve-outs provided for professionals retained by the debtor in possession or trustee. (*See* ¶ C. 11)

13. Provisions that provide an inadequate carve-out for a subsequently appointed trustee in the case, whether before or after conversion. (*See* ¶ C. 11)

F. The court will ordinarily approve the following:

1. Withdrawal of consent to use cash collateral or termination of further financing, upon occurrence of a default or conversion to Chapter 7.

2. Securing any postpetition diminution in the value of the secured party's collateral with a lien on postpetition collateral of the same type as the secured party had prepetition, if such lien is subordinated to the compensation and expense reimbursement (excluding professional fees) allowed to any trustee thereafter appointed in the case.

3. Securing new advances or value diminution with a lien on other assets of the estate, but only if the lien is subordinated to all the expenses of administration (including professional fees) of a superseding Chapter 7 case.

4. Reservations of rights under Bankruptcy Code § 507(b), unless the stipulation calls for modification of the Code's priorities in the event of a conversion to Chapter 7. (See Bankruptcy Code § 726(b))

5. Reasonable reporting requirements.

6. Reasonable budgets and use restrictions.

7. Expiration date for the stipulation.

G. Certification.

Each unopposed motion or stipulation for the use of cash collateral or post petition financing must include a certification signed by counsel for the debtor in possession or trustee ("Certifying Professional") regarding compliance with these Guidelines. The certification must appear as part of the Introductory Statement and be signed by the Certifying Professional. The certification is as follows:

> **Certification – The undersigned Certifying Professional has read the accompanying motion or stipulation and the Cash Collateral - Post Petition Financing Introductory Statement; to the best of my knowledge, information and belief, formed after reasonable inquiry, the terms of the relief sought in the motion or stipulation are in conformity with the Court's Guidelines For Cash Collateral And Financing Motions and Stipulations except as set forth above. I understand and have advised the debtor in possession or trustee that the court may grant appropriate relief under Fed. R. Bankr. P. 9024 if the court determines that a material element of the motion or stipulation was not adequately disclosed in the Introductory Statement.**

____

(Certifying Professional's Name)

C. Guidelines for Compensation and Expense Reimbursement of Professionals and Trustees

GUIDELINES FOR COMPENSATION AND EXPENSE REIMBURSEMENT OF PROFESSIONALS AND TRUSTEES

The following guidelines are promulgated pursuant to B.L.R. 9029-1 and govern the most significant issues related to applications for compensation and expense reimbursement. The guidelines cover the narrative portion of an application, time records and expenses. They apply in their entirety to professionals seeking compensation under 11 U.S.C. § 330 and, where indicated, to Chapter 7 and Chapter 11 trustees. The guidelines are not intended to cover every situation. The court is advised that compliance with these guidelines will satisfy the requirements of the United States Trustee.

I. GUIDELINES APPLICABLE TO ATTORNEYS AND OTHER PROFESSIONALS

The Narrative

The professional may use reasonable discretion in defining projects for this purpose, provided that the application provides meaningful guidance to the Court as to the complexity and difficulty of the task, the professional's efficiency, and the results achieved. The number of billing categories created should take account of the total amount of fees and expenses sought in the case. Thus, for example, an application totaling $100,000 should generally be broken into more categories than an application totaling $10,000, even if the nature of the work represented in the two applications is otherwise similar.

There is no minimum amount necessary to justify the creation of a new billing category. The maximum amount that should be included in a single category should generally be $20,000. This cap may be exceeded where further breakdown is impractical (e.g., courtroom time in a long trial). Generally, each category should contain less than $20,000. Miscellaneous items may be included in a category such as case administration, but such a category should not generally represent more than 15% of the fee request.

Work in a main case should be broken into categories appropriate to the size, chapter, and complexity of the case, and the role of the professional. Generally, each adversary proceeding should be set forth in a separate category. Within each adversary proceeding, subcategories should be created for pleadings, discovery, motions, and trial. In complex adversary proceedings, additional categories may be appropriate.

With respect to each project or task, the number of hours spent, the results obtained, and the amount of compensation and expenses requested should be set forth at the conclusion of the discussion of that project or task. Please also note the requirement in Guideline 11 relating to time records by project.

1. Employment and Prior Compensation—The application should disclose the date of the order approving applicant's employment and contain a clear statement itemizing the date of each prior request for compensation, the amount requested, the amount approved and the amount paid.

2. Case Status—With respect to interim requests, the application should briefly explain the history and the present posture of the case.

In Chapter 11 cases, the information furnished should describe the general operations of the debtor; whether the business of the debtor, if any, is being operated at a profit or loss; the debtor's cash flow; whether a plan has been filed, and if not, what the prospects are for reorganization and when it is anticipated that a plan will be filed and a hearing set on the disclosure statement.

In Chapter 7 cases, the application should contain a report of the administration of the case including the disposition of property of the estate; what property remains to be disposed of; why the estate is not in a position to be closed; and whether it is feasible to pay an interim dividend to creditors.

In both Chapter 7 and Chapter 11 cases, the application should state the amount of money on hand in the estate and the estimated amount of other accrued expenses of administration. On applications for interim fees, the applicant should orally supplement the application at the hearing to inform the Court of any changes in the current financial status of the debtor's estate since the filing of the application.

With respect to final requests, applications should meet the same criteria except, where a Chapter 7 Trustee's final account is being heard at the same time, the financial information in the final account need not be repeated.

Fee applications submitted by special counsel seeking compensation from a fund generated directly by their efforts, auctioneers, real estate brokers, or appraisers do not have to comply with the above. For all other applications, when more than one application is noticed for the same hearing, they may, to the extent appropriate, incorporate by reference the narrative history furnished in a contemporaneous application.

3. Project Billing—In any application exceeding $10,000, or when the professional's anticipated services for the case will exceed $20,000, the narrative should categorize by subject matter and separately discuss each project or task. All work for which compensation is requested should be in a category.

4. Billing Summary—Hours and total compensation requested in each application should be aggregated and itemized as to each professional and paraprofessional who provided compensable services.

5. Paraprofessionals—Fees may be sought for paralegals, professional assistants and law clerks only if identified as such and if the following requirements are met:

a. The services for which compensation is sought would have had to be done by the professional if not done by the paraprofessional, and would have been compensable under these guidelines;

b. The person who performed the services is specially trained or is a law school student, and is not primarily a secretary or clerical worker; and

c. The application includes a resume or summary of the paraprofessional's qualifications.

6. Preparation of Application—Reasonable fees for preparation of a fee application may be requested. Fees for preparation of a fee application ***may not exceed five percent*** of the total amount of fees and costs requested in the application. This five percent guideline is a ceiling rather than a floor; preparation expenses equaling five percent are not

presumptively reasonable. The aggregate number of hours spent, the amount requested and the percentage of the total request which the amount represents must be disclosed. If the actual time spent will be reflected and charged in a future fee application, this fact should be stated but an estimate nevertheless provided.

7. Client Review of Billing Statement—A debtor in possession, trustee or official committee shall exercise reasonable business judgment in monitoring the fees and expenses of the estate's professionals. Billing statements should be sent to the employing entity (debtor in possession, trustee or official committee) on a monthly basis. A fee application shall be sent to the employing entity at least ***20 days prior*** to the scheduled hearing date. The application shall be transmitted with a cover letter that contains the following statement:

> *The court's Guidelines for Compensation and Expense Reimbursement of Professionals and Trustees provide that a debtor in possession, a trustee or an official committee must exercise reasonable business judgment in monitoring the fees and expenses of the estate's professionals. We invite you to discuss any objections, concerns or questions you may have with us. The Office of the United States Trustee will also accept your comments. The court will also consider timely filed objections by any party in interest at the time of the hearing.*

A copy of the transmittal letter shall be attached to the application.

8. Certification—Each application for compensation and expense reimbursement must contain a certification by the professional designated by the applicant with the responsibility in the particular case for compliance with these guidelines ("Certifying Professional") that: (a) the Certifying Professional has read the application; (b) to the best of the Certifying Professional's knowledge, information and belief, formed after reasonable inquiry, the compensation and expense reimbursement sought is in conformity with these guidelines, except as specifically noted in the certification application; and (c) the compensation and expense reimbursement requested are billed at rates, in accordance with practices, no less favorable than those customarily employed by the applicant and generally accepted by the applicant's clients.

9. Short Form Applications—Where the professional is filing only a final request for compensation in a Chapter 7 case and the request, exclusive of costs, ***does not exceed $15,000*** for the case, and has not charged in excess of one hour of time for preparation of the application, the professional has the option of utilizing the approved Chapter 7 form application.

In a Chapter 13 case, where the professional has utilized and filed the Rights and Responsibilities of Chapter 13 Debtors and their Attorneys, the professional has the option of utilizing the approved Chapter 13 form application when seeking compensation in excess of that approved at the time of confirmation.

Copies of the approved form applications are available in the Clerk's Office.

Time Records

10. Time Records Required—All professionals, except auctioneers, real estate brokers, appraisers and those employed on a contingency fee basis, must keep accurate contemporaneous time records. The Court may, however, specifically direct that time records be kept on a contingent fee matter.

11. Time Records By Project—In any application ***exceeding $10,000***, or where the professional's anticipated services for the case ***will exceed $20,000***, time records should be kept by categories as described in Paragraph 3 relating to Project Billing above. Time records should be sorted, assembled and attached to the application by category corresponding to the discussion in the narrative.

12. Increments—Professionals are required to keep time records in minimum increments ***no greater than six minutes***. Professionals who utilize a minimum billing increment ***greater than .1 hour*** are subject to a substantial reduction of their requests.

13. Descriptions—At a minimum, the time entries should identify the person performing the services, the date performed, what was done and the subject involved. Mere notations of telephone calls, conferences, research, drafting, etc., without identifying the matter involved, may result in disallowance of the time covered by the entries.

14. Clumping—If a number of separate tasks are performed on a single day, the fee application should disclose the time spent for each such task (i.e., no "grouping" or "clumping").

15. Conferences—Professionals should be prepared to explain time spent in conferences with other professionals or paraprofessionals in the same firm. Failure to justify this time may result in disallowance of all fees related to such conferences.

16. Multiple Professionals—Professionals should be prepared to explain the need for more than one professional or para-professional from the same firm at the same court hearing, deposition or meeting. Failure to justify this time may result in compensation for only the person with the lowest billing rate.

17. Airplane Travel Time—Airplane travel time is not compensable, but work actually done during a flight is compensable. If significant airplane travel time is expected in a case, specific guidelines should be obtained for that case.

18. Administrative Tasks—Time spent in addressing, stamping and stuffing envelopes, filing, photocopying or "supervising" any of the foregoing is not compensable, whether performed by a professional, paraprofessional or secretary.

Expenses

19. Firm Practice—All expenses for which reimbursement is sought must be of the kind, and at the least expensive rate, the applicant customarily charges nonbankruptcy/insolvency clients.

20. Actual Cost—Is defined as the amount paid to a third party provider of goods or services without enhancement for handling or other administrative charge.

21. Documentation—Must be retained and made available upon request for all expenditures in ***excess of $50.00***. Where possible, receipts should be obtained for all expenditures.

22. Office Overhead—Not reimbursable. Overhead includes: secretarial time, secretarial overtime, word processing time, charges for after-hour and weekend air conditioning and other utilities, and cost of meals or transportation provided to professionals and staff who work late or on weekends.

23. Word Processing—Not reimbursable.

24. Computerized Research—Actual cost.

25. Paraprofessional Services—May be compensated as a paraprofessional under § 330 but not charged or reimbursed as an expense.

26. Professional Services—A professional employed under § 327 may not employ, and charge as an expense, another professional (e.g., special litigation counsel employing an expert witness) unless the employment of the second professional is approved by the Court prior to the rendering of services.

27. Photocopies (Internal)—Charges must be disclosed on an aggregate and per page basis. If the per page cost ***exceeds 20 cents***, the professional must demonstrate to the satisfaction of the Court, with data, that the per page cost represents a good faith estimate of the actual cost of the copies, based upon the purchase or lease cost of the copy machine and supplies therefor including the space occupied by the machine, but not including time spent in operating the machine.

28. Photocopies (Outside)—Actual cost.

29. Postage—Actual cost.

30. Overnight Delivery—Actual cost where shown to be necessary.

31. Messenger Service—Actual cost where shown to be necessary. An in-house messenger service is reimbursable but the estate cannot be charged more than the cost of comparable services available outside the firm.

32. Facsimile Transmission—Actual cost of telephone charges for outgoing transmissions are reimbursable. Transmissions received are reimbursable on a per page basis. If the per page cost exceeds 20 cents, the professional must demonstrate to the satisfaction of the Court, with data, that the per page cost represents a good faith estimate of the actual cost of the copies, based upon the purchase or lease cost of the facsimile machine and supplies therefor including the space occupied by the machine, but not including time spent in operating the machine.

33. Long Distance Telephone—Actual cost.

34. Automotive Transportation—Travel of one hour or less round-trip is not reimbursable. Travel expense for trips in excess of one hour round-trip is reimbursable in accordance with the amount allowed by the Internal Revenue Service. (IRC § 274(d) and the current applicable I.R.B. Announcement. At this date the amount is 31 cents per mile.) Travel by a professional, paraprofessional or other staff member between his or her residence and principal place of business is not reimbursable regardless of the day of the week or time of day.

35. Parking—Actual cost, provided that parking for professionals, paraprofessionals or other staff member at their principal place of business is not reimbursable regardless of the day of the week or time of day.

36. Air Transportation—Air travel is expected to be at regular coach fare for all flights.

37. Hotels—Due to wide variation in hotel costs in various cities, it is not

possible to establish a single guideline for this type of expense. All persons will be required to exercise discretion and prudence in connection with hotel expenditures.

38. Meals-Travel—The cost of lunches while a party is away from the Bay Area, or in the Bay Area from another city, is not reimbursable. Reimbursement may be sought for the reasonable cost of breakfast and dinner while traveling.

39. Meals-Working—Working meals at restaurants or private clubs are not reimbursable. Reimbursement may be sought for working meals only where food is catered to the professional's office in the course of a meeting with clients, such as a Creditors Committee, for the purpose of allowing the meeting to continue through a normal meal period.

40. Amenities—Charges for entertainment, alcoholic beverages, newspapers, dry cleaning, shoe shines, etc. are not reimbursable.

41. Filing Fees—Actual cost.

42. Court Reporter Fees—Actual cost.

43. Witness Fees—Actual cost.

44. Process Service—Actual cost.

45. UCC Searches—Actual cost.

II. GUIDELINES APPLICABLE TO TRUSTEES

Chapter 7 and Chapter 11 trustees must maintain contemporaneous time records in every case. Time records must be maintained by project categories. At a minimum, project categories should include: (1) Assets Recap (asset analysis and recovery/asset disposition); (2) Investigation of Financial Affairs of the Debtor; (3) Claims Administration and Objections; and (4) Fee Applications. Trustees may add additional categories at their discretion. Trustees are also subject to Guidelines 4, 5 (subject to § 326), 10, 12, 13 and 19 - 45 dealing with expenses.

In cases in which the trustee's compensation request is anticipated to be ***$15,000*** or less, the trustee may submit a brief narrative description of the services performed and a statement of the amount of time spent. In cases in which the final compensation exceeds ***$15,000***, or where an interim request is made and it is anticipated that the total compensation requested will exceed ***$15,000***, the trustee's application must include time records as well as a narrative description of the services performed and comply with the guidelines referenced above.

The guidelines regarding trustee time records shall apply only to cases filed on or after January 1, 1997.

D. Guidelines for Early Disposition of Assets in Chapter 11 Cases, Pre-Packaged Plans, and the Sale of Substantially All Assets Under § 363

GUIDELINES FOR EARLY DISPOSITION OF ASSETS IN CHAPTER 11 CASES, PRE-PACKAGED PLANS, AND THE SALE OF SUBSTANTIALLY ALL ASSETS UNDER § 363

The following guidelines are promulgated as a result of the increasing use of pre-packaged plans or § 363 sales to dispose of substantially all assets of a Chapter 11 debtor shortly after the filing of the petition. The court will consider all requests to modify the guidelines to fit the circumstances of a particular case.

PRE-PACKAGED PLANS

1. Declaration of Counsel for Debtor-In-Possession – In connection with any request for the special setting of a hearing to approve a disclosure statement or a combined hearing to approve a disclosure statement and confirm a plan, in addition to any other required papers, counsel for the debtor-in-possession should submit a declaration covering the following points:

a. Retention of counsel. The date counsel was retained by the debtor, the approximate number of hours of professional time expended pre-petition, compensation paid to counsel pre-petition including source of payment and the approximate amount of accrued but unpaid compensation.

b. Communications with creditors. A description of any written communications of the debtor with creditors during the pre-petition reorganization process. Copies of letters should be attached. If letters contain confidential information, they need not be attached but the court may require in-camera inspection.

c. Communications with shareholders or partners. A description of any written communications with shareholders or partners of a partnership during the pre-petition reorganization process. Copies of letters should be attached. If letters contain confidential information, they need not be attached but the court may require in-camera inspection.

d. Creditors' Committee. If a Creditors' Committee existed pre-petition, indicate the date and manner in which the committee was formed.

e. Counsel for Committee. If the pre-petition Creditors' Committee retained counsel, indicate the date counsel was engaged and the selection process.

f. Position of United States Trustee. It is expected that the United States Trustee will be consulted prior to, or simultaneously with, the filing. Set forth the position of the United States Trustee regarding the request for a special setting, if known.

2. Declaration of Counsel for Creditors' Committee – Where counsel has represented a pre-petition Creditors' Committee and anticipates representing the Official

Creditors' Committee when appointed, counsel should submit a declaration covering the following points:

a. Retention of counsel. The date counsel was retained by the Committee, the approximate number of hours of professional time expended pre-petition, compensation paid to counsel pre-petition including source of payment and the approximate amount of accrued but unpaid compensation.

b. Investigation of Committee and Counsel. A description of the scope and results of any investigation into the debtor's affairs conducted by the Committee and/or its counsel.

c. Communication with creditors. A description of any written communications of the Committee or its counsel with creditors during the pre-petition reorganization process. Copies should be attached. If letters contain confidential information, they need not be attached but the court may require in-camera inspection.

d. Involvement in formulation of plan and disclosure statement. A description of the Committee's and counsel's involvement in the formulation of the plan and disclosure statement.

THE SALE OF SUBSTANTIALLY ALL ASSETS UNDER § 363 WITHIN 60 DAYS OF THE FILING OF THE PETITION

3. Declaration of Counsel for Debtor-In-Possession – In connection with any hearing to approve the sale of substantially all assets within 60 days of the filing of the petition, the request for the special setting of a hearing or the sale motion itself when regularly noticed, should be supported by a separate declaration by counsel for the debtor-in-possession covering the following points:

a. Retention of counsel. Same as ¶ 1.a. Above.

b. Communications with creditors. Same as ¶ 1.b. Above.

c. Communications with shareholders or partners. Same as ¶ 1.c. Above.

d. Creditors' Committee. Same as ¶ 1.d. Above.

e. Counsel for Committee. Same as ¶ 1.e. Above.

f. Sale Contingencies. Statement of all contingencies to the sale agreement together with a copy of the agreement.

g. Creditor Contact List. If no committee has been formed, a list of contact persons together with fax and phone numbers for each of the largest 20 unsecured creditors.

h. Administrative Debts. Assuming the sale is approved, an estimate of administrative debts to be incurred prior to closing and the source of payment for such debts.

i. Proceeds of sale. An estimate of the gross proceeds anticipated from the sale together with an estimate of the net proceeds coming to the estate with an explanation of the items making up the difference.

j. Debt Structure of debtor. A brief description of the debtor's debt structure including the amount of the debtor's secured debt, priority claims and general unsecured claims.

k. Disposition of Proceeds. A statement setting forth, to the best of declarant's knowledge, the likely distribution of proceeds to secured claimants, administrative claimants, priority claimants and general unsecured creditors.

4. Declaration of Responsible Individual for Debtor-In-Possession – Counsel's declaration referred to in ¶ 3 above should be accompanied by a declaration from the responsible individual covering the following matters:

a. Alternatives to Sale. A description of the efforts, if any, to pursue other alternatives such as financing, capital infusion, etc., including the period of time involved and the results achieved.

b. Marketing of Assets. A description of the manner in which the assets were marketed for sale including the period of time involved and the results achieved.

c. Decision to Sell. The date on which the debtor accepted the offer to purchase the assets.

d. Asset Valuation. Disclosure of the debtor's prior valuations, within the last year, of the assets to be sold, if any. (i.e., book value, appraisals, financial statements, etc.)

e. Relationship of Buyer. A statement identifying the buyer and setting forth, to the best of declarant's knowledge, all of the buyer's (including its officers, directors and shareholders) connections with the debtor, creditors, any other party in interest, their respective attorneys, accountants, the United States Trustee or any person employed in the office of the United States Trustee.

f. Post Sale Relationship with Debtor. A statement setting forth, to the best of declarant's knowledge, any relationship or connection the debtor (including its officers, directors, shareholders, and employees) will have with the buyer after the consummation of the sale, assuming it is approved.

g. Relationship with Secured Creditors. If the sale involves the payment of all or a portion of secured debt(s), a statement of all connections between debtor's officers, directors, employees or other insiders and each secured creditor involved (for example, release of insider's guaranty).

h. Insider Compensation. Disclosure of current compensation received by officers, directors, key employees or other insiders pending approval of the sale.

5. Declaration of Counsel for Creditors' Committee – Where counsel has represented a pre-petition Creditors' Committee and anticipates representing the Official Creditors' Committee when appointed, counsel should submit a declaration covering the following points:

a. Retention of counsel. Same as ¶ 2.a. Above.

b. Investigation of Committee and Counsel. Same as ¶ 2.b. Above.

c. Communication with creditors. Same as ¶ 2.c. Above.

d. Involvement in sale. A description of the Committee's and counsel's involvement in the negotiation of the sale.

6. Hearing and Notice Regarding Sale – Unless the court orders otherwise, all sales governed by these guidelines, including auctions or the presentation of competing bids, will occur at the hearing before the court.

The notice sent to creditors and other parties in interest regarding the sale should contain the information required by ¶¶ 3. h - k and 4. a - g above, in addition to any other matters normally set forth in a notice of sale.

7. Proposed Order Approving Sale – A proposed order approving the sale should be provided to chambers 24 hours prior to the hearing.

8. Good Faith Finding – There must be an evidentiary basis for a finding of good faith under § 363(m). Evidence can be presented in the form of a declaration from the prospective purchaser.

9. Competing Bids – Unless the court orders otherwise, competing bids can be presented at the time of the hearing.

10. Financial Ability to Close – Unless the court orders otherwise, any competing bidder must be prepared to demonstrate to the satisfaction of the court its ability to consummate the transaction if it is the successful bidder.

11. Overbids – Unless the court orders otherwise, each overbid must be at least 5% more than the amount of the original offer. The amount of the original offer is determined without regard to any commission or payment to a broker or agent.

12. Damages Payable to Prospective Purchaser – Whether denominated liquidated damages, breakup fee, topping fee or other designation, no damages of any kind are payable to a prospective purchaser or its agents absent approval of the court.

If a provision for damages is contained in the original purchase agreement, and the parties intend to seek court approval for the provision separately, the provision should provide that it can be approved separately from the agreement itself.

A request for the approval of a damage provision shall be supported by, in addition to any other required papers, a declaration from counsel for the debtor-in-possession setting forth the precise conditions under which damages would be payable and the factual basis on which the seller determined the provision was reasonable. Counsel for the proposed buyer may, but is not required to, submit a similar declaration.

E. Guidelines for Legal Services to be Provided by Debtors' Attorney in Chapter 7 Cases

GUIDELINES FOR LEGAL SERVICES TO BE PROVIDED BY DEBTORS' ATTORNEY IN CHAPTER 7 CASES

To assist individuals who are chapter 7 debtors and their attorneys in arriving at a mutual understanding of the services that will be included in the process of filing and concluding a chapter 7 bankruptcy case, a description of the standard services provided by an attorney in the District is set forth below. Use of the term "the attorney" means an attorney in the law firm representing the debtor, who is admitted to practice law before the U.S. District Court for the Northern District of California. Inherent in these Guidelines is the concept that due to the complexities and unpredictable aspects of most such cases, it is not appropriate to set a minimum or maximum attorneys' fee for chapter 7 cases. The following services to be provided by the attorney assume that the debtor has fully, accurately and honestly disclosed all assets, debts, and all other financial information requested by the attorney or required by the United States Trustee, the chapter 7 trustee, the official bankruptcy forms or by law. In addition, the performance of these services by the attorney is understood to be completely dependent upon the continued timely cooperation of the debtor with regard to paying required court fees, providing information and documentation, and executing documents necessitated by the unfolding legal process and the requirements of the attorney in representing the debtor effectively. If the debtor fails to perform any of the debtor's obligations under these Guidelines, including the fulfillment of financial commitments made to the attorney, the attorney may move to withdraw from the case. If the attorney fails to perform the legal services described herein, which are not intended as an exclusive list, the debtor may bring the omission to the attention of the court or pursue other available remedies.

A. Services Always Included in the Pre-Petition Fee

1. The attorney provides a copy of these Guidelines to the debtor.

2. The attorney meets personally with the debtor and explains the options available under both chapter 7 and chapter 13 before the debtor selects the chapter to be filed.

3. The attorney reviews the final petition, schedules, statement of financial affairs, and statement of social security number, prior to having them filed with the court.

4. The attorney, with staff assistance, reviews the debtor's proof of identification and social security number and advises the debtor to provide documentation thereof or a written statement that such documentation does not exist, at the § 341 meeting.

5. The attorney personally attends the § 341 meeting. However, if the attorney is unable to attend the meeting, he/she may arrange for another attorney to appear, subject to the provisions of 6.

6. The attorney provides an "outside contract services attorney" representing the debtor at legal proceedings (such as § 341 meetings and other meetings, depositions and court appearances) with all of the information necessary to fully and competently represent the debtor. The attorney must also take precautions to assure that the information imparted to the outside contract services attorney is held in confidence. Where use of an outside contract

services attorney is anticipated at the time of retention, the attorney must obtain the debtor's consent to the employment of an outside contract services attorney in a written agreement that names the outside contract services attorney or a list of possible outside contract services attorneys, and must fully disclose the compensation for services to be performed. Where the use of an outside contract services attorney is unanticipated at the time of retention but becomes necessary, the outside contract services attorney may be employed, provided that all of the following circumstances have been met: a) the attorney informs the client of the name, address and telephone number of the outside contract services attorney and obtains the prior written consent to use of an outside contract services attorney whenever possible; b) the attorney fully discloses the compensation for services to be performed by the outside contract services attorney; and, c) the attorney has attempted to obtain a continuance of the matter without success, unless it is in the debtor's best interests to proceed with the matter.

7. The attorney explains to the debtor with secured debts all of the following rights:

a. to retain the security with continued ongoing payments in accordance with applicable case law;

b. to redeem the security by motion or negotiation;

c. to reaffirm the underlying debt, along with the risks of incurring future deficiency claims; and

d. to surrender the security.

8. The attorney files changes of the debtor's mailing address, as necessary.

9. The attorney represents the debtor in matters brought under 11 U.S.C. § 707(a).

10. The attorney, with staff assistance, informs the debtor of all chapter 7 trustee and U.S. Trustee requests for documents or other information and assists the debtor in transmitting available information to the requesting trustee. However, the debtor is solely responsible for locating such documentation and providing it to the attorney on a timely basis.

11. The attorney, with staff assistance, responds to reasonable creditor inquiries to confirm the case filing.

12. The attorney, with staff assistance, assists the debtor in:

a. ensuring that creditors, collection agents, and attorneys provided by the debtor are notified of the case filing; and

b. notifying levying officers or agencies in order to stop evictions, foreclosures, wage garnishments, bank levies, and other asset seizures in effect on the petition filing date, as appropriate.

B. Services Always Included, But Additional Fee May Be Charged Pre- or Post-Petition, as Mutually Agreed

13. The attorney, as appropriate and necessary, where requested by the debtor:

a. negotiates with a secured creditor to confirm the enforceability of the security interest and the redemption value of said security;

b. files a motion to set the value and redeem said security; or

c. negotiates a reaffirmation agreement having fully advised the debtor of the legal effect and consequences of the agreement and any default thereunder, including the possibility of a future deficiency claim against the debtor, and being persuaded that such agreement represents a fully informed and voluntary agreement by the debtor and does not impose an undue hardship on the debtor or a dependent of the debtor.

14. The attorney, based upon new information provided by the debtor or confirmed by the debtor, files signed amendments to the petition, schedules, statement of financial affairs, or statement of social security number.

15. The attorney reviews motions for relief from the automatic stay, with staff assistance communicates with the debtor regarding them, responds to such motions where necessary, and appears in court on behalf of the debtor where necessary.

16. The attorney represents the debtor with regard to objections to claims of exemption.

17. The attorney represents the debtor in matters brought under 11 U.S.C. § 707(b), as well as related Rule 2004 examinations.

C. Optional Services Not Included in the Pre-Petition Fee – Subject To Separate Agreement, If Any

18. The attorney files motions for abandonment of estate property.

19. The attorney files motions to avoid judicial liens on real property and other liens that impair exemptions.

20. The attorney files or defends, on behalf of the debtor, any dischargeability complaints.

21. The attorney defends objections to discharge pursuant to 11 U.S.C. § 727.

22. The attorney files or defends, on behalf of the debtor, other adversary proceedings including ancillary matters such as Rule 2004 examinations and document requests.

23. The attorney files, prosecutes, or defends appeals on behalf of the debtor.

24. The attorney moves to re-open the debtor's closed case.

Effective 3/15/2005

F. *Guidelines for Valuing and Avoiding Liens in Individual Chapter 11 Cases and Chapter 13 Cases*

GUIDELINES FOR VALUING AND AVOIDING LIENS IN INDIVIDUAL CHAPTER 11 CASES AND CHAPTER 13 CASES

A debtor may be able to eliminate a lien through a chapter 11 or chapter 13 plan to the extent the lien is "out of the money," meaning there is no value (after senior liens and property taxes) to secure the amount owed to the lienholder. Counsel for debtors have raised various questions regarding the procedure to be employed when the debtor seeks to "strip" liens exceeding the value of the collateral. Despite the convenient label of lien "stripping," motions described in these Guidelines are motions to value security under FRBP 3012. These guidelines address questions concerning procedure and do not purport to address questions of substantive law. These guidelines apply to the valuation and avoidance of liens on both personal and real property.

1. **Motion**. Although an adversary proceeding may be utilized under FRBP 7001(2), the court will permit the debtor to obtain a valuation of a secured creditor's claim by motion served upon the affected lienholder. Although the actual "stripping" of the amount by which the lien exceeds the value of the collateral is accomplished through the confirmation and performance of the debtor's chapter 11 or chapter 13 plan, valuing the lien must occur first. The court requires debtor to file and serve a separate motion in order to provide clear notice to the affected lienholder, and to specify a well-established way for the debtor to submit evidence and legal argument in support of the proposed treatment of the lien.

2. **Notice**. Because a motion to strip lien seeks relief against a specific, identifiable party, debtor must comply with B.L.R. 9014-1(b) & (c). Debtor should take care to serve the affected lienholder in the manner required by the FRBP, and in particular FRBP 7004(b) and 7004(h) as to certain lenders.

3. **Time for Filing Motion**. Because a motion to strip lien is in aid of the confirmation of the plan and works through the confirmation of the plan, the motion must be resolved before the plan is confirmed.

4. **Supporting Papers**. A motion to strip lien shall be supported by a memorandum of points and authorities, and by declarations under penalty of perjury establishing all facts necessary to entitle debtor to the relief requested. At minimum, required declarations include statements by competent witnesses regarding the value of the collateral and the balance due on each lien relevant to the motion.

5. **Actual Hearing Not Required**. Debtor may utilize any of the options permitted under Bankruptcy Local Rule 9014-1: actual hearing, notice and opportunity for hearing with tentative hearing date, or notice and opportunity for hearing without tentative hearing date.

6. **Evidentiary Hearing**. If the affected lienholder effectively contests any issue of fact material to the motion, the court will conduct an evidentiary hearing to resolve that dispute of fact. The notice of motion shall specify that, except as otherwise ordered by the court, the initial hearing on the motion will not be an evidentiary hearing, and will serve as a status conference at which the court may schedule any evidentiary hearing necessary.

7. **Standard-form Orders**. If the court determines that a motion to strip lien should

be granted, the court will employ the standard-form ORDER VALUING LIEN OF [NAME OF LIENHOLDER], attached hereto as Appendix A. If the debtor's plan is confirmed and completed or debtor receives a discharge, on request of debtor the court will enter the standard-form JUDGMENT VOIDING LIEN OF [NAME OF LIENHOLDER], attached hereto as Appendix B, after 10 days notice to the affected lienholder and opportunity for a hearing. If the debtor's chapter 11 or chapter 13 case is dismissed or converted before debtor receives a discharge or completes the plan, on request of the "stripped" lienholder or other party in interest, the court will enter the standard-form ORDER RESTORING LIEN OF [NAME OF LIENHOLDER], attached hereto as Appendix C, after 10 days notice to debtor and opportunity for a hearing. NOTE: The standard-form orders attached contain language typically used to identify real property collateral. Where the motion concerns personal property, the debtor should complete the standard-form order with a description appropriate to the type of collateral (e.g., for vehicle, use manufacturer, model, year, and vehicle identification number).

8. **Questions of Substantive Law**. As these guidelines do not purport to decide questions of substantive law, the language in paragraph 7, and in the standard-form orders set forth below, stating that judgment voiding a lien may be entered when debtor either completes plan payments or receives a discharge should not be construed as a ruling that entry of judgment voiding a lien is appropriate where debtor is barred from receiving a discharge or where debtor receives a discharge without completing plan payments.

APPENDIX A

(Version 1: hearing held)

ORDER VALUING LIEN OF ________________

On [date], the court held a hearing on Debtor's motion to value the lien of [name of lienholder] against the property commonly known as [street address] and more fully described in Exhibit A hereto, which lien was recorded in [name of county] on or about [date] as document [number] (hereinafter the Lien).

[Name] appeared for Debtor. [Name] appeared for [name of lienholder].

The court finds that notice of the motion was proper. Upon due consideration, and for the reasons stated [on the record at the hearing / in the accompanying memorandum decision / in the accompanying opinion], the court hereby orders as follows.

(1) For purposes of Debtor's chapter [11/13] plan only, the Lien is valued at zero, [name of lienholder] does not have a secured claim, and the Lien may not be enforced, pursuant to 11 U.S.C. [§§ 506, 1123(b)(5) and 1141 / §§ 506, 1322 (b)(2) and 1327].

(2) This order shall become part of Debtor's confirmed chapter [11/13] plan.

(3) Upon entry of a discharge or completion of plan payments in Debtor's chapter [11/13] case, the Lien shall be voided for all purposes, and upon application by Debtor, the court will enter an appropriate form of judgment voiding the Lien.

(4) If Debtor's chapter [11/13] case is dismissed or converted to one under another chapter before Debtor obtains a discharge or completes plan payments, this order shall cease to be effective and the Lien shall be retained to the extent recognized by applicable nonbankruptcy

law, and upon application by the lienholder, the court will enter an appropriate form of order restoring the Lien.

(5) Except as provided by separate, subsequent order of this court, the Lien may not be enforced so long as this order remains in effect.

APPENDIX A

(Version 2: no hearing held)

ORDER VALUING LIEN OF ________________

On [date], Debtor filed a motion to value the lien of [name of lienholder] (hereinafter Lienholder) against the property commonly known as [street address] and more fully described in Exhibit A hereto, which lien was recorded in [name of county] on or about [date] as document [number] (hereinafter the Lien).

The court finds that notice of the motion upon Lienholder was proper. Lienholder having failed to file timely opposition to Debtor's motion, the court hereby orders as follows.

(1) For purposes of Debtor's chapter [11/13] plan only, the Lien is valued at zero, [name of lienholder] does not have a secured claim, and the Lien may not be enforced, pursuant to 11 U.S.C. [§§ 506, 1123(b)(5) and 1141 / §§ 506, 1322 (b)(2) and 1327].

(2) This order shall become part of Debtor's confirmed chapter [11/13] plan.

(3) Upon entry of a discharge or completion of plan payments in Debtor's chapter [11/13] case, the Lien shall be voided for all purposes, and upon application by Debtor, the court will enter an appropriate form of judgment voiding the Lien.

(4) If Debtor's chapter [11/13] case is dismissed or converted to one under another chapter before Debtor obtains a discharge or completes plan payments, this order shall cease to be effective and the Lien shall be retained to the extent recognized by applicable nonbankruptcy law, and upon application by the lienholder, the court will enter an appropriate form of order restoring the Lien.

(5) Except as provided by separate, subsequent order of this court, the Lien may not be enforced so long as this order remains in effect.

APPENDIX B

JUDGMENT VOIDING LIEN OF ______________

On [date], this court entered an ORDER VALUING LIEN OF [NAME OF LIENHOLDER] against certain property of Debtor for purposes of this chapter [11/13] case. That order was subject to being set aside until Debtor obtained a discharge or completed plan payments in this chapter [11/13] case. Debtor having [obtained discharge/completed plan payments], the court now therefore enters the following judgment.

The lien of [name of lienholder] regarding the property commonly known as [address] and more fully described in Exhibit A hereto, and which was recorded in [name of county] on or about [date] as document [number], is hereby determined to be entirely, permanently, and for all purposes void and unenforceable.

APPENDIX C

ORDER RESTORING LIEN OF ________________

On [date], this court entered an ORDER VALUING LIEN OF [NAME OF LIENHOLDER] against certain property of Debtor for purposes of Debtor's plan in this chapter [11/13] case. That order was subject to being set aside if Debtor's chapter [11/13] case was dismissed or converted to another chapter before Debtor obtained a discharge or completed plan payments in this chapter [11 / 13] case. Because Debtor's chapter [11/13] case was [dismissed / converted] before Debtor obtained a discharge or completed plan payments, the court now therefore enters the following order.

This court's [date] ORDER VALUING LIEN OF [NAME OF LIENHOLDER] is hereby vacated. The lien of [name of lienholder] regarding the property commonly known as [address] and more fully described in Exhibit A hereto, and which was recorded in [name of county] on or about [date] as document [number] shall have the validity, priority, and amount recognized under applicable nonbankruptcy law.

Lien Avoidance Guidelines September 9, 2010

G. Guidelines Regarding Sale Orders

GUIDELINES RE SALE ORDERS

A. Introduction

The bankruptcy judges of the Northern District of California have become increasingly concerned about the orders they are being asked to sign on motions to approve sales of property of the estate under section 363(b) and 363(f). Many of the proposed orders submitted: (a) seek relief beyond the scope of the motion before the court; (b) seek to affect parties not before the court; (c) seek advisory rulings where there is no case or controversy; (d) include findings of fact that should be stated orally or in a separate memorandum; and (e) are so wordy and complex that the court has difficulty determining their meaning.

The crafting of orders is a judicial function. Accordingly, the judges have approved a model order for motions seeking authority to sell property of the estate and motions to sell such property free and clear of liens. The following guidelines are intended to explain how to use the model order, and what provisions the court will and will not generally approve as additions to the model order or where the parties draft their own order. These guidelines do not apply to any separate orders approving bidding procedures, break-up fees or other matters related to the sale of property. In addition, these guidelines do not apply in Chapter 13 cases.

The model order is not mandatory, but the judges will use the model order on their own motion where parties vary from these guidelines without sufficient cause and explanation.

In the event that a party submits a sale order that deviates from these guidelines, the party shall, unless otherwise instructed by the court, submit a declaration to the court in which the party identifies the provisions that vary from these guidelines and sets forth the justification therefore.

B. Motions for Authority to Sell Property of the Estate

1. A motion to sell property of the estate outside the ordinary course of business under section 363(b) merely seeks authority to take such action on behalf of the estate. Accordingly, the order should be very simple and need identify only the property to be sold, the purchaser, and the general terms of sale.

2. Other than as set forth herein, the order should not include findings of fact or conclusions of law. All necessary findings and conclusions should be stated orally on the record or in a separate statement of findings of fact and conclusions of law, memorandum or opinion. Generally, the court will state its findings orally on the record. Accordingly, parties should not prepare separate proposed findings and conclusions unless invited to do so by the court.

3. The court acknowledges that the purchaser may seek to review or approve the form of the sale order and may seek to condition its purchase upon the entry of a sale order that is satisfactory to the purchaser. In general, the court will not permit the purchaser to exercise any such condition to obtain entry of an order that does not comply with these guidelines.

4. The court will generally approve the following in the sale order:

   a. A finding that notice of the motion was proper and adequate given the circumstances;

b. A finding that a purchaser is in good faith and entitled to the protections of section 363(m), where such a request is supported by competent evidence, where creditors have been given notice that such a finding will be requested, and where there are no objections to the request or all objections have been overruled;

c. A provision approving the sale as the highest and best offer;

d. A provision addressing any back-up bids, as necessary or appropriate;

e. A provision granting the motion and authorizing the debtor in possession or trustee to enter into the purchase and sale agreement on behalf of the estate;

f. A provision authorizing the debtor in possession or trustee to execute the purchase and sale agreement and to undertake such other actions as may be reasonably necessary to complete the sale;

g. A provision authorizing the debtor in possession or trustee to pay any closing costs, broker's fees or commissions as requested in the motion;

h. A provision authorizing the debtor in possession or trustee to pay the amounts secured by any liens which are not in dispute and authorizing the debtor in possession or trustee to file or record termination statements, instruments of satisfaction, releases of liens and any other documents necessary for the purpose of documenting the release of specified liens;

i. A provision that the sale is on an "as is, where is" and "with all faults" basis;

j. A provision that the purchase and sale agreement and related documents or instruments may be modified, amended or supplemented by the parties without further order of the court, provided that such modification, amendment or supplement does not have a material adverse effect on the estate;

k. A provision waiving any applicable stay under Rule 6004(h) of the Federal Rules of Bankruptcy Procedure, upon a proper showing of cause; and

l. A provision reserving bankruptcy court jurisdiction to implement the sale, enforce the sale order or to resolve any disputes arising in connection with or related to the sale.

5. Any bidder that intends to request that the court make a finding under Bankruptcy Code section 363(m) that such bidder's purchase of the assets or the assignment to it of an executory contract or unexpired lease is in good faith, shall, by a date established by the court, file with the court and serve as required by the court, a written declaration of a competent witness demonstrating (1) the bidder's good faith and (2) the absence of fraud or collusion between the bidder and any other bidder or between the bidder and the debtor's or the estate's agents or employees. The declaration shall also disclose any facts material to the good faith determination, including:

a. The bidder's pre- and post-petition relationships with (i) any other bidder, (ii) the debtor or the debtor's current or former officers, directors, agents or employees, and (iii) any of the debtor's major creditors or equity security holders;

b. The bidder's anticipated relationship after the sale with any of the debtor's current or former officers, directors, agents or employees;

c. Whether any offers of employment or compensation have been or will be made to any of the debtor's current or former officers, directors, agents or employees; and

d. Whether the bidder has paid or contemplates paying consideration in connection with the sale to any person other than the debtor.

6. The court generally will not approve any of the following:

a. Any provision that incorporates the terms of any written or oral agreement into the order, or directs the debtor in possession or trustee to perform any act, except as provided in paragraph 4, f. As noted above, an order under section 363(b) merely authorizes the debtor-in-possession to act.

b. Any provision that purports to exempt the transaction from transfer taxes under section 1146(c). By its own terms, that section applies only to a sale pursuant to a plan of reorganization, not a sale outside of a plan under section 363(b).

c. Any provision that purports to grant a purchaser an administrative claim with respect to a breach of the purchase and sale agreement by the debtor in possession or trustee. Though a purchaser may be entitled to an administrative claim for any damages resulting from such breach, the court is unwilling to give an advisory ruling on the potential recourse available to a purchaser in the event of a breach.

d. Except as otherwise provided herein, any provision that purports to grant declarative or injunctive relief.

e. Any provision that purports to excuse any party from complying with applicable state or federal law.

C. Motions for Sale Free and Clear of Liens, Claims, and Interests

1. A motion to sell free and clear of liens, claims, or interests pursuant to section 363(f) may be added to a motion for authority to sell under section 363(b).

2. The motion must identify each lienholder or other party claiming a property right in the assets to be sold, must be served on each lienholder or party that is to be affected, and must expressly state the grounds for relief under section 363(f) with respect to each lien, claim, or interest to be affected, and must comply with B.L.R. 6004-1.

3. The court will grant a motion to sell free and clear only where there is a genuine case or controversy. That is, there must be evidence that the party to be affected actually asserts a lien, claim, or other interest that would follow the property into the hands of the purchaser absent an order from the court. This requirement is generally satisfied by any

written instrument purporting to be a security interest, whether recorded or not, and generally will be satisfied with respect to all scheduled creditors who do not assert a security interest or lien in the property to be sold and any party that has filed a proof of claim or a request for notice and who does not assert a security interest or lien in the property to be sold. Other types of liens, claims, and interests may require more detailed proof.

4. An order for sale free and clear of liens must identify with particularity the parties to be affected and the liens, claims, and interests to be affected. The order must also provide that any affected property interest such as a lien or other interest is transferred to the proceeds of the sale with the same force, effect, validity and priority that such property interest had against the assets sold.

5. The court will generally not approve a blanket order that purports to provide for a sale free and clear of all liens, claims and interests, or free and clear of all liens, claims and interests of all parties that were served with the motion.

6. An order authorizing a sale free and clear of liens may contain language providing that pursuant to the order and Bankruptcy Code section 363(f), completion of the sale will vest the property in the purchaser free and clear of the liens, claims, and interests of the affected parties, and providing that the affected parties are barred from asserting their affected liens, claims and interests against the purchaser or the property.

7. The court will generally not approve any of the following in an order for sale free and clear.

   a. Any provision that purports to disallow a lien, claim, or interest (as opposed to ordering sale free and clear with the lien, claim, or interest to attach to the proceeds).

   b. Any provision that purports to bar successor liability claims without a showing of a specific threat of such a claim by an identified party.

   c. Any provision for injunctive relief.

D. Motions to Value Secured Claims

1. Not all courts allow a debtor-in-possession to sell overencumbered property free and clear of liens under section 363(f). An alternative basis to sell overencumbered property is a motion to value claims secured by lien on property under Fed. R. Bankr. P. 3012 to the extent the liens exceed the fair market value of the property to be sold.

2. A motion to value claims secured by lien on property under Fed. R. Bankr. P. 3012 to the extent they exceed the sale price may be added to a motion for authority to sell the property under section 363(b) and a motion to sell free and clear of liens under section 363(f).

3. The motion must be served on each affected lienholder, must identify the relief sought regarding that lienholder, and must state grounds for relief under Fed. R. Bankr. P. 3012 regarding that lienholder.

E. Motions to Assume and Assign Executory Contracts or Unexpired Leases

1. The hearing on a motion to assume and assign executory contracts or unexpired leases pursuant to Bankruptcy Code section 365 may be combined with a separate motion for authority to sell under section 363(b) and must comply with B.L.R. 6006-1.

2. The motion must be served on each affected party to the contract, unexpired lease or other agreement to be assumed and assigned.

3. The court will generally approve the following:

a. A provision identifying the contracts, leases or other agreements that are the subject of the motion;

b. Provided that proper notice has been given and the other requirements of section 365 are satisfied, a provision determining the cure amount for each such contract, lease or other agreement or establishing a procedure for the determination of such cure amounts;

c. A provision that relieves the estate from any liability for any breach or an assigned contract, lease or other agreement that occurs after the assignment in accordance with Bankruptcy Code section 365(k); and

d. A provision waiving any applicable stay under Rule 6006(d) of the Federal Rules of Bankruptcy Procedure, upon a proper showing of cause.

Revised 3-19-09

PART II

Court Divisions

Procedures and Practices of the
Oakland Division
San Francisco Division
San Jose Division
Santa Rosa Division

Oakland Division

I. OAKLAND DIVISION

A. Cell Phone Policy

CELL PHONE POLICY

The Oakland Division will now permit the use of cell phones on the second floor at 1300 Clay Street, Oakland, CA, but **only** in the special areas designated for that purpose.

If cell phone users do not restrict their use to the designated areas, or if users fail to turn their cell phones off when they are not in the designated areas (especially in the courtrooms), then the court's permission to use cell phones on the second floor will be withdrawn.

B. *Chapter 7 Fee Application and Final Account Hearings*

IN THE UNITED STATES BANKRUPTCY COURT
FOR THE NORTHERN DISTRICT OF CALIFORNIA
Oakland Division
1300 Clay St., 2nd Floor
Oakland, CA 94612

February 2, 2012

MEMORANDUM

To: Lois Brady
Michael G. Kasolas
John Kendall
Paul Mansdorf
Tevis Thompson

cc: United States Trustee Carr, McClellan, Ingersoll, Thompson & Horn Goldberg, Stinnett, Davis, & Linchey Kornfield, Paul, Nyberg & Kuhner Marshall & Ramos Pinnacle Law Group Stromsheim & Associates Wendel, Rosen, Black & Dean Bachecki, Crom & Co. Kokjer, Pierotti, Maiocco & Duck

From: Judge Roger L. Efremsky
Judge M. Elaine Hammond
Judge William J. Lafferty

Subject: Chapter 7 Fee Application and Final Account Hearings

---

In the interest of saving you and your professionals valuable time, we have decided to implement the following procedures. If we have failed to copy any of your regularly employed professionals, please forward a copy of this memorandum to them.

Effective July 14, 2008, Chapter 7 Trustees and their professionals may, but need not, personally appear at fee application and final account hearings in Oakland Division, unless an objection is on file or you receive notice from the court to appear, in which case you must appear. However, you must be available by telephone at the time of the hearing, in case an objecting party appears or the court has questions. Any person wishing to utilize this telephone standby procedure must contact the Courtroom Deputy by telephone or fax at least 24 hours in advance and provide your direct line. Absent this information, you will be required to attend the hearing.

C. Distribution of Funds in Chapter 13 Cases

Distribution of Funds in Chapter 13 Cases

Payments shall be disbursed in the following order:

1. To secured creditors and the balance of attorney's fees. Those secured creditors which are specified in the plan to receive fixed monthly payments will be paid the amount specified. If fixed monthly payments are specified in the plan for all secured creditors, the balance of the plan payment will be disbursed toward attorney's fees.

2. To priority creditors in the order prescribed by the Bankruptcy Code;

3. To unsecured creditors.

D. Guidelines for Payment of Attorney Fees in Chapter 13 Cases

GUIDELINES FOR PAYMENT OF ATTORNEYS' FEES IN CHAPTER 13 CASES – OAKLAND DIVISION

The following are guidelines for the circumstances under which a detailed fee application need not be filed in Chapter 13 cases and the manner in which the Chapter 13 Trustee will disburse fees which are approved.

A. FEE APPLICATIONS

1. Counsel may receive an order approving fees up to the amounts set forth in **Paragraph 2** without filing a detailed application if:

(a) Counsel has filed an executed copy of the "Rights and Responsibilities of Chapter 13 Debtors and Their Attorneys," copies of which are available in the Clerk's Office and in the Office of the Chapter 13 Trustee; and

(b) No objection to the requested fees has been raised.

2. The maximum fee which can be approved through the procedure described in **Paragraph 1** is: $4,800 in nonbusiness cases and $6,000 in business cases. Retainers of more than $2,000 will be closely scrutinized by both the Chapter 13 Trustee and the Court. An additional flat fee of $1,500 for Motions or Adversary proceedings to strip liens pursuant to 11 USC § 506 requires an ex parte application and order signed off by the Chapter 13 Trustee.

3. If an executed copy of the "Rights and Responsibilities of Chapter 13 Debtors and Their Attorneys" is not filed, or there is an objection, an order will not be entered automatically pursuant to these Guidelines. In such cases, counsel must apply for all fees, and shall comply with Bankruptcy Rules 2002 and 2016 as well as the "Guidelines for Compensation and Expense Reimbursement of Professionals" adopted by the Bankruptcy Judges of the Northern District of California.

4. If counsel has filed an executed copy of the "Rights and Responsibilities of Chapter 13 Debtors and Their Attorneys," but the initial fee is not sufficient to fully compensate counsel for the legal services rendered in the case, the attorney may apply for additional fees. The form application attached hereto may be used in place of the procedures set forth in the "Guidelines for Compensation and Expense Reimbursement for Professionals." The necessity for a hearing on the application shall be governed by Bankruptcy Rule 2002(a)(6) and Local Bankruptcy Rule 9014-1(b)(l)(B).

5. Any fees owed after payment of the retainer shall be paid through the plan unless otherwise ordered. The Chapter 13 Trustee shall pay counsel pro-rata with the secured claims. If there are no secured claims, counsel shall be paid in full prior to payment of priority and unsecured claims.

6. On its own motion or the motion of any party in interest, the Court may order a hearing to review any fee paid.

E. Notice Regarding Proposed Orders Filed with Motions

IN THE UNITED STATES BANKRUPTCY COURT
FOR NORTHERN DISTRICT OF CALIFORNIA
Oakland Division

Amendments to the Federal Rules of Bankruptcy Procedure went into effect on December 1. The below procedures is applicable for the **Oakland** and **San Jose divisions** ***only***. The following rules require the filing of proposed forms of order with the motions:

- Rule 4001(b) — Use of Cash Collateral;
- Rule 4001(c) — Obtaining credit; and
- Rule 4001(d) — Agreement relating to relief from the automatic stay, prohibiting or conditioning the use, sale, or lease of property, providing adequate protection, use of cash collateral, and obtaining credit.

Please ensure that every proposed forms of order is clearly marked ***Proposed***, is filed only as an exhibit or attachment to a motion, and ***is not*** docketed in such a manner that may mislead the parties or public to believe that it is an order of the court.

Please note, that proposed forms of order filed along with motions ***will not*** be executed by the Court. In order to have an order signed, you ***must*** upload a PDF version of the order via CM/ECF. ***Please do not put Proposed on an order which is submitted for the Court's signature***.

If you have any questions, please contact the **Oakland** or **San Jose** divisions.

F. *Notice Regarding Reduction in Attorney Fees*

IN THE UNITED STATES BANKRUPTCY COURT
FOR NORTHERN DISTRICT OF CALIFORNIA
Oakland Division

NOTICE REGARDING REDUCTION IN ATTORNEY FEES

TO: ALL CHAPTER 13 DEBTORS' ATTORNEYS

FROM: THE JUDGES OF THE UNITED STATES BANKRUPTCY COURT, OAKLAND DIVISION

RE: APPEARANCE AT MEETINGS OF CREDITORS/ATTORNEY FEES

Effective December 1, 2010, failure by the debtor's attorney to appear at an initial meeting of creditors or continued meeting of creditors will result in an automatic reduction of $300 to the fee being paid to the debtor's attorney through the chapter 13 trustee's office.

Upon failure to appear by the attorney of record or an attorney authorized to appear specially, the chapter 13 trustee shall submit a declaration regarding the failure and an order authorizing the reduction in the attorney's fee for the signature of the court.

The chapter 13 trustee shall take into account emergency circumstances such as car accidents or sudden illness and may in her discretion refrain from submitting a declaration and order.

Notwithstanding the foregoing, any attorney may, at his or her option, contest the reduction by setting the matter for hearing in accordance with the rules of this court, on notice to the chapter 13 trustee and debtor. Nothing contained herein shall be construed to limit the authority of the court to reduce fees in an amount other than $300, or impose other sanctions as the circumstances may warrant.

Dated: February 2, 2012

____
Roger L. Efremsky
United States Bankruptcy Judge

____
William J. Lafferty
United States Bankruptcy Judge

____
M. Elaine Hammond
United States Bankruptcy Judge

G. *Order Clarifying Model Chapter 13 Plan*

IN THE UNITED STATES BANKRUPTCY COURT
FOR THE NORTHERN DISTRICT OF CALIFORNIA
Oakland Division

ORDER RE FORM CHAPTER 13 PLAN

Certain members of the bar have expressed confusion and concern over the intended meaning of the boxes in Paragraph 2(b) of the form of Chapter 13 Plan approved for use in the Oakland Division of this court. Those boxes read, respectively, "§ 506" and "Non § 506." The "plain language" of these boxes is meaningless. It follows that the confusion is justified.

Although it is in no-way apparent from the plan, the court understands that the boxes were intended for a very narrow purpose, specifically, to indicate whether or not a debtor incurred a debt secured by a motor vehicle within the 910 days prior to the date of the petition. If so, then pursuant to the "hanging paragraph" of Bankruptcy Code § 1325(a), Bankruptcy Code § 506(a)'s method of valuing secured claims would not apply, and the debtor would be required to pay the full amount of such a secured debt without regard to the value of the vehicle securing the claim.

The problem, however, apart from the meaningless language of the boxes, is that the model plan language below the boxes states, in relevant part:

> With respect to secured claims per § 506, valuation stated shall bind unless a timely objection to confirmation is filed. With respect to a non § 506 claim as referenced in § 1325, the claim, to the extent allowed, shall control.

Chapter 13 debtors may not modify a debt secured only by a first deed of trust on a residence, or a junior deed of trust that attaches to some equity (both hereinafter referred to as "secured deed of trust") by reducing the amount of the creditor's claim based on the value of the property. See Bankruptcy Code § 1322(b)(2).

However, if the debtor checks the "§ 506" box, a creditor whose claim is secured only by a secured deed of trust may be bound by a property valuation that is not germane to the issue of confirmation. Similarly, if a debtor were to check the "Non § 506 box," list a claim thereafter that is a claim secured by a secured deed of trust, then the plan, taking into account the language below the boxes, might reasonably be construed as binding a creditor by a value and claim amount listed by the debtor that is less than what might be the actual amount of an undersecured debt secured by a secured deed of trust.

Generally, documents should be construed in a manner that is legal, rather than illegal. Even so, and to avoid any confusion or misunderstanding while the ambiguity in Oakland's form chapter 13 plan exists, it is

ORDERED AS FOLLOWS, applicable to all chapter 13 cases filed in the Oakland Division of this court:

1. Except to the extent that the collateral listed in paragraph 2(b) of the model chapter 13 plan approved for use in the Oakland division of this court is a motor vehicle, the court will pay no regard to whether the above-referenced "§ 506" and "Non § 506" boxes are checked, and if checked, to which of the boxes has been checked.

2. In cases where the collateral listed is a motor vehicle, and the "§ 506" box in the plan is checked, the court will construe the checking of the box as a representation by the debtor that the debtor incurred the debt secured by a motor vehicle more than 910 days prior to the filing of the petition.

3. If any ambiguity is present in paragraph 2(b) or any other provision of any chapter 13 plan filed on the approved form, the court will construe the plan in a manner consistent with the provisions of Bankruptcy Code § 1322(b)(2), and all other applicable provisions of the Bankruptcy Code.

Dated: April 21, 2011

____

Edward D. Jellen
United States Bankruptcy Judge

____

Roger L. Efremsky
United States Bankruptcy Judge

____

William J. Lafferty
United States Bankruptcy Court

H. Order Regarding Filing of Payment Advices

IN THE UNITED STATES BANKRUPTCY COURT
FOR NORTHERN DISTRICT OF CALIFORNIA
Oakland Division

ORDER RE FILING OF PAYMENT ADVICES

(1) In lieu of filing payment advices with the court, as required by 11 U.S.C. § 521(a)(1)(B)(iv), unless otherwise ordered by the court, the debtor shall provide the required payment advices (or an alternative described in subsection (2) below) directly to the trustee at least seven days prior to the first date set for the meeting of creditors under 11 U.S.C. § 341.

(2) A debtor who is unable to provide the required payment advices to the trustee may provide the trustee, in the alternative, with a certification setting forth the reasons that the required information is unavailable. The certification should state the debtor's estimate of payments received within the 60 days before the petition date and provide other evidence, if any is available, of the payments received.

Good cause appearing therefor, it is

SO ORDERED

Dated: February 2, 2012

____
Roger L. Efremsky
United States Bankruptcy Judge

____
William J. Lafferty
United States Bankruptcy Judge

____
M. Elaine Hammond
United States Bankruptcy Judge

I. Order Regarding Initial Disclosures and Discovery Conference

ORDER RE INITIAL DISCLOSURES AND DISCOVERY CONFERENCE

The Oakland and San Francisco Divisions of the United States Bankruptcy Court for the Northern District of California have promulgated a form of order dealing with the requirements of Federal Rule of Bankruptcy Procedure 7026, incorporating Federal Rule of Civil Procedure 26.

The clerk will issue this order on behalf of the court concurrently with the filing of a complaint initiating an adversary proceeding and the issuance of a summons. The order modifies the Rule 7026 requirements in some respects and directs plaintiffs to serve a copy along with the summons and complaint.

Counsel (and *pro se* plaintiffs) are directed to submit to the clerk an original and two copies of this form of order, completed to show the names of the parties, when filing the complaint. The clerk will insert the adversary proceeding number and return a copy to the plaintiff.

Attached is the form of Order Re Initial Disclosures and Discovery Conference.

IN THE UNITED STATES BANKRUPTCY COURT
FOR THE NORTHERN DISTRICT OF CALIFORNIA
Oakland Division

In re:) No. ____________
) Adv No. ____________
Debtor(s).)
______________________________)
)
Plaintiff(s),)
v.)
Defendant(s).)
______________________________)

ORDER RE INITIAL DISCLOSURES AND DISCOVERY CONFERENCE

The purpose of this order is: (1) to notify the parties of their obligation under Fed. R. Civ. P. 26, as incorporated by Fed. R. Bankr. P. 7026, to make Initial Disclosures and meet for a Discovery Conference; and (2) to modify those Rule 26 requirements in certain respects. As such, this order has no effect in any proceeding exempted under Rule 26(a)(1)(E) and (f) from the Initial Disclosure and Discovery Conference requirements.

1. The Discovery Conference. At least 21 calendar days before the status conference scheduled in the summons, the parties shall confer (in person or by telephone) at a "Discovery Conference." Plaintiff shall initiate contact regarding arrangement of the Discovery Conference. Defendant shall cooperate in fixing the time and place of the Discovery Conference. Except to the extent the parties stipulate otherwise, no party shall initiate or conduct any formal discovery prior to the Discovery Conference. The parties may conduct informal discovery.

2. **Settlement.** At the Discovery Conference, the parties shall consider the nature and basis of their claims and defenses and the possibility of an early settlement. The parties shall also discuss ADR options, as required by B.L.R. 9040-3.

3. **Initial Disclosures.** At the Discovery Conference, the parties shall arrange to make the "Initial Disclosures" required by Rule 26(a), without necessity of a formal discovery request. The Disclosures shall be made at or within 14 calendar days after the Discovery Conference. All disclosures shall be in writing, signed by the party or his or her attorney, and served on all other parties.

4. **Discovery Plan.** Unless:

(a) the proceeding is exempt under Rule 26(f);

(b) the proceeding seeks to recover money or property, or except a debt from discharge pursuant to 11 U.S.C. § 523(a), of no more than $15,000, excluding interest, attorneys, fees, and costs; or

(c) the parties stipulate to the contrary in a writing filed with the court; the parties shall, at the Discovery Conference, also develop a written Discovery Plan signed by all parties or their counsel, that reflects the parties' views and proposals concerning:

(i) what changes, if any, should be made in the timing, form, or requirements of the Initial Disclosures;

(ii) the timing, subject matter, and limitations, if any, of discovery to be conducted after the initial disclosures; and

(iii) the subject of any orders that the court should enter under Fed.R.Bankr.P. 7016(b) and (c) and 7026(a)(1).

The Discovery Plan shall be filed within 14 calendar days after the Discovery Conference.

5. **Pretrial Disclosures.** Notwithstanding Rule 26(a)(3), pretrial disclosures shall be made in accordance with further order of the court.

6. **Service hereof.** The summons, complaint, and this order shall be served by the plaintiff within 10 days of the date of this order. A return or proof of service shall be filed within 5 days after service.

SO ORDERED.

Dated: ____________________

FOR THE COURT

____

Clerk of Court

I certify that a copy of this Order was returned to the plaintiff at the time the original summons was issued.

Dated: ________________

____

Deputy Clerk of Court

J. Order Regarding Joint Prehearing Conference Statements on Objections to Confirmation of Chapter 13 Plans

IN THE UNITED STATES BANKRUPTCY COURT
FOR NORTHERN DISTRICT OF CALIFORNIA
Oakland Division

ORDER REGARDING JOINT PREHEARING CONFERENCE STATEMENTS ON OBJECTIONS TO CONFIRMATION OF CHAPTER 13 PLANS

This order applies to all cases that are calendared for a chapter 13 plan confirmation hearing as a result of an objection to confirmation being filed by a creditor.

THE DEBTOR'S ATTORNEY OR DEBTOR IN *PRO PER* AND THE OBJECTING CREDITOR OR CREDITOR'S ATTORNEY ARE ORDERED to confer by telephone at least 14 days prior to the date set for hearing regarding confirmation of the chapter 13 plan. At least 7 days prior to the confirmation hearing, the parties shall file and serve a joint prehearing statement with the court, not to exceed 2 pages in length, addressing the following:

1. A statement of the date and time of the telephone conference required by this order. If a telephone conference is not held, an explanation as to why it did not occur is required.
2. A precise and separate statement of each factual and legal issue, that must be determined to resolve the objection to confirmation and a brief statement of the facts in support thereof.
3. An estimate of the time needed to resolve the issues surrounding the objection. Failure to conduct a conference to resolve objection and/or failure to file a prehearing conference statement may result in sanctions against the parties.

If, however, one side fails and/or refuses to cooperate in the preparation of the joint prehearing conference statement, all parties must still file a timely prehearing conference statement. Failure to comply with this order may result in sanctions being levied against a party(s) and/or counsel.

Dated: February 2, 2012

____
Roger L. Efremsky
United States Bankruptcy Judge

____
William J. Lafferty
United States Bankruptcy Judge

____
M. Elaine Hammond
United States Bankruptcy Judge

K. Order Regarding Payment of Pre-Confirmation Adequate Protection Payments

IN THE UNITED STATES BANKRUPTCY COURT
FOR THE NORTHERN DISTRICT OF CALIFORNIA
Oakland Division

ORDER RE PAYMENT OF PRE-CONFIRMATION ADEQUATE PROTECTION PAYMENTS PURSUANT TO 11 U.S.C. § 1326 IN CHAPTER 13 CASES FILED ON OR AFTER OCTOBER 17, 2005 IN THE NORTHERN DISTRICT OF CALIFORNIA, OAKLAND DIVISION

Unless the Court orders otherwise, the debtor shall commence making payments not later than 30 days after the filing of the plan or entry of the Order of Relief or Order of Conversion, whichever is earlier, and every month thereafter in the amount -

a. Proposed by the plan to the Trustee. This amount shall also specifically provide a monthly amount to be paid as adequate protection to each creditor holding an allowed claim secured by personal property to the extent the claim is attributable to the purchase of such property by the debtor for that portion of the obligation that became due after the filing of the plan or entry of the Order of Relief or the Order of Conversion whichever is earlier.

b. With respect to payments for the lease of personal property that became due after the filing of the plan or entry of the Order For Relief or the Order of Conversion, whichever is earlier, said payments shall be paid by the debtor directly to the lessor, reducing the payments under Paragraph (a) above by the amount so paid and providing the Trustee with evidence of such payment, including the amount and date of payment, at least 3 court days prior to the Confirmation Hearing date.

c. Pursuant to the Trustee's next monthly disbursement cycle, after 30 days of the filing of the plan or entry of the Order for Relief or the Order of Conversion, whichever is earlier, and every 30 days thereafter pending confirmation of the plan, the Trustee shall make the adequate protection payments to each creditor as provided in Paragraph (a) above to the extent the Trustee has such funds on hand.

d. For purposes of Paragraph (a) above, an allowed claim secured by personal property shall be a proof of claim that complies with Rule 3001, F.R.B.P.

e. Upon dismissal of a case prior to confirmation of the plan, the Trustee shall first make such payments required by Paragraph (a) above, then any unpaid claims allowed under 11 U.S.C. § 503(b), before returning the balance of the funds being held by the Trustee to the debtor.

f. The Trustee may assess an administrative fee for affecting the payments required by Paragraph (a) above and shall collect such fee at the time of making the payment from the funds on hand in the case. The allowed expense fee shall be equal to the percentage fee established by the Attorney General pursuant to 28 U.S.C. § 586(e)(1)(B) in effect at the time of distribution.

Dated: February 2, 2012

____
Roger L. Efremsky
United States Bankruptcy Judge

____
William J. Lafferty
United States Bankruptcy Judge

____
M. Elaine Hammond
United States Bankruptcy Judge

L. Order Regarding Procedures for Approval of Reaffirmation Agreements Where Debtor Is Represented by Counsel

IN THE UNITED STATES BANKRUPTCY COURT
FOR NORTHERN DISTRICT OF CALIFORNIA
Oakland Division

ORDER RE PROCEDURES FOR APPROVAL OF REAFFIRMATION AGREEMENTS WHERE DEBTOR IS REPRESENTED BY COUNSEL

In cases filed on or after October 17, 2005, a reaffirmation agreement subject to 11 U.S.C. § 524(c)(3) (i.e., accompanied by the declaration of the attorney that represented the debtor during the course of negotiating the agreement) is presumed to be an undue hardship where the difference between the debtor's monthly income and the debtor's monthly expenses, as shown on the statement required under 11 U.S.C. § 524(k)(6)(A), is less than the scheduled payments on the reaffirmed debt. The debtor may attempt to rebut this presumption by filing a statement identifying additional sources of funds to make the payments required by the reaffirmation agreement. See 11 U.S.C. § 524(m)(1).

If the debtor files such a statement, the Court will review the agreement and decide whether to approve or disapprove it at a hearing on a motion initiated by either debtor or the creditor, on notice to the other party to the agreement.

Good cause appearing therefor, it is

SO ORDERED.

Dated: February 2, 2012

____
Roger L. Efremsky
United States Bankruptcy Judge

____
William J. Lafferty
United States Bankruptcy Judge

____
M. Elaine Hammond
United States Bankruptcy Judge

M. *Order Regarding Procedures for Dismissal of Chapter 13 Case on Chapter 13 Trustee's Motion for Lack of Feasibility of Plan After Audit*

IN THE UNITED STATES BANKRUPTCY COURT
FOR NORTHERN DISTRICT OF CALIFORNIA
Oakland Division

ORDER RE PROCEDURES FOR DISMISSAL OF CHAPTER 13 CASE ON CHAPTER 13 TRUSTEE'S MOTION FOR LACK OF FEASIBILITY OF PLAN AFTER AUDIT

In cases filed under Chapter 13 in the Oakland Division of the Northern District of California, a Chapter 13 Trustee's motion to dismiss a case for lack of feasibility of the plan following a post-confirmation audit shall be permitted to be filed on a default basis, as permitted by B.L.R. 9014-1 and this Order.

In addition to the exception provided for in B.L.R. 9014-1(b)(1)(C) that no actual hearing is required for a Chapter 13 Trustee's motion to dismiss brought under 11 U.S.C. § 1307(c); in the Oakland Division, B.L.R. 9014-1(b)(1)(C) shall be supplemented to except from the actual hearing requirement a Chapter 13 Trustee's motion to dismiss for lack of feasibility of the plan after audit.

Good cause appearing therefor, it is

SO ORDERED.

Dated: February 2, 2012

____
Roger L. Efremsky
United States Bankruptcy Judge

____
William J. Lafferty
United States Bankruptcy Judge

____
M. Elaine Hammond
United States Bankruptcy Judge

N. Rights and Responsibilities of Chapter 13 Debtors and Their Attorneys

IN THE UNITED STATES BANKRUPTCY COURT
FOR THE NORTHERN DISTRICT OF CALIFORNIA
Oakland Division

RIGHTS AND RESPONSIBILITIES OF CHAPTER 13 DEBTORS AND THEIR ATTORNEYS

It is important for debtors who file a bankruptcy case under Chapter 13 to understand their rights and responsibilities. It is also important that the debtors know what their attorneys' responsibilities are, and understand the importance of communicating with their attorney to make the case successful. Debtors should know that they may expect certain services to be performed by their attorney. In order to assure that debtors and their attorneys understand their rights and responsibilities in the bankruptcy process, the following guidelines provided by the court are hereby agreed to by the debtors and their attorneys. Unless the Court orders otherwise:

BEFORE THE CASE IS FILED

The debtor agrees to:

1. Provide the attorney with accurate financial information.

2. Discuss with the attorney the debtor's objectives in filing the case.

The attorney agrees to:

1. Meet with the debtor to review the debtor's debts, assets, liabilities, income and expenses.

2. Counsel the debtor regarding the advisability of filing either a chapter 7 or Chapter 13 case, discuss both procedures with the debtor, and answer the debtor's questions.

3. Explain what payments will be made directly by the debtor and what payments will be made through the debtor's Chapter 13 Plan, with particular attention to mortgage and vehicle loan payments, as well as any other claims which accrue interest.

4. Explain to the debtor how, when and where to make the Chapter 13 plan payment.

5. Explain to the debtor how the attorney fees and trustee fees are paid and provide an executed copy of this document to the debtor.

6. Explain to the debtor that the first plan payment must be made to the Trustee within 30 days after the date of the filing of the plan or order for relief, whichever is earlier.

7. Advise the debtor of the requirement to attend the 341 Meeting of Creditors, and instruct the debtor as to the date, time and place of the meeting.

8. Advise the debtor of the necessity of maintaining liability, collision and comprehensive insurance on vehicles securing loans or lease.

9. Timely prepare and file the debtor's petition, plan statements and schedules.

10. Accept a retainer of no more than $2,000, unless the attorney makes a special application to the court for approval of a larger retainer.

AFTER THE CASE IS FILED

The debtor agrees to:

1. Keep the Trustee and attorney informed of the debtor's address and telephone number.

2. Inform the attorney of any wage garnishments or attachment of assets which occur or continue after the filing of the case.

3. Contact the attorney promptly if the debtor loses his/her job or has other financial problems.

4. Let the attorney know if the debtor is sued during the case.

5. Inform the attorney if any tax refunds the debtor is entitled to are seized or not returned to the debtor by the IRS or Franchise Tax Board.

6. Contact the attorney before buying, refinancing, or selling real property or before entering into any long-term loan agreements to find out what approvals are required.

7. Pay any filing fees and expenses that may be incurred directly to the attorney.

The attorney agrees to provide the following legal services:

1. Appear at the 341 Meeting of Creditors with the debtor.

2. Respond to objections to plan confirmation, and where necessary, prepare an amended plan.

3. Prepare, file and serve necessary modifications to the plan which may include suspending, lowering or increasing plan payments.

4. Prepare, file and serve necessary amended statements and schedules, in accordance with information provided by the debtor.

5. Prepare, file and serve necessary motions to buy, sell or refinance real property when appropriate.

6. Object to improper or invalid claims, if necessary, based upon documentation provided by the debtor.

7. Represent the debtor in motions for relief from stay.

8. Where appropriate, prepare, file and serve necessary motions to avoid liens on real or personal property.

9. Provide such other legal services as are necessary for the

administration of the present case before the Bankruptcy Court.

The Guidelines for Payment of Attorneys fees in Chapter 13 Cases for the Oakland Division provide for maximum initial fees in the following amounts: $4,800 in non-business cases and $6,000 in business Cases. Any retainer of more than $2,000 will be closely scrutinized by both the Chapter 13 Trustee and the Court."

Initial fees charged in this case are $________________.

If the initial fees ordered by the court are not sufficient to compensate the attorney for the legal services rendered in this case, the attorney further agrees to apply to the court for any additional fees. Fees shall be paid through the plan unless otherwise ordered. The attorney may not receive fees directly from the debtor other than the initial retainer.

If the debtor disputes the legal services provided or the fees charged by the attorney, an objection may be filed with the court and the matter set for hearing. The attorney may move to withdraw or the debtor may discharge the attorney at any time.

Dated: ____________________ ____________________
Debtor

Dated: ____________________ ____________________
Debtor

Dated: ____________________ ____________________
Attorney for Debtor(s)

San Francisco Division

II. San Francisco Division

A. *Chapter 13 Calendar Procedures*

IN THE UNITED STATES BANKRUPTCY COURT
FOR THE NORTHERN DISTRICT OF CALIFORNIA
San Francisco Division

CHAPTER 13 CALENDAR PROCEDURES
Effective January 2011

INTRODUCTION

When a Chapter 13 case is filed, the '341 Notice will include a date and time for the confirmation hearing. If the Basic Steps discussed below have been completed prior to the first date set for the confirmation hearing, the '341 meeting of creditors has concluded and no objections to confirmation have been filed or such objections have been resolved and withdrawn without judicial intervention, the Trustee will transfer the case to the Chapter13 Case Confirmation List ("Confirmation List"), taking the matter off calendar. A text entry reporting the transfer to the Confirmation List will be docketed and ECF Registered Users will receive a Notice of Electronic Filing to that effect. The Trustee will give written notice to pro se debtors or non-ECF Registered Users. The Confirmation List will also be posted on the Trustee's website.

Plans in cases on the Confirmation List will be confirmed as of the next regularly scheduled Chapter 13 calendar.

If the Basic Steps have not been completed, the '341 meeting of creditors has not been concluded or other Trustee's issues have not been resolvedin time for transfer of a case to the Confirmation List, the Trustee will transfer the case to the Trustee's Case Pending List ("TPL"), taking the case off calendar. A text entry reporting the transfer to the TPL will be docketed and ECF Registered Users will receive a Notice of Electronic Filing to that effect. The Trustee will give written notice to pro se debtors or non-ECF Registered Users. The TPL will alsobe posted on the Trustee's website.

BASIC STEPS

A case will not be moved from the TPL to the Confirmation List until all objections are resolved and the documents listed below have been delivered to the Trustee and the '341 meeting of creditors has been concluded. The basic documents are:

- Copy of federal income tax return or tax transcript for the prior calendar year;
- Income declaration and required income advices;
- Completed Business Questionnaire (if requested by the Trustee);
- Declaration regarding any pending loan modification application.

If these documents (and other documents that the Trustee may request) are not provided to the Trustee at least seven (7) days prior to the '341 meeting of creditors, that meeting will be continued and the case will remain on the TPL.

CHAPTER 13 CONTESTED MATTER CALENDAR

Pending chapter 13 cases in which the plan has not yet been confirmed by the first date set for confirmation will not come before the court unless and until action by a judge is required to resolve factual or legal issues. Generally, the Chapter 13 Contested Matter Calendar ("Contested Matter Calendar") will consist of a few contested matters fully ready for judicial resolution and a few trial-setting conferences ready for trial on matters such as objections to confirmation, objections to claims and motions to value liens. This will not normally occur until the Basic Steps have been completed and all documents and information requested by the parties (including Trustee) have been provided; negotiations in a good faith attempt to resolve the dispute have been completed; and the parties are ready to submit the dispute for resolution by the court or to have the matter set for trial on a later date.

Contested matters that do not require the taking of testimony may be placed on the Contested Matter Calendar provided the issue is properly served and noticed by giving twenty-eight (28) days notice of the regular Chapter 13 calendar date as posted on the Trustee's website.

Alternatively,the Court encourages the parties to use the notice-and-opportunity-for-a-hearing option of BLR 9014-1 for motions to value liens, and not to set such matters for hearing unless the lienholder files an objection to the motion.

Any evidentiary hearing must be scheduled by the court. Time for trial-setting conferences will be made available on the Contested Matter Calendar, but the parties must meet and confer beforehand to attempt toagree upon a schedule. If the parties are able to agree upon a schedule, and if the trial will be a day or less, counsel are requested to obtain a trial date through the appropriate courtroom deputy, rather than set the matter on the Contested Matter Calendar.

PROCEDURE FOR PLACING MATTERS ON CONTESTED MATTER CALENDAR

A party who believes a legal or factual dispute in a case should be set on the Contested Matter Calendar must file and serve a proper Notice of Chapter 13 Contested Matter (a newly created docket event) at least twenty-eight (28) days before the hearing. The notice must specify what relief is sought from the court. Chambers copies should be sent to the assigned judge's chambers. At least ten (10) days before the hearing date a party should remove their case from the Contested Matter Calendar or continue it to a future Contested Matter Calendar for any matter that is not ready to be submitted for decision or trial scheduling.

PRE-CONFIRMATION DISMISSAL CALENDAR

The court will no longer conduct status conferences regarding cases on the TPL to monitor debtors' progress in completing the Basic Steps, complying with Trustee's requests for declarations, documents, amendments to the schedules or the plan, filing objections to claims, filing motions to value lien, providing details of pending loan modifications, etc. Instead, the Trustee will afford debtor a reasonable time to take the action requested, and will file a Motion to Dismiss if debtor does not timely comply.

In those cases where the debtor's attorney appears to have not provided prompt responses to the Trustee's request or otherwise is responsible for unreasonable delay, the Motion to Dismiss may include a request for disgorgement of the attorney's retainer.

Any such Motion to Dismiss will be placed on the Pre-Confirmation Dismissal Calendar. Trustee will serve a Motion to Dismiss twenty-eight (28) days before the Pre-Confirmation Dismissal Calendar unless the court shortens time on the Trustee's request.

Debtors should not expect to avoid dismissal through last-minute compliance that Trustee is unable to confirm. Debtors should not assume that compliance effected less than fourteen (14) days before the Motion to Dismiss hearing date will cause Trustee to withdraw or continue, or the court to deny or continue such a motion. Unless there has been timely compliance, opposition to a Motion to Dismiss must be filed and served fourteen days before the hearing or the case may be dismissed and the matter dropped from calendar without further notice.

POST-CONFIRMATION DISMISSAL CALENDAR

After plans have been confirmed, if payments are delinquent, the plan is over-term, or other grounds exist for the Trustee to seek dismissal of the case, the Trustee may file a Motion to Dismiss and place the motion on the Post-Confirmation Dismissal Calendar. Trustee will serve a Motion to Dismiss twenty-eight (28) days before the Post-Confirmation Dismissal Calendar unless the court shortens time on the Trustee's request.

2011 CALENDAR DATES AND TIMES

Judge Carlson's calendar will be called at 9:30 A.M. and begin with the Confirmation List and the Post-Confirmation Dismissal Calendar. His Pre-Confirmation Dismissal Calendar will be called at 9:35 A.M. His Chapter 13 Contested Matter will be called at 9:40 A.M.

Judge Montali's calendar will be called at 1:30 P.M. and begin with the Confirmation List and the Post-Confirmation Dismissal Calendar. His Pre-Confirmation Dismissal Calendar will be called at 1:35 P.M. His Chapter 13 Contested Matter will be called at 1:40 P.M.

The 2011 Chapter 13 Calendar dates are:

- January 19
- February 16
- March 16
- April 20
- May 18
- June 15
- July 20
- August 22
- September 21
- October 19
- November 16
- December 21

B. Chapter 13 Motions to Dismiss

IN THE UNITED STATES BANKRUPTCY COURT
FOR THE NORTHERN DISTRICT OF CALIFORNIA
San Francisco Division

Chapter 13 Motions to Dismiss

The San Francisco Judges issue the following notice regarding the practices they will employ in resolving pre-confirmation motions to dismiss filed by the Chapter 13 Trustee.

1. Such motions are in substance motions to dismiss for failure to prosecute the case to confirmation without undue delay. The Trustee's motion will list the deficiencies in the plan or schedules, or the failure to provide other information that Trustee asserts as the basis for the motion.

2. To oppose the motion, the debtor must do all of the following:

(a) File written opposition not later than the later of

(i) 14 days after service of the motion; or

(ii) 14 days before the hearing on the motion.

(b) In the opposition, address separately each deficiency asserted by the Trustee in the motion; and

(i) Cure such deficiency as of the date of the opposition, and state in the opposition that such deficiency has already been cured; or

(ii) Explain in detail why the deficiency has not been cured as of the date of the opposition, and state when such deficiency will be cured.

(c) Where the case has been pending for a substantial period of time, the court will presume that there is undue delay unless the debtor provides an explanation that is both detailed and persuasive as to why the deficiency was not cured by the date opposition is due.

(d) Failure to file a timely opposition to a motion to dismiss will normally result in the matter being dropped from calendar and the case being dismissed without further notice to the debtor.

C. E-Orders Procedures

San Francisco Division

E-ORDERS PROCEDURES

I. Uploading Orders

When a proposed order is uploaded in CM/ECF (Bankruptcy/Order Upload), counsel should link it to the appropriate motion. (Do not link the order to a request for default). Counsel submitting orders generally do not need to include any form of transmittal letter. A proof of service of proposed orders in accordance with B.L.R. 9021-1 should be docketed separately. The proof of service should be docketed in CM/ECF before the Order is uploaded (**Bankruptcy/Miscellaneous/Certificate of Service/add to text "*regarding proposed order,*" and reference the original motion entry**). Similarly, any declarations of default or other documents necessary for the review of an order should be docketed before uploading the order. Do not put "proposed" in the title of the order.

II. Communicating with Chambers Regarding Proposed Orders

Occasionally counsel desire expedited handling of orders in the case of bona fide emergencies (e.g., sale of property; issuance of a temporary restraining order). After such an order has been uploaded into the ECF system, counsel may notify chambers by telephone or via an e-mail to the assigned judge's designated email addresses below. Do not send the order itself to the e-mail addresses.

JUDGE MONTALI	Montali_Orders@canb.uscourts.gov	**AND**
	Peggy_Brister@canb.uscourts.gov	
JUDGE CARLSON	Carlson_Orders@canb.uscourts.gov	**AND**
	Jennifer_Hayes@canb.uscourts.gov	**AND**
	Jane_Galvani@canb.uscourts.gov	

When counsel believe it necessary to advise the court about a matter pertaining to a submitted order (e.g., that opposing counsel has agreed to the form; that opposing counsel has disagreed as to the form and will submit an alternate form, etc.), they may notify the chambers of the assigned judge at the e-mail addresses above (with a copy to opposing counsel and other parties as appropriate). Alternatively, counsel may docket (as a separate document) a letter with proof of service in CM/ECF (**Bankruptcy/Miscellaneous/Document: include in the text "*Letter to Court regarding proposed order*"**). The letter will become and remain a permanent part of the record in the case. Please notify the appropriate chambers by e-mail when the letter is docketed.

III. Court Service List

In general, orders should be served only on specified respondents or on parties opposing the relief granted (or seeking the relief denied). As indicated in B.L.R. 9022-1, counsel who are Registered Participants in the Court's ECF system who have appeared in the case or adversary proceeding will receive a Notice of Electronic Filing of the order. Accordingly, the court service list at the end of orders **shall only** include the names of counsel and/or parties who are not registered CM/ECF Participants in the case or proceeding. (To view a list of Registered Participants in a particular case or adversary proceeding, go to UTILITIES in ECF; click on "Mailings . . ."; click on "Mailing Info for a Case No."; insert the case number; then click SUBMIT. The list shall include counsel and/or parties who are currently registered participants and who will receive e-mail notice/service for the particular case or adversary proceeding.

In addition, the names on the court service list **shall be** alphabetized by **first name**. In cases where the court service list contains more than fifty names, the court will not serve the order. Rather, promptly upon entry of the order, counsel must serve the signed order and thereafter file a proof of service with the court.

D. *Guidelines for Payment of Attorney's Fees in Chapter 13 Cases*

GUIDELINES FOR PAYMENT OF ATTORNEY'S FEES IN CHAPTER 13 CASES

The following guidelines determine presumptively reasonable fees for Chapter 13 cases, describe simplified procedures for seeking such fees, and determine the manner in which the Chapter 13 Trustee will disburse approved fees.

This court has issued guidelines regarding the "Rights and Responsibilities of Chapter 13 Debtors and Their Attorneys." Parts I and II of those guidelines describe certain legal services that an attorney agrees to perform for the attorney's clients (the Basic Services). Through these fee guidelines, the court determines the fees that an attorney may recover for performing the Basic Services (the Guideline Fees) and sets forth a simplified procedure for applying for Guideline Fees.

A. Fees & Fee Applications.

1. Counsel may receive an order approving fees and costs up to the amounts set forth in Paragraph 2 without filing a detailed application if:

    a. Counsel has filed and served the Chapter 13 Trustee with an executed copy of the current San Francisco Division "Rights and Responsibilities of Chapter 13 Debtors and Their Attorneys," copies of which are available on the Court's website;

    b. No objection to the requested fees has been made.

2. The maximum fee that can be approved through the procedure described in Paragraph 1 is:

$3,500 for the basic case; and an additional
$850 if the case involves real property claims;
$500 for each additional parcel of real property with an encumbrance of at least $10,000;
$700 if the case involves unfiled tax returns or objections to claims of taxing agencies;
$500 if the case involves vehicle loans or leases;
$1,500 if the case involves an operating business;
$300 if the Debtor has twenty-five or more creditors;
$800 if the case involves domestic support claims;
$300 if the case involves student loans;
$500 if case involves Motions to Extend Stay;
$600 if case involves Motions to Avoid Lien.

3. Additional flat fees for services rendered will be automatically approved upon application by counsel, without requiring the submission of time records and without a hearing, as follows:

    a. Plan modifications filed after one year from the petition date: $400

    b. Permission to sell or refinance real property (unless the order confirming the plan permits sale or refinance without an order of the court), or for one or more motions to avoid judicial lien(s):

i. Not requiring court hearing: $300

ii. Requiring court hearing: $450

c. New motions for relief from the automatic stay, excluding unopposed motions, filed after one year from the petition date:

i. Regarding personal property: $200

ii. Regarding real property: $350

d. Motions to dismiss, convert, or reconvert, excluding Chapter 13 Trustee's motions to dismiss regarding plan payments and also excluding unopposed motions: $450

e. Assistance with preparation of tax returns: $200

f. Motions for plan modifications filed by the Chapter 13 Trustee more than one year after the petition date based on trustee's review of post-confirmation income, excluding unopposed motions: $400

g. Chapter 13 Trustee's motions to dismiss regarding plan payments filed more than one year after the petition date, but only if counsel appears at the hearing, the motion is later withdrawn and the Debtor has not filed a motion to modify the plan: $200

4. The Guideline Fees set forth above in Paragraphs A.2 and 3 are viewed by the court as the maximum reasonable fees for Basic Services, and are intended to be the only allowed compensation for such services absent unexpected and unusual circumstances.

5. The simplified procedures for awarding fees in accordance with Paragraphs A.1, 2 and 3 will not be available for Chapter 13 debtor's counsel if:

a. An executed copy of the current San Francisco Division "Rights and Responsibilities of Chapter 13 Debtors and Their Attorneys" is not filed as of the date first set for the meeting of creditors under 11 U.S.C. § 341; or

b. A timely objection to the attorneys fees has been filed.

6. If counsel seeks fees for Basic Services in excess of the Guideline Fees, seeks fees for services other than Basic Services, chooses not to utilize these fee procedures, or if the simplified procedures are not available because of either of the conditions described in Paragraph 5, then:

(a) all fees including the retainer must be approved by the court following a hearing and proper application, whether or not the fees are payable through the Chapter 13 Trustee's Office and whether or not fees are paid for services in connection with the Chapter 13 case; and

(b) counsel must comply with Rules 2002 and 2016 of the Federal Rules of Bankruptcy Procedure, as well as the "Guidelines for Compensation and Expense Reimbursement of Professionals" adopted by the Bankruptcy Judges of the Northern District of California.

7. Counsel may request reimbursement of out-of-pocket court filing fees advanced, even if counsel elects to receive the automatic fees available in accordance with

Paragraph 2.

8. On its own motion or the motion of any party in interest, the court may order a hearing to review any fee, whether paid or unpaid.

B. Distribution of Funds in Chapter 13 Cases.

Payments shall be disbursed as set forth in the Model Plan effective January 01, 2009.

E. *Guidelines Regarding Residential Loan Modifications on Relief from Stay Motions and in Chapter 11 and Chapter 13 Plans*

GUIDELINES REGARDING RESIDENTIAL LOAN MODIFICATIONS ON RELIEF FROM STAY MOTIONS AND IN CHAPTER 11 AND CHAPTER 13 PLANS

(San Francisco and San Jose Divisions)

Introduction

The court has numerous Chapter 11 and 13 cases in which creditors holding first lien mortgage loans secured by borrower-occupied principal residences file motions for relief from stay and/or debtors have filed or will file applications to modify the terms of such home mortgage loans. Debtors in Chapter 7 frequently appeal to the court for extension of the automatic stay while they seek loan modifications without appreciating that the court can afford them little relief if the trustee does not oppose relief from stay.

The following are guidelines that are applicable to creditors filing such motions for relief from stay and for debtors who hope to modify their principal residence first lien mortgage loans by agreement with their first lien mortgage lender.[1] They do not apply to non-consensual modifications of secured creditors' liens.

NOTE: CREDITORS ARE NOT VIOLATING THE AUTOMATIC STAY WHEN THEY ARE NEGOTIATING LOAN MODIFICATIONS WITH DEBTORS IN BANKRUPTCY.

Motions for Relief from Stay (Chapter 11 or 13)

1. Creditors must state on the cover sheet accompanying their motion whether or not debtor(s) have requested a loan modification prior to bankruptcy and/or prior to the date the motion is filed.

2. If debtor(s) have made such a request, the creditor must also indicate on the cover sheet the status of the request (e.g., request pending, no decision yet; modification in trial period; denied in writing (attaching a copy of the denial), etc.).

3. If debtor(s) have not made a request for a loan modification prior to the date of filing the motion for relief from stay, but intend to do so, or have done so after that date and the creditor has not so indicated in its motion for relief from stay, then they should advise the court accordingly at the hearing on the motion for relief from stay. As one form of adequate protection, the court may set a deadline for the debtor(s) to file and serve on the creditor (and in Chapter 13, on the trustee) a declaration stating under penalty of perjury:(1) the date of such a request and to whom it was sent (attaching a true copy of any transmittal letter or cover sheet, without exhibits); (2) if known, the status of the request (e.g., request pending but no decision yet; modification in trial period; denied in writing, etc.); and (3) the amount that is

---

[1] While many loan modifications are under the Home Affordable Modification Program (HAMP), these guidelines apply to any program available to debtors seeking relief on their first lien mortgage loans. Under HAMP, eligible loans must have been originated prior to January 1, 2009, on which the unpaid principal balances do not exceed $729,750 for a single unit dwelling, $934,200 for 2 units, $1,129,250 for 3 units, and $1,403,400 for 4 units.

31% of the debtor(s)' monthly gross income as shown on Schedule I.

4. As additional adequate protection of the creditor's interest in the debtor(s)' principal residence pending consideration of the loan modification request by the creditor, the court will set an appropriate monthly payment amount, and in doing so may consider as adequate a monthly amount that is 31% of the debtor(s)' monthly gross income, with payments beginning in the month that follows the first hearing on the motion for relief from stay or at the end of the contractual grace period in the month that follows after the motion was filed.

5. The court's adequate protection order will normally provide that if the creditor in its sole discretion denies the loan modification request in writing provided to debtor(s) and counsel, if any, either (1) the adequate protection payments will revert to the amount provided in the loan documents in the next calendar month after the denial or (2) the creditor will be permitted to restore the matter to calendar on ten (10) days notice.

Motions for Relief from Stay (Chapter 7)

6. Chapter 7 does not provide a debtor rights greater than those available under non-bankruptcy law to cure a default on secured debt or otherwise to modify the terms of secured debt. Chapter 7 offers debtor only a discharge of unsecured debt. Accordingly, the court will almost always grant relief from stay to the holder of secured debt in a chapter 7 case unless the trustee objects on some basis, such as that the collateral should be sold by trustee for the benefit of all creditors. Because Chapter 7 does not permit the debtor to alter the terms of secured debt without the consent of the lender, and because none of the loan modification programs currently in effect give the debtor any legal right to have a loan modified, the court will normally not deny or delay relief from stay in a chapter 7 case on the basis that a loan modification application is pending.

Chapter 11 and 13 Plans

7. If the debtor(s)' Chapter 13 plan is premised upon a modification of a first mortgage loan secured by the principal residence, no later than the § 341 meeting of creditors debtor(s) must file and serve on the Chapter 13 trustee a declaration stating under penalty of perjury: (1) the date of such a request, to whom it was sent (attaching a true copy of any transmittal letter or cover sheet, without exhibits); (2) if known, the status of the request (e.g., request pending but no decision yet; modification in trial period; denied in writing, etc.); and (3) the present (unmodified) balances and total monthly payments on all claims secured by the debtor(s)' principal residence.

8. For a Chapter 11 plan premised upon a modification of a first mortgage loan secured by the debtor(s)' principal residence, the same information required in ¶ 7 for a Chapter 13 case should be included in the debtor(s)' disclosure statement.

9. No plan referred to in ¶¶ 7 and 8 that proposes the loan modification payment terms for treatment of the first lien mortgage creditor's claim will be confirmed until the modification has been approved by the first mortgage lender, with proof of such approval provided to the Chapter 13 trustee, where applicable, or to the court in a Chapter 11 case.

10. Notwithstanding paragraph 9, the court may confirm a plan while a loan modification request is pending, if the language of the plan provides clearly that plan payment terms in

conformity with a not-yet-approved loan modification request shall by the terms of the plan itself revert to the terms provided in the operative loan documents if the loan modification request is denied. If a loan modification request remains pending when all other plan payments have been made, the case may be closed without a discharge.

SF & SJ Loan Modification Guidelines
(Effective December 1, 2010)

F. *Open Calendar Procedure*

OPEN CALENDAR PROCEDURE

The San Francisco Division will now permit counsel to utilize an Open Calendar Procedure for the scheduling of certain matters. This procedure will allow counsel to self-select an available date and time on the appropriate San Francisco division judge's calendar and serve notice of that date and time without first having to obtain the date and time from the calendar clerk.

The Open Calendar Procedure will operate as follows:

1. Types of proceedings that may be set in accordance with the Open Calendar Procedure:
   - Law and Motion matters in adversary proceedings.
   - "Main case motions" such as sales of property free and clear of liens, motions to assume or reject executory contracts, and similar contested matters.
   - Relief from stay preliminary hearings.
   - Fee applications, except: in Chapter 7 cases, applications must be set on the calendar dates reserved for the particular case trustees; in Chapter 13 cases, applications must be set on the regular Chapter 13 calendar dates maintained by the Chapter 13 Trustee for the respective judge.
   - Status conferences on objections to claims and objections to exemptions.
   - United States Trustee motions to convert or dismiss Chapter 11 cases.
2. The Open Calendar Procedure will not be available for the following:
   - Trials in adversary proceedings.
   - Status conferences in adversary proceedings, except where a prior status conference was dropped from calendar.
   - Any matter requiring an order shortening time.
   - Temporary restraining orders.
   - Chapter 11 Plan confirmation or disclosure statement approval.
   - Matters set pursuant to an order to show cause.
   - Chapter 13 calendar matters (except fee applications).
3. Procedure

a. In order to utilize the Open Calendar Procedure, counsel should select an available date and time as shown on the appropriate attached list for the judge assigned the main case. The lists of available dates will be updated regularly and will be placed on bulletin boards in the clerk's office and outside of each judge's courtroom. The lists will also be posted on the court's Internet website at http://www.canb.uscourts.gov. The date selected must be no earlier than as required by applicable national or local rules, as nothing in this Open Calendar Procedure alters applicable time limits.

b. After selecting an available date and time, counsel should serve proper notice of the matter in accordance with applicable rules.

Note: If a motion for relief from stay is set by a party in accordance with this Open

Calendar Procedure more than thirty days after the date the motion is filed, the party will be deemed to waive the thirty day limitation of 11 U.S.C. § 362(e).

c. No later than **three** days after the service on other parties, counsel should file all appropriate papers with the court, including chambers copies. The chambers copies should be accompanied by a transmittal letter addressed specifically to the calendar clerk of the assigned judge, indicating that the particular hearing has been set pursuant to the San Francisco Division's Open Calendar Procedure.

d. Once a matter is set by the Open Calendar Procedure, continuances must be handled through the assigned judge's calendar clerk.

e. Counsel **must not** request that the calendar clerk call back to confirm that the matter has been placed on the calendar. Counsel desiring confirmation that a matter has been placed on the calendar by the Open Calendar Procedure may include an extra copy of the transmittal letter with a stamped self-addressed envelope for the calendar clerk to return. Alternatively, counsel should watch the published calendars in the local legal newspapers or posted outside the division's courtrooms. (In the near future the San Francisco Division hopes to place its calendar on the bankruptcy court's Internet site.)

f. Failure to comply with the foregoing Open Calendar Procedure will result in the matter not being placed on calendar.

Note: Occasionally there may be a need to reschedule matters that have been placed on the calendar in accordance with this Open Calendar Procedure. Typically this will be because of calendar congestion or unforeseen schedule changes. In those instances the judge's calendar clerk will contact the moving party as soon as possible so that a notice of a rescheduled hearing may be disseminated.

G. Order Establishing San Francisco Division Procedures for Chapter 13 Pre-Confirmation Adequate Protection Payments

IN THE UNITED STATES BANKRUPTCY COURT
FOR THE NORTHERN DISTRICT OF CALIFORNIA
San Francisco Division

ORDER ESTABLISHING SAN FRANCISCO DIVISION PROCEDURES FOR CHAPTER 13 PRE-CONFIRMATION ADEQUATE PROTECTION PAYMENTS

Unless the Court orders otherwise,

a. The provisions of Paragraph 2 of the Chapter 13 Model Plan for this division, entitled Pre-Confirmation Adequate Protection Payments, shall apply prior to confirmation in Chapter 13 cases filed on or after October 17, 2005.

b. The Debtor shall not reduce plan payments to the Trustee under §1326 (a)(l)(B) & (C) without entry of an order of the Court. A Creditor may file a motion requesting a change in the amount of the pre-confirmation payments. Until the Creditor's motion is resolved, the Chapter 13 Trustee shall continue to make the payments proposed to such creditor as set forth in the plan.

c. The Chapter 13 Trustee is authorized to pay pre-confirmation payments set forth in the proposed plan without entry of an Order by the Court. No payments shall be made to a Creditor until the proof of claim is filed. The Chapter 13 Trustee is authorized to deduct from an allowed claim, as of the date of each payment, the pre-confirmation payment paid to the Creditor.

d. Prior to confirmation, the Creditor shall receive from the Trustee any payments due and owing upon dismissal of the case, from funds collected by the Trustee, less statutory Trustee fees and Debtor's attorney fees.

Dated: January 5, 2006

THOMAS E. CARLSON
United States Bankruptcy Judge

Dated: January 5, 2006

DENNIS MONTALI
United States Bankruptcy Judge

H. *Order Regarding Model Chapter 13 Requirements*

IN THE UNITED STATES BANKRUPTCY COURT
FOR THE NORTHERN DISTRICT OF CALIFORNIA
San Francisco Division

ORDER RE MODEL CHAPTER 13 PLAN REQUIREMENTS

(1) Format Requirements:

The San Francisco Division requires all Chapter 13 debtors to file their Chapter 13 Plans using the Model Chapter 13 Plan available on the court's website, at the SF Division Office or the Office of the Chapter 13 Trustee.

Registered users in the Court's Electronic Case Filing (ECF) System must create the Model Chapter 13 Plan in a word processing application (Word or Wordperfect) and directly convert the plan to PDF Format. The document image size must not exceed 8.5 x 11 inches. A registered user is required to check the page size prior to attempting to upload the PDF into the ECF system. PDF files exceeding the page size limit must be modified before uploading the document (refer to the court's website).

Pro Se filers or attorneys who are exempt from mandatory ECF must submit the Model Chapter 13 Plan in hard copy in the court's approved form of the Model Chapter 13 Plan.

(2) Noticing Requirements:

If the Model Chapter 13 Plan ***is filed within 15 days*** from the filing of the petition, the Court will generate the *Notice of Chapter 13 Case, Meeting of Creditors, and Deadlines*, attach a copy of the plan, and transmit the notice to all creditors and parties in interest through the Court's Bankruptcy Noticing Center.

If the Model Chapter 13 Plan ***is not filed within 15 days*** from the filing of the petition, the Court will generate the *Notice of Chapter 13 Case, Meeting of Creditors, and Deadlines* without the Chapter 13 Plan. The attorney for the debtor(s) or pro se debtor(s) must transmit a copy of the Model Chapter 13 Plan to all creditors and parties in interest and file a Certificate of Service with the court.

Failure to comply with the requirements listed above may result in the Chapter 13 case being dismissed for non-compliance.

IT IS SO ORDERED.

Dated: October 10, 2006

THOMAS E. CARLSON
United States Bankruptcy Judge

DENNIS MONTALI
United States Bankruptcy Judge

I. *Order Regarding Reporting Income in Chapter 13 Cases*

IN THE UNITED STATES BANKRUPTCY COURT
FOR THE NORTHERN DISTRICT OF CALIFORNIA
San Francisco Division

ORDER RE REPORTING INCOME IN CHAPTER 13 CASES

(1) Chapter 13 debtors are hereby **excused from filing with the court** payment advices or other evidence of payment received by the debtor from any employer of the debtor within 60 days before the date of filing a Chapter 13 petition 11 U.S.C. § 521(a). Instead, Chapter 13 debtors are hereby ordered to file the applicable declaration(s) regarding income in the forms available on the court's or the Chapter 13 trustee's website at least seven days prior to the first date set for the meeting of creditors under 11 U.S.C. § 341. Copies of the applicable declaration(s) should be served on the Chapter 13 Trustee.

(2) Any debtor who does not provide the declaration(s) as required in paragraph (1) by the deadline stated above must file, prior to that deadline, a request of the court for an extension of time to do so.

(3) Failure to comply with paragraphs (1) or (2) may result in the case being dismissed following a hearing on a motion to dismiss filed by the Chapter 13 Trustee, the United States Trustee or any party in interest.

(4) This court's Order Re Payment Advices in Chapter 13 Cases dated September 26, 2006, is hereby abrogated.

IT IS SO ORDERED.

Dated: December 7, 2009

THOMAS E. CARLSON
United States Bankruptcy Judge

DENNIS MONTALI
United States Bankruptcy Judge

J. *Policy and Procedures for Appearances By Telephone*

IN THE UNITED STATES BANKRUPTCY COURT
FOR THE NORTHERN DISTRICT OF CALIFORNIA
San Francisco Division

POLICY AND PROCEDURES FOR APPEARANCES BY TELEPHONE
Judge Thomas Carlson
Judge Dennis Montali

The following procedures apply in the San Francisco Division for telephone appearances by counsel or parties appearing in propria persona:

1. Permitted Appearances.

In general, telephonic appearances are permitted except in situations where the party or counsel:

will be examining witnesses;
is the proponent of a chapter 11 disclosure statement or plan;
is counsel for a client who is present in court; or
is directed by the court to appear personally.

There are no restrictions on eligibility to appear by telephone based upon the geographic location of the counsel or the party. **The Court does not require advance permission for telephonic appearances.**

2. Procedure for Arranging for Telephonic Appearances.

Telephonic appearances are arranged through CourtCall. All parties/counsel using this service **must have an account or make arrangements to set one up well in advance of the hearing.**

Appearances are arranged by reservation. To make a reservation, a participant should call **1-866-582-6878** no later than **4:00 p.m. PT the day before the appearance.** (Failure to make a reservation no later than 4:00 PM the day before the hearing may result in the inability of CourtCall to arrange for the appearance.) Note however, CourtCall will not process telephonic appearances unless an account has been set up. The coordinator will need:

court date and time;
name of judge;
case name and number;
name and phone number of the attorney appearing;
verification that a CourtCall account has been set up.

After scheduling a reservation, attorneys will receive a confirmation, either by fax or e-mail, providing the party with dial-in information and telephonic instructions. Attorneys are required to notify CourtCall of any appearance substitutions.

Telephonic appearances are connected directly with the courtroom's public address system and electronic recording equipment so that a normal record is produced. To ensure a quality record, the court prohibits the use of car phones, cellular phones, public telephone booths, or phones in other public places except in emergencies or unless the presiding judge has consented. Participants should be able to hear all parties without difficulty or echo.

At the time of the hearing, a participant may initially be able to hear the matter(s) preceding his or her case. After a call is connected to the courtroom, the courtroom deputy will call the case. The presiding judge will ask for appearances and direct the manner in which the hearing proceeds. Each time a participant speaks, he or she should identify himself or herself for the record. The court's teleconferencing system allows more than one speaker to be heard so that the judge can interrupt a speaker to ask a question or redirect the discussion. When the judge informs the participants that the hearing is completed, the participants may disconnect and the next case will be called.

Failure to comply with these procedures may result in the imposition of sanctions. Sanctions may include dropping the matter from the calendar, continuing the hearing, proceeding in the absence of an unavailable participant, a monetary sanction, or a temporary or permanent prohibition against a person/firm appearing telephonically.

When the court conducts a telephone conference on short notice and uses CourtCall, it may designate one party to bear the entire cost of the conference call. The court may on occasion initiate calls to one or two persons directly without use of a conference operator. In those instances, the courtroom deputy will contact parties to inform them of the arrangements.

Because the courtroom deputy is usually in court prior to the initiation of any particular call, last minute changes are generally impossible to handle and are discouraged.

Judge Carlson's Courtroom Deputy is Mr. Gordon Hom (415-268-2362 or Gordon_Hom@canb.uscourts.gov). Judge Montali's Courtroom Deputy is Ms. Lorena Parada (415-268-2323 or Lorena_Parada@canb.uscourts.gov).

Revised January 27, 2011

K. Policy for Chamber Copies of ECF Filed Documents

IN THE UNITED STATES BANKRUPTCY COURT
FOR THE NORTHERN DISTRICT OF CALIFORNIA
San Francisco Division

POLICY FOR CHAMBER COPIES OF ECF FILED DOCUMENTS

The following are the San Francisco Division's requirements for submission of courtesy "Chambers Copies" of papers filed through the court's Electronic Case Filing ("ECF") system. All copies must be:

- Delivered to the Division's intake desk promptly after the papers have been filed electronically and
- Marked "Chambers Copy."

Adversary Proceedings

Chambers Copies Required: All papers relating to scheduled future hearings, (e.g., a noticed motion to dismiss a complaint, summary judgment motion) other than the initial status conference and attachments to supporting declarations. For trials, pre-trial and post-trial briefs.

Chambers Copies Not Required: Status conference statements; trial exhibit lists or witness designations.

Contested Matters

Chambers Copies Required: All papers relating to future hearings scheduled with the initial filing, whether or not there is a designated respondent (e.g., motion to assume an executory contract; debtor's motion to dismiss case)other than attachments to supporting declarations. Chapter 11 Plans, Chapter 11 Disclosure Statements, and related notices should be provided when the matters have been set for hearing.

All papers relating to hearings scheduled after hearing requested (see below).

Even though there may be no opposition:

- Fee Applications
- Cash Collateral Stipulations and Motions; Borrowing Motions;
- First Day Orders pertaining to bonuses, severance and retention plans, payroll and utilities
- Objections to any of the above.

Chambers Copies Not Required: Matters initiated under B.L.R 9014-1 "scream or die" procedures. If a party requests a hearing, (e.g., on objection to claim; motion to sell, etc.) the party setting the hearing must provide Courtesy Copies of the moving papers and any oppositon papers.

Motions for Relief From Stay

Chambers Copies Required: Opposition to motions or replies to oppositions.

Chambers Copies Not Required: Motions for relief from stay.

L. Rights and Responsibilities of Chapter 13 Debtors and Their Attorneys

RIGHTS AND RESPONSIBILITIES OF CHAPTER 13 DEBTORS AND THEIR ATTORNEYS

It is important for debtors who file a bankruptcy case under Chapter 13 to understand their rights and responsibilities. It is also important that the debtors know what their attorney's responsibilities are, and understand the importance of communicating with their attorney to make the case successful. Debtors should also know that they may expect certain services to be performed by their attorney. In order to assure that debtors and their attorney understand their rights and responsibilities in the bankruptcy process, the following guidelines provided by the court are hereby agreed to by the debtors and their attorneys. Unless the Court orders otherwise,

I. BEFORE THE CASE IS FILED

A. The debtor agrees to:

1. Provide the attorney with accurate financial information concerning income and expenses, and assets and liabilities.

2. Discuss with the attorney the debtor's objectives in filing the case.

B. The attorney agrees to perform the following "Basic Services":

1. Meet with the debtor to review the debtor's assets, liabilities, income, and expenses.

2. Counsel the debtor regarding the advisability of filing either a Chapter 7 or Chapter 13 case, discuss both procedures with the debtor, and answer the debtor's questions.

3. Advise the debtor of the requirement (and procedures involved) for obtaining a credit counseling certificate and completing the debtor education course.

4. Advise the debtor of the requirement for providing documentation on income and tax return filings.

5. Explain what payments will be made directly by the debtor and what payments will be made through the debtor's Chapter 13 plan, with particular attention to mortgage and vehicle loan payments, as well as any other claims which accrue interest.

6. Explain to the debtor how, when, and where to make the Chapter 13 plan payments.

7. Explain to the debtor how the attorney's fees and trustee's fees are paid and provide an executed copy of this document to the debtor.

8. Explain to the debtor that the first plan payment must be made to the Chapter 13 Trustee within 30 days of the date the plan is filed.

9. Advise the debtor of the requirement to attend the 341 Meeting of

Creditors, and instruct the debtor as to the date, time and place of the meeting.

10. Advise the debtor of the necessity of maintaining liability, collision and comprehensive insurance on vehicles securing loans or leases.

11. Timely prepare and file the debtor's petition, plan, statements and schedules.

II. AFTER THE CASE IS FILED

A. *The debtor agrees to:*

1. Keep the Chapter 13 Trustee and attorney informed of the debtor's address and telephone number.

2. Inform the attorney of any wage garnishments or attachments of assets which occur or continue after the filing of the case.

3. Contact the attorney promptly if the debtor loses his/her job or has other financial problems.

4. Let the attorney know if the debtor is sued during the case.

5. Inform the attorney if any tax refunds the debtor is entitled to are seized or not returned to the debtor by the IRS or Franchise Tax Board.

6. Contact the attorney before buying, refinancing, or selling real property or before entering into any long-term loan agreements, to find out what approvals are required.

7. Pay directly to the attorney any filing fees and expenses that may be incurred.

B. *The attorney agrees to provide the following "Basic Services":*

1. Appear at the 341 Meeting of Creditors with the debtor.

2. Respond to objections to plan confirmation, and where necessary, prepare an amended plan.

3. Prepare, file, and serve necessary modifications to the plan which may include suspending, lowering, or increasing plan payments.

4. Prepare, file, and serve necessary amended statements and schedules, in accordance with information provided by the debtor.

5. Prepare, file, and serve necessary motions to sell or refinance real property when appropriate.

6. Object to improper or invalid claims, if necessary, based upon documentation provided by the debtor.

7. Represent the debtor in motions for relief from stay.

8. Represent the debtor in motions to dismiss or convert.

9. Where appropriate, prepare, file, and serve necessary motions to avoid liens on real or personal property.

10. Review annual reports received from the Chapter 13 Trustee.

11. Monitor debtors' submission of annual tax returns to Chapter 13 Trustee.

12. Respond to continuing creditor inquiries.

13. Maintain contact with debtors regarding changes in financial situations during Chapter 13 case.

14. Assist with and ensure debtor's submission of appropriate declarations and other requirements for obtaining discharge.

15. Provide such other legal services as are necessary for the administration of the present case before the Bankruptcy Court..

III. GUIDELINE FEES

The "Guidelines for Payment of Attorney's Fees in Chapter 13 Cases" for the San Francisco Division provide for maximum initial fees in the following amounts:

$3,500 for the basic case; and an additional
$850 if the case involves real property claims;
$500 for each additional parcel of real property with an encumbrance of at least $10,000;
$700 if the case involves unfiled tax returns or objections to claims of taxing agencies;
$500 if the case involves vehicle loans or leases;
$1,500 if the case involves an operating business;
$300 if the Debtor has twenty-five or more creditors;
$800 if the case involves domestic support claims;
$300 if the case involves student loans;
$500 if case involves Motions to Extend Stay;
$600 if case involves Motions to Avoid Lien.

Additional flat fees for services rendered will be automatically approved upon application by counsel, without requiring the submission of time records and without a hearing, as follows:

a. Plan modifications filed after one year from the petition date: $400

b. Permission to sell or refinance real property (unless the order confirming the plan permits sale or refinance without an order of the court), or for one or more motions to avoid judicial lien(s):

i. Not requiring court hearing: $300

ii. Requiring court hearing: $450

c. New motions for relief from the automatic stay, excluding unopposed motions, filed after one year from the petition date:

i. Regarding personal property: $200

ii. Regarding real property: $350

d. Motions to dismiss, convert, or reconvert, excluding Chapter 13 Trustee's motions to dismiss regarding plan payments and also excluding unopposed motions: $450

e. Assistance with preparation of tax returns: $200

f. Motions for plan modifications filed by the Chapter 13 Trustee more than one year after the petition date based on trustee's review of post-confirmation income, excluding unopposed motions: $400

g. Chapter 13 Trustee's motions to dismiss regarding plan payments filed more than one year after the petition date, but only if counsel appears at the hearing, the motion is later withdrawn and the Debtor has not filed a motion to modify the plan: $200

IV. ADDITIONAL FEES

Absent unexpected and unusual circumstances, the Guideline Fees described in Part III are intended to be the only allowed compensation for all those services the attorney agrees to perform under Parts I and II, above. An attorney who seeks fees in excess of the Guideline Fees agrees to apply to the court for approval of such fees and costs, attaching a supporting declaration (with time records) justifying that those fees and costs are merited and have not been compensated through the amounts previously ordered. Reimbursement of advanced court fees shall be awarded independently of other fees and costs. Fees shall be paid through the plan unless otherwise ordered. The attorney may not receive fees directly from the debtor other than the initial retainer.

If the debtor disputes the legal services provided or the fees charged by the attorney, an objection may be filed with the court and the matter set for hearing. The attorney may move to withdraw, or the client may discharge the attorney, at any time.

Dated: ________________ ________________________
Debtor

Dated: ________________ ________________________
Debtor

Dated: ________________ ________________________
Attorney for Debtor(s)

M. *San Francisco Digital Audio Announcement*

SAN FRANCISCO DIGITAL AUDIO ANNOUNCEMENT

Effective June 27, 2011, the San Francisco Division will create digital audio recordings of certain court proceedings and make those recordings available to the public through the Case Management Electronic Case Filing (CM/ECF) System. Unless otherwise ordered, recordings of the following types of hearings will be available: Law and Motion Hearings; Chapter 11 Status Conference and Chapter 11 Disclosure Statement Hearings; Formal Pretrial Conferences; Discovery Hearings and Conferences; or any other hearing the judge presiding may specify. Prior to the commencement of any other type of hearing, any party may ask the judge presiding to order that a recording of the hearing be made available via CM/ECF.

San Jose Division

III. San Jose Division

A. Changes to San Jose Division's Filing Procedure for Adversary Proceedings

Effective August 1, 2005, the San Jose Division will require a statement of the ***complete name(s) and address(es) for all defendant(s) when opening a new adversary proceeding***.

Specifically, when an adversary proceeding is filed, the attorney will search the database in order to eliminate duplicate records in the system. If the name and address of the defendant appears and is exactly the same, the information can be accepted for that party. If the party is not already in the database, the attorney would enter the Name and Address information in the appropriate boxes for the party defendant who is being added. The name of each party who is a defendant in the case along with their mailing address must be entered. If the address is not entered at the time the complaint is filed, the court will send notification of an error by the filing party.

If you have any questions regarding this issue, you may contact the **San Jose Help Desk at 408-278-7500**.

B. Chapter 13 Calendar Procedures

IN THE UNITED STATES BANKRUPTCY COURT
FOR THE NORTHERN DISTRICT OF CALIFORNIA
San Jose Division

CHAPTER 13 CALENDAR PROCEDURES
Effective August 1, 2011

INTRODUCTION

These procedures are being established to improve the processing of chapter 13 cases in the San Jose Division and are intended (1) to facilitate the timely resolution of Chapter 13 cases, (2) to reduce time spent by counsel and the court on Chapter 13 cases, and (3) to provide access to the court for parties who need judicial intervention. In general, these procedures provide that Chapter 13 cases ready for confirmation will be confirmed expeditiously. Debtor(s) whose cases require further work will have time to complete that work and will have judicial assistance when appropriate. Cases not eligible for Chapter 13 or not making appropriate progress in Chapter 13 will be subject to dismissal.

CHAPTER 13 UNCONTESTED CONFIRMATION CALENDAR

When a Chapter 13 case is filed, the § 341(a) notice will include the date and time of the confirmation hearing and will state that the deadline for objections to a Chapter 13 plan is the same date as the first set § 341(a) meeting (see B.L.R. 3015-1(b)(3)). The confirmation hearing will be set on a Chapter 13 Uncontested Confirmation Calendar ("Uncontested Confirmation Calendar"). Absent timely objection and upon finding that the requirements of § 1325(a) are satisfied, the court will confirm the plan at the confirmation hearing. Cases will be considered ready for confirmation when (1) the § 341(a) meeting of creditors has concluded; (2) no objections to confirmation have been filed, or such objections have been resolved or withdrawn without judicial intervention; (3) payments under the proposed plan are current; and (4) there are no other unresolved deficiencies.

CASES NOT READY FOR CONFIRMATION:
PROCEDURES AND THE TRUSTEE'S PENDING LIST

For cases that are not ready for confirmation, ten (10) days before the date originally set for confirmation, the Trustee shall file a Statement of Non-Readiness for Confirmation, which will place the case on the Trustee's Pending List ("TPL"). When the Trustee dockets the Statement of Non-Readiness for Confirmation, the court's ECF system will automatically generate these notices:

1. A text entry reporting that (1) the case has been added to the Trustee's Pending List, and (2) parties in interest need not attend the first date set for the confirmation hearing, the plan will not be confirmed at that time, and the case will be taken off calendar at the hearing;

2. A Notice of Electronic Filing (the "NEF") notifying ECF Registered Users of the information in paragraph 1.

The NEF will provide instructions for restoring a case to the confirmation calendar.

A case can be restored to the confirmation calendar as follows: (1) the Trustee may file a Statement of Resolution, placing the matter back on the Uncontested Confirmation Calendar, or (2) a party in interest (debtor(s) or other party in interest) may file a Notice of Hearing, placing the case on a Chapter 13 Contested Confirmation Calendar in conformity with the procedures set forth below; and

3. A written notice of the foregoing information to pro se debtor(s) and non-ECF Registered Users.

At the scheduled confirmation hearing, the court will announce the case has been placed on the TPL. All cases on the TPL will be identified on a list which will be posted on the court's website. Cases will remain on the TPL until confirmation, dismissal, or conversion.

It will be the Trustee's duty to monitor and track the progress of the cases on the TPL. While cases are on the TPL, the parties should meet and confer and work toward resolution of the cases. The goal is to ensure that every case capable of being confirmed is returned to the Uncontested Confirmation Calendar as soon as possible.

RESTORING CASES TO UNCONTESTED CONFIRMATION CALENDAR

The Trustee should recommend confirmation when all deficiencies have been cured, outstanding objections have been resolved, and payments are current. When this occurs, the Trustee shall file a Trustee's Statement of Resolution. The court will generate and serve a Notice of Hearing, restoring the confirmation hearing to the next available Uncontested Confirmation Calendar. The court will give notice to the debtor(s), debtor(s)' counsel, the Trustee, other parties that have objected to the plan, and parties requesting special notice. The Notice of Hearing will automatically generate a Notice of Electronic Filing alerting ECF Registered Users of the restored confirmation hearing and a written notice to unrepresented debtor(s), other unrepresented parties, and non-ECF Registered Users of the same.

CHAPTER 13 CONTESTED CONFIRMATION CALENDAR

In some cases, the parties will need access to the court to resolve factual or legal issues pertaining to the Chapter 13 case, such as feasibility, disposable income, and eligibility matters. In these situations, a party may set such matters on the Chapter 13 Contested Confirmation Calendar ("Contested Confirmation Calendar"). However, parties may set a matter on the Contested Confirmation Calendar only if these three conditions are satisfied:

- The § 341(a) meeting has been concluded;
- The parties have met and conferred in good faith (in person or by telephone) but cannot resolve their dispute; and
- The parties are ready to submit the dispute for resolution by the court or to have the matter set for trial, evidentiary hearing, or briefing.

To set a matter on the Contested Confirmation Calendar, parties should follow the same rules that apply to any motion in a bankruptcy case as provided by B.L.R. 9014-1(a). Matters may be set for hearing on any available Contested Confirmation Calendar date. Parties are urged to consult the court's website to obtain available dates. To set a matter, the moving party should file and serve a Notice of Hearing and Certificate of Service on twenty-eight (28) days' notice to parties in interest (generally, debtor(s), debtor(s)' counsel, the Trustee, parties that have objected to the plan, and parties requesting special notice). Responses and objections are governed by B.L.R. 9014-1(c). The court expects that the Contested Confirmation Calendar will consist only of matters ready for judicial resolution or status conference.

In addition, any party setting a matter on the Contested Confirmation Calendar must file a Chapter 13 Status Conference Statement at least fourteen (14) days before an actual hearing. The Chapter 13 Status Conference Statement shall indicate: (1) the unresolved disputed factual and legal issues that require judicial determination; (2) the time estimate for trial or argument and the proposed trial and/or briefing dates; and (3) the date and time of the conference between the parties.

If the noticing party does not timely file a Chapter 13 Status Conference Statement, the matter will be stricken from the Contested Confirmation Calendar and an appropriate notice will be docketed by the court. If a matter is stricken from the Contested Confirmation Calendar, it must be re-noticed for hearing with a new Notice of Hearing, Certificate of Service, and Chapter 13 Status Conference Statement.

When multiple objections to confirmation are pending in a case, one party's Notice of Hearing will place only the noticed objection on the Contested Confirmation Calendar. At the court's discretion, however, any objection filed by the Trustee may be heard at the same time. The court retains discretion pursuant to Fed. R. Bankr. P. 7042 to consolidate or sever multiple objections for hearing as appropriate.

CHAPTER 13 MOTIONS

In some cases, the parties will need access to the court to resolve factual or legal issues which are not Chapter 13 plan driven, such as motions to value, fee applications, and claims objections. These matters also should be set on the Chapter 13 Motions Calendar. To set non-plan related matters on the Chapter 13 Motions Calendar, parties should follow the same rules that apply to any motion in a bankruptcy case, under B.L.R. 9014-1(a). Matters may be set for hearing on any available Chapter 13 Motions Calendar date. Parties are urged to consult the court's website to obtain an available date. To set a matter, the moving party should file and serve a Notice of Hearing and Certificate of Service to any party affected by the motion. Responses and objections are governed by B.L.R. 9014-1.

Parties are encouraged to use the "notice and opportunity for hearing" procedure available under B.L.R. 9014-1(b)(3) to obtain an order by default if no objection is raised. If an objection is raised, the parties shall notice it for hearing as indicated above.

TRUSTEE'S MOTIONS TO DISMISS

The court will no longer conduct pre-hearing conferences on objections to confirmation in cases on the TPL simply to monitor the debtor(s)' progress in fulfilling the debtor(s)' obligations. Instead, if outstanding issues are not resolved and deficiencies are not cured on a timely basis, the case may become subject to a Motion to Dismiss by the Trustee. The Trustee will exercise her discretion in bringing such motions, but she is expected to afford the debtor(s) a reasonable period of time to bring a case to confirmation.

Pre-confirmation Motions to Dismiss

When making a motion to dismiss, the Trustee is encouraged to use the "notice and opportunity for hearing" procedure available under B.L.R. 9014-1(b)(3). In cases assigned to Judge Weissbrodt, motions to dismiss the chapter 13 cases of pro per debtor(s) should be set for hearing on the Chapter 13 Motions Calendar. In those cases where the debtor(s)' attorney fails to provide timely responses to the Trustee's requests or otherwise is responsible for unreasonable delay, the Motion to Dismiss may include a request for disgorgement of the attorney's retainer. Responses and objections are governed by B.L.R. 9014-1(c). The court may issue default orders dismissing the case pre-confirmation and dealing with disgorgement as appropriate, per B.L.R. 9014-1(b)(4). If a request for hearing is made, pre-confirmation motions to dismiss should be placed on a Chapter 13 Motions Calendar.

Counsel and debtor(s) should take special notice that the court will carefully review any response to a motion to dismiss brought by the Trustee. To avoid dismissal, debtor(s) must provide detailed information explaining why the Chapter 13 plan has not been confirmed, addressing, in particular, the debtor(s)' efforts to comply with the requirements of the Bankruptcy Code and the Trustee's requests, and why the delay in the case is not prejudicial to creditors under 11 U.S.C. § 1307(c). The debtor(s) should not expect that last-minute compliance will cause the Trustee to withdraw the motion or continue the hearing, or the court to deny the motion or continue the hearing. Untimely opposition to a motion to dismiss may not be considered. Cases may be dismissed on default.

Post-confirmation Motions to Dismiss

Upon the debtor(s)' failure to tender a plan payment to the Trustee (or otherwise comply with any other plan provision) in a timely manner, the Trustee may serve written notice of default on the debtor(s) and debtor(s)' counsel. Within twenty (20) days of the notice of default, the debtor(s) shall: (1) cure the default; (2) meet and confer with the Trustee and enter into an agreement resolving the default on terms acceptable to the Trustee; or (3) file and serve an Application to Modify Plan that proposes terms under which the plan is not in default and provides for plan completion within sixty (60) months of the date the first plan payment was due. Absent timely compliance by the debtor(s) with any of the foregoing, the court likely will issue a dismissal order upon application of the Trustee supported by a declaration.

A post-confirmation Motion to Dismiss based upon grounds other than a material default by the debtor(s) with respect to a confirmed plan should be filed using the notice and opportunity for a hearing procedure of B.L.R. 9014-1(b)(3). In cases assigned to Judge Weissbrodt, motions to dismiss the chapter 13 cases of pro per debtor(s) should be set for hearing on the Chapter 13 Motions Calendar. Absent a timely objection or request for a hearing, the Trustee may request the entry of a post-confirmation dismissal order by default. An actual hearing on a post-confirmation Motion to Dismiss should be noticed for the Chapter 13 Motions Calendar.

C. Disbursement of Funds in Chapter 13 Cases

IN THE UNITED STATES BANKRUPTCY COURT
FOR THE NORTHERN DISTRICT OF CALIFORNIA
San Jose Division

DISBURSEMENT OF FUNDS IN CHAPTER 13 CASES

In all Chapter 13 cases assigned to the undersigned Judge, disbursement of funds shall be in the following order:

1. To creditors specified in the plan to receive adequate protection payments in the amounts specified in the plan as adequate protection.

2. After disbursement for adequate protection payments, funds shall be disbursed in the order prescribed by the Bankruptcy Code.

IT IS SO ORDERED.

Dated: 10-15-2010

____
CHARLES NOVACK
United States Bankruptcy Judge

____
STEPHEN L. JOHNSON
United States Bankruptcy Judge

D. *Guidelines Regarding Residential Loan Modifications on Relief from Stay Motions and in Chapter 11 and Chapter 13 Plans*

GUIDELINES REGARDING RESIDENTIAL LOAN MODIFICATIONS ON RELIEF FROM STAY MOTIONS AND IN CHAPTER 11 AND CHAPTER 13 PLANS

(San Francisco and San Jose Divisions)

Introduction

The court has numerous Chapter 11 and 13 cases in which creditors holding first lien mortgage loans secured by borrower-occupied principal residences file motions for relief from stay and/or debtors have filed or will file applications to modify the terms of such home mortgage loans. Debtors in Chapter 7 frequently appeal to the court for extension of the automatic stay while they seek loan modifications without appreciating that the court can afford them little relief if the trustee does not oppose relief from stay.

The following are guidelines that are applicable to creditors filing such motions for relief from stay and for debtors who hope to modify their principal residence first lien mortgage loans by agreement with their first lien mortgage lender.[1] They do not apply to non-consensual modifications of secured creditors' liens.

NOTE: CREDITORS ARE NOT VIOLATING THE AUTOMATIC STAY WHEN THEY ARE NEGOTIATING LOAN MODIFICATIONS WITH DEBTORS IN BANKRUPTCY.

Motions for Relief from Stay (Chapter 11 or 13)

1. Creditors must state on the cover sheet accompanying their motion whether or not debtor(s) have requested a loan modification prior to bankruptcy and/or prior to the date the motion is filed.

2. If debtor(s) have made such a request, the creditor must also indicate on the cover sheet the status of the request (e.g., request pending, no decision yet; modification in trial period; denied in writing (attaching a copy of the denial), etc.).

3. If debtor(s) have not made a request for a loan modification prior to the date of filing the motion for relief from stay, but intend to do so, or have done so after that date and the creditor has not so indicated in its motion for relief from stay, then they should advise the court accordingly at the hearing on the motion for relief from stay. As one form of adequate protection, the court may set a deadline for the debtor(s) to file and serve on the creditor (and in Chapter 13, on the trustee) a declaration stating under penalty of perjury:(1) the date of such a request and to whom it was sent (attaching a true copy of any transmittal letter or cover sheet, without exhibits); (2) if known, the status of the request (e.g., request pending but no decision yet; modification in trial period; denied in writing, etc.); and (3) the amount that is

[1] While many loan modifications are under the Home Affordable Modification Program (HAMP), these guidelines apply to any program available to debtors seeking relief on their first lien mortgage loans. Under HAMP, eligible loans must have been originated prior to January 1, 2009, on which the unpaid principal balances do not exceed $729,750 for a single unit dwelling, $934,200 for 2 units, $1,129,250 for 3 units, and $1,403,400 for 4 units.

31% of the debtor(s)' monthly gross income as shown on Schedule I.

4. As additional adequate protection of the creditor's interest in the debtor(s)' principal residence pending consideration of the loan modification request by the creditor, the court will set an appropriate monthly payment amount, and in doing so may consider as adequate a monthly amount that is 31% of the debtor(s)' monthly gross income, with payments beginning in the month that follows the first hearing on the motion for relief from stay or at the end of the contractual grace period in the month that follows after the motion was filed.

5. The court's adequate protection order will normally provide that if the creditor in its sole discretion denies the loan modification request in writing provided to debtor(s) and counsel, if any, either (1) the adequate protection payments will revert to the amount provided in the loan documents in the next calendar month after the denial or (2) the creditor will be permitted to restore the matter to calendar on ten (10) days notice.

Motions for Relief from Stay (Chapter 7)

6. Chapter 7 does not provide a debtor rights greater than those available under non-bankruptcy law to cure a default on secured debt or otherwise to modify the terms of secured debt. Chapter 7 offers debtor only a discharge of unsecured debt. Accordingly, the court will almost always grant relief from stay to the holder of secured debt in a chapter 7 case unless the trustee objects on some basis, such as that the collateral should be sold by trustee for the benefit of all creditors. Because Chapter 7 does not permit the debtor to alter the terms of secured debt without the consent of the lender, and because none of the loan modification programs currently in effect give the debtor any legal right to have a loan modified, the court will normally not deny or delay relief from stay in a chapter 7 case on the basis that a loan modification application is pending.

Chapter 11 and 13 Plans

7. If the debtor(s)' Chapter 13 plan is premised upon a modification of a first mortgage loan secured by the principal residence, no later than the § 341 meeting of creditors debtor(s) must file and serve on the Chapter 13 trustee a declaration stating under penalty of perjury: (1) the date of such a request, to whom it was sent (attaching a true copy of any transmittal letter or cover sheet, without exhibits); (2) if known, the status of the request (e.g., request pending but no decision yet; modification in trial period; denied in writing, etc.); and (3) the present (unmodified) balances and total monthly payments on all claims secured by the debtor(s)' principal residence.

8. For a Chapter 11 plan premised upon a modification of a first mortgage loan secured by the debtor(s)' principal residence, the same information required in ¶ 7 for a Chapter 13 case should be included in the debtor(s)' disclosure statement.

9. No plan referred to in ¶¶ 7 and 8 that proposes the loan modification payment terms for treatment of the first lien mortgage creditor's claim will be confirmed until the modification has been approved by the first mortgage lender, with proof of such approval provided to the Chapter 13 trustee, where applicable, or to the court in a Chapter 11 case.

10. Notwithstanding paragraph 9, the court may confirm a plan while a loan modification request is pending, if the language of the plan provides clearly that plan payment terms in

conformity with a not-yet-approved loan modification request shall by the terms of the plan itself revert to the terms provided in the operative loan documents if the loan modification request is denied. If a loan modification request remains pending when all other plan payments have been made, the case may be closed without a discharge.

SF & SJ Loan Modification Guidelines
(Effective December 1, 2010)

E. Notice of Procedures to Restore to Confirmation Calendar

NOTICE OF PROCEDURES TO RESTORE TO CONFIRMATION CALENDAR

Based on the Trustee's Statement of Non-Readiness for Confirmation, this case is hereby placed on the Trustee's Pending List ("TPL") pursuant to the Chapter 13 Calendar Procedures for the San Jose Division, which may be found at http://www.canb.uscourts.gov/procedures/sj. Parties in interest do not need to attend the scheduled confirmation hearing since the plan will not be confirmed, and the case will be taken off calendar at that time.

Procedures to Restore to Uncontested Confirmation Calendar

While on the TPL, the case may be restored at the appropriate time to either the Uncontested Confirmation Calendar or the Contested Confirmation Calendar for disposition by the court. To restore the matter to the Uncontested Confirmation Calendar, the Trustee will file a Trustee's Statement of Resolution when all outstanding objections are resolved, deficiencies have been cured, and the debtor(s) is current on plan payments. The Trustee's docketing of the Statement of Resolution will cause the court to issue a notice that the restored confirmation hearing is set on the date of the next available Uncontested Confirmation Calendar and to serve the notice on parties in interest.

Procedures to Restore to Contested Confirmation Calendar

To restore a contested confirmation matter to calendar so the court can resolve factual or legal issues, any party in interest (including the debtor(s)) may file and serve in conformity with B.L.R. 9014-1(a) a Notice of Hearing and Certificate of Service on 28 days' notice to parties in interest. The matter may be set on any Contested Confirmation Calendar date posted on the court's website, but only if these three conditions are met: (1) the § 341 meeting has concluded; (2) the parties have met and conferred in good faith (in person or by telephone); and (3) the dispute is ready to be submitted for resolution, trial setting, evidentiary hearing, or briefing. No later than 14 days before the hearing, the noticing party shall file a Chapter 13 Status Conference Statement identifying: (a) the disputed factual and legal issues; (b) the date and time when the parties conferred; and (c) the time estimate for trial or argument. If the Chapter 13 Status Conference Statement is not timely filed, the matter will be stricken from calendar. Matters stricken from the Contested Confirmation Calendar must be re-noticed for hearing by submitting a new Notice of Hearing, Certificate of Service, and Chapter 13 Status Conference Statement.

F. Order Establishing Procedures for Objection to Confirmation

Order Establishing Procedures for Objection to Confirmation

1. **Placement on Trustee's Pending List and Hearing Taken Off Calendar.** If an objection to confirmation is filed or a case is otherwise not ready for confirmation based on deficiencies, such as defaults on plan payments, the Trustee will file a Trustee's Statement of Non-Readiness for Confirmation at least 10 days before the confirmation hearing. The court will serve a notice indicating that the case has been placed on the Trustee's Pending List ("TPL") and that no appearances are expected, the plan will not be confirmed, and the matter will be taken off calendar at the confirmation hearing.

2. **Procedures for Restoring Matter to Confirmation Calendar.** A case that is on the TPL may be restored to the confirmation calendar as follows:

   a. To restore the matter to the Uncontested Confirmation Calendar, the Trustee will file a Trustee's Statement of Resolution when all outstanding objections are resolved, deficiencies have been cured, and the debtor(s) is current on plan payments. The Trustee's docketing of the Statement of Resolution will cause the court to issue a notice that the restored confirmation hearing is set on the date of the next available Uncontested Confirmation Calendar and to serve the notice on parties in interest.

   b. To restore a contested confirmation matter to calendar so the court can resolve factual or legal issues, any party in interest (including the debtor(s)) may file and serve in conformity with B.L.R. 9014-1(a) a Notice of Hearing and Certificate of Service on 28 days' notice to the parties in interest. The matter may be set on any Contested Confirmation Calendar date posted on the court's website, but only if these three conditions are met: (1) the § 341 meeting has concluded; (2) the parties have met and conferred in good faith (in person or by telephone); and (3) the dispute is ready to be submitted for resolution, trial setting, evidentiary hearing, or briefing.

   No later than 14 days before the hearing, the noticing party shall file a Chapter 13 Status Conference Statement identifying: (a) the disputed factual and legal issues; (b) the date and time when the parties conferred; and (c) the time estimate for trial or argument. If the Chapter 13 Status Conference Statement is not timely filed, the matter will be stricken from calendar. Matters stricken from the Contested Confirmation Calendar must be re-noticed for hearing by submitting a new Notice of Hearing, Certificate of Service, and Chapter 13 Status Conference Statement.

IT IS SO ORDERED.

ARTHUR S. WEISSBRODT
United States Bankruptcy Judge

CHARLES NOVACK
United States Bankruptcy Judge

STEPHEN L. JOHNSON
United States Bankruptcy Judge

G. Order for the Reassignment of Cases

IN THE UNITED STATES BANKRUPTCY COURT
FOR THE NORTHERN DISTRICT OF CALIFORNIA
San Jose Division

ORDER FOR THE REASSIGNMENT OF CASES

Upon the retirement of the undersigned judge and the appointment of Charles Novack as successor bankruptcy judge for the United States Bankruptcy Court for the Northern District of California, San Jose Division, all bankruptcy cases and related adversary proceedings assigned to the undersigned judge are hereby reassigned to the Honorable Charles Novack effective May 13, 2010.

All matters that are currently scheduled for hearing before Judge Morgan on or after May 13,2010 will be heard by Judge Novack in Courtroom 3070, except for those chapter 13 matters that are scheduled forhearing in The Quadrangle, 1000 S. Main Street, Room 214, Salinas, California.

DATED: May 7, 2010

MARILYN MORGAN
United States Bankruptcy Judge

H. *Order Regarding Delayed Discharged of Individuals in Chapter 13 Cases*

IN THE UNITED STATES BANKRUPTCY COURT
FOR THE NORTHERN DISTRICT OF CALIFORNIA
San Jose Division

ORDER RE: DELAYED DISCHARGED OF INDIVIDUALS IN CHAPTER 13 CASES

(a) Chapter 13 debtors who have claimed exemptions in excess of the adjusted amount set forth in 11 U.S.C. § 522(q)(1) must file a statement pursuant to Rule 1007(b)(8), not earlier than the date of the last payment under the plan or the date of filing a motion for a discharge under 11 U.S.C. § 1328(b).

(b) Unless otherwise ordered, upon plan completion:

(1) All Chapter 13 debtors must file a certification in support of discharge stating whether or not the debtor:

(A) has completed an instructional course concerning personal financial management described in 11 U.S.C. § 111 prior to making the last plan payment and has filed a certificate of completion of that course;

(B) has been required to pay, and has paid, a domestic support obligation as that term is defined in 11 U.S.C. § 101(14A);

(C) has received a discharge in a Chapter 7, 11, 12 bankruptcy case filed within four years prior to filing the present Chapter 13 case, or in a Chapter 13 case filed within two years prior to filing the present Chapter 13 case.

(2) If a Chapter 13 debtor has been required to pay a domestic support obligation as that term is defined in 11 U.S.C. § 101(14A), the debtor's certification in support of discharge shall be served by the Chapter 13 Trustee on all domestic support obligation payees for whom the Chapter 13 Trustee has an address, including those payees who have filed a proof of claim.

(c) (1) The Clerk shall serve the statement required in Subparagraph (a) by mail on all parties in interest.

(2) Any party requesting a delay in the entry of the discharge must file a written response no later than twenty (20) days from the date of service of the debtor's statement and the response must be served by mail on the Chapter 13 Trustee, the debtor and the debtor's attorney.

(3) If the delay request is timely filed, the debtor must schedule a hearing on the request and advise the Chapter 13 Trustee, and the party requesting the delay, of the date and time of the hearing. The hearing must be held not more than ten (10) days before the date of the entry of the discharge order.

(4) If either no delay request is filed or if the delay request is not timely filed, the Court may enter a discharge order in the case, but not earlier than thirty (30) days after the filing of the statement.

(d) Debtors shall make the statements and certifications required by this order on forms approved by the Court in accordance with B.L.R. 1007-1. Those forms shall be available on the Court's website and at the offices and on the websites of the district's Chapter 13 Trustees.

IT IS SO ORDERED.

Dated: 10-15-2010

ARTHUR S. WEISSBRODT
United States Bankruptcy Judge

CHARLES NOVACK
United States Bankruptcy Judge

STEPHEN L. JOHNSON
United States Bankruptcy Judge

I. Order Regarding Filing of Payment Advices

IN THE UNITED STATES BANKRUPTCY COURT
FOR THE NORTHERN DISTRICT OF CALIFORNIA
San Jose Division

ORDER RE: FILING OF PAYMENT ADVICES

(1) A debtor will have satisfied the filing requirement described in 11 U.S.C. § 521(a)(1)(B)(iv) by providing the required payment advices (or an alternative described in subsection (2) below) directly to the trustee at least seven days prior to the first date set for the meeting of creditors under 11 U.S.C. § 341.

(2) A debtor with unavailable payment advices may provide to the trustee, in the alternative, a certification setting forth the reasons that the required information is unavailable. The certification should state the debtor's estimate of payments received within the 60 days before the petition date and provide other evidence, if any, of the payments received.

IT IS SO ORDERED.

Dated: 10-15-2010

____
ARTHUR S. WEISSBRODT
United States Bankruptcy Judge

____
CHARLES NOVACK
United States Bankruptcy Judge

____
STEPHEN L. JOHNSON
United States Bankruptcy Judge

J. Order Regarding Motion for Order Confirming that No Stay Is in Effect

IN THE UNITED STATES BANKRUPTCY COURT
FOR THE NORTHERN DISTRICT OF CALIFORNIA
San Jose Division

ORDER RE: MOTION FOR ORDER CONFIRMING THAT NO STAY IS IN EFFECT

To obtain an order confirming that no stay is in effect pursuant to 11 U.S.C. § 362(c)(4)(A)(i), a party must notice a motion in accordance with B.L.R. 4001-1.

IT IS SO ORDERED.

Dated: 10-15-2010

ARTHUR S. WEISSBRODT
United States Bankruptcy Judge

CHARLES NOVACK
United States Bankruptcy Judge

STEPHEN L. JOHNSON
United States Bankruptcy Judge

K. Order Regarding Payment of Attorney's Fees in Chapter 13 Cases

IN THE UNITED STATES BANKRUPTCY COURT
FOR THE NORTHERN DISTRICT OF CALIFORNIA
San Jose Division

ORDER RE PAYMENT OF ATTORNEY'S FEES IN CHAPTER 13 CASES

1. For attorney's fees sought under the Court's Guidelines for Payment of Attorney's Fees in Chapter 13 Cases (the "No-Look Fees"), the trustee shall not make disbursements from plan payments until entry of orders confirming a plan and approving the No-Look Fees.

2. For attorney's fees sought under any provision other than the No-Look Fees, the trustee may make disbursements for payment of attorney's fees from plan payments prior to entry of an order confirming a plan only after entry of an order approving a fee application.

3. The trustee shall make disbursements under this Order according to her normal monthly disbursement cycle and only to the extent there are funds on hand after making disbursements for adequate protection payments under 11 U.S.C. § 1325(a)(5)(B)(iii)(II) and/or § 1326(a).

4. The trustee is entitled to collect the percentage fee established by 28 U.S.C. § 586(e)(1)(B) in effect at the time of disbursement of attorney's fees and adequate protection payments.

IT IS SO ORDERED.

Dated: January 1, 2011

____
ARTHUR S. WEISSBRODT
United States Bankruptcy Judge

____
CHARLES NOVACK
United States Bankruptcy Judge

____
STEPHEN L. JOHNSON
United States Bankruptcy Judge

L. *Order Regarding Pre-Confirmation Adequate Protection Payments in Chapter 13 Cases*

IN THE UNITED STATES BANKRUPTCY COURT
FOR THE NORTHERN DISTRICT OF CALIFORNIA
San Jose Division

ORDER RE PRE-CONFIRMATION ADEQUATE PROTECTION PAYMENTS IN CHAPTER 13 CASES

1. If a proposed Chapter 13 plan provides a specific amount to be paid on a periodic basis as adequate protection pursuant to 11 U.S.C. § 1326(a)(1)(C), the trustee shall make disbursements on any such payment from plan payments prior to confirmation.

2. Subject to the trustee's monthly disbursement cycle, the trustee shall commence making disbursement on any such payments within 30 days after a party claiming a right to an adequate protection payment files a proof of claim.

3. The trustee is entitled to collect the percentage fee established by 28 U.S.C. § 5 86(e) (1)(B) in effect at the time of disbursement of adequate protection payments.

IT IS SO ORDERED.

Dated: 10-15-2010

CHARLES NOVACK
United States Bankruptcy Judge

STEPHEN L. JOHNSON
United States Bankruptcy Judge

M. Order Setting Telephonic Hearing for Relief from Stay

IN THE UNITED STATES BANKRUPTCY COURT
FOR THE NORTHERN DISTRICT OF CALIFORNIA
San Jose Division

ORDER SETTING TELEPHONIC HEARING FOR RELIEF FROM STAY

IT IS HEREBY ORDERED that a preliminary hearing will be held telephonically on ____________________ at _____ _.m., or as soon thereafter as the matter may be heard, to consider the attached motion for relief from stay. This Order modifies Bankruptcy Local Rule 4001-1 by requiring telephonic, rather than personal appearances, by the parties on a motion for relief from stay. The moving party shall complete the information in this Order, serve a copy of this Order with the moving papers and file all pleadings as well as proof of service at least fourteen days before the noticed hearing date.

All telephonic appearances shall be through Court Conference. Any questions regarding procedures for the telephonic hearing may be directed to Court Conference at 1-800-538-7633.

The parties shall, in good faith, confer before the hearing regarding the issues raised by the motion and resolution of the motion. If debtor's counsel or the debtor does not appear telephonically, the Court may presume there is no opposition to the motion. If either counsel or the parties abuse the process for telephonic hearings, the Court may order sanctions as appropriate, which may include removing the matter from the calendar, granting relief from the automatic stay, or awarding monetary sanctions.

____

CHARLES NOVACK
United States Bankruptcy Judge

N. Procedures for Suspending Payments in Chapter 13

IN THE UNITED STATES BANKRUPTCY COURT
FOR THE NORTHERN DISTRICT OF CALIFORNIA
San Jose Division

PROCEDURES FOR SUSPENDING PAYMENTS IN CHAPTER 13

1. If a debtor is delinquent with Chapter 13 payments post-confirmation, the Chapter 13 Standing Trustee may, in her discretion, allow the debtor to suspend a payment without notice to creditors. *Creditors are not bound by the agreement between the debtor and Trustee.* The agreement will not be reduced to a written stipulation, but will be noted in the debtor's case by the Trustee's staff. Creditors can access the Trustee's website www.13network.com and view a field to track the number of suspensions a debtor receives. The Trustee may allow no more than three (3) suspended payments in a case.

2. If a fourth suspension is requested, the debtor must file a modification with notice to all interested parties, as well as those requesting special notice. In the modification, the debtor must account for all prior missed payments. The terms of the modification must clearly indicate that all prior suspended payments are being included in the modification and it must set forth the total dollar amount of payments to be suspended.

3. After a modification that addresses prior suspended payments is ordered, the Trustee may, in her discretion, resume payment suspensions following the procedures set forth in paragraph 1 above.

Approved:

Dated: 10-15-2010

ARTHUR .WEISSBRODT
United States Bankruptcy Judge

CHARLES NOVACK
United States Bankruptcy Judge

STEPHEN L. JOHNSON
United States Bankruptcy Judge

O. Rights and Responsibilities of Chapter 13 Debtors and Their Attorneys

IN THE UNITED STATES BANKRUPTCY COURT
FOR THE NORTHERN DISTRICT OF CALIFORNIA
San Jose Division

RIGHTS AND RESPONSIBILITIES OF CHAPTER 13 DEBTORS AND THEIR ATTORNEYS

It is important for debtors who file a bankruptcy case under Chapter 13 to understand their rights and responsibilities. It is also important that the debtors know what their attorney's responsibilities are, and understand the importance of communicating with their attorney to make the case successful. Debtors should also know that they may expect certain services to be performed by their attorney. In order to assure that debtors and their attorney understand their rights and responsibilities in the bankruptcy process, the following guidelines provided by the court are hereby agreed to by the debtors and their attorneys. Unless the Court orders otherwise,

BEFORE THE CASE IS FILED

The debtor agrees to:

1. Provide the attorney with accurate financial information.
2. Discuss with the attorney the debtor's objectives in filing the case.

The attorney agrees to:

1. Meet with the debtor to review the debtor's debts assets, liabilities, income, and expenses.
2. Counsel the debtor regarding the advisability of filing either a Chapter 7 or Chapter 13 case, discuss both procedures with the debtor, and answer the debtor's questions.
3. Explain what payments will be made directly by the debtor and what payments will be made through the debtor's Chapter 13 plan, with particular attention to mortgage and vehicle loan payments, as well as any other claims which accrue interest.
4. Explain to the debtor how, when, and where to make the Chapter 13 plan payments.
5. Explain to the debtor how the attorney's fees and trustee's fees are paid and provide an executed copy of this document to the debtor.
6. Explain to the debtor that the first plan payment must be made to the Trustee within 30 days of the date the plan is filed.
7. Advise the debtor of the requirement to attend the 341 Meeting of Creditors, and instruct the debtor as to the date, time and place of the meeting.
8. Advise the debtor of the necessity of maintaining liability, collision and comprehensive insurance on vehicles securing loans or leases.
9. Timely prepare and file the debtor's petition, plan, statements and schedules.

AFTER THE CASE IS FILED

The debtor agrees to:

1. Keep the trustee and attorney informed of the debtor's address and telephone number.
2. Inform the attorney of any wage garnishments or attachments of assets which

occur or continue after the filing of the case.

3. Contact the attorney promptly if the debtor loses his/her job or has other financial problems.

4. Let the attorney know if the debtor is sued during the case.

5. Inform the attorney if any tax refunds the debtor is entitled to are seized or not returned to the debtor by the IRS or Franchise Tax Board.

6. Contact the attorney before buying, refinancing, or selling real property or before entering into any long-term loan agreements to find out what approvals are required.

7. Pay any filing fees and expenses that may be incurred directly to the attorney.

The attorney agrees to provide the following legal services:

1. Appear at the 341 Meeting of Creditors with the debtor.

2. Respond to objections to plan confirmation, and where necessary, prepare an amended plan.

3. Prepare, file, and serve necessary modifications to the plan which may include suspending, lowering, or increasing plan payments.

4. Prepare, file, and serve necessary amended statements and schedules, in accordance with information provided by the debtor.

5. Prepare, file, and serve necessary motions to buy, sell, or refinance real property when appropriate.

6. Object to improper or invalid claims, if necessary, based upon documentation provided by the debtor.

7. Represent the debtor in motions for relief from stay.

8. Where appropriate, prepare, file, and serve necessary motions to avoid liens on real or personal property.

9. Provide such other legal services as are necessary for the administration of the present case before the Bankruptcy Court.

The "Guidelines for Payment of Attorney's Fees in Chapter 13 Cases for the San Jose Division" provides for maximum initial fees in the following amounts:

- $2,750 for the basic case: and an additional $300 only if the compromise plan is used in cases assigned to the Hon. Arthur S. Weissbrodt;
- $850 if the case involves real property claims;
- $500 per each additional piece of real property with an encumberance of at least $10,000;
- $700 if the case involves state or federal tax claims;
- $700 if the case involves vehicle loans or leases;
- $1,500 if the case involves an operating business;
- $800 if the case involves support arrears claims;
- $300 if the case involves student loans;
- $300 if the case involves 25 or more creditors, including collection agencies and attorneys;
- $450 if the case involves motions to commence or extend the automatic stay;

Initial fees charged in this case are $______. In addition to these initial fees, in the following situations the attorney may apply to the court for the additional fees shown below which shall be approved upon application:

For filed post-confirmation plan modifications:

- not requiring amended Schedules I & J ($400)
- requiring amended Schedules I & J ($600)

For permission to sell, refinance, or purchase real property, or if one or more motions to avoid judicial liens, has been filed:

- not requiring court hearing ($500)
- requiring court hearing ($750)

For new motions for relief from the automatic stay, excluding unopposed motions, filed after one year from the petition date:

- regarding personal property ($400)
- regarding real property ($600)

For motions to dismiss, convert, or reconvert,excluding Trustee's Notices of Default regarding plan payments ($450) (This additional $450 will not apply to pre-confirmation motions to dismiss in cases assigned to the Hon. Roger L. Efremsky or the Hon. Charles Novack.)

For motion or adversary proceeding to value and/or avoid real property liens ($800)

For preparation of tax returns: This is not required by debtor's counsel, but is optional. ($200 each year)

In addition, if the above fees ordered by the court are not sufficient to compensate the attorney for the legal services rendered and costs incurred in the case, the attorney further agrees to apply to the court for approval of such fees and costs, attaching a supporting declaration with time records justifying that said fees and costs are merited and have not been compensated within the amounts previously ordered. Reimbursement of advanced court fees shall be awarded independently of other fees and costs. Fees shall be paid through the plan unless otherwise ordered. The attorney may not receive fees directly from the debtor other than the initial retainer.

If the debtor disputes the legal services provided or the fees charged by the attorney, an objection may be filed with the court and the matter set for hearing. The attorney may move to withdraw or the client may discharge the attorney at any time.

Dated:____________________ ____________________
Debtor

Dated:____________________ ____________________
Debtor

Dated:____________________ ____________________
Attorney for Debtor(s)

(rev. 09/01/10)

Santa Rosa Division

IV. Santa Rosa Division

A. Electronic Filing Requirements

ELECTRONIC FILING REQUIREMENTS

Effective January 1, 2005

All pleadings in this division shall be filed electronically with **only** the following exceptions:

1. Attorneys or law firms which did not file any pleading in this division in the previous calendar year may file one pleading in paper in this calendar year. If the pleading is more than 10 pages in length, it shall be accompanied by a disk containing the entire pleading in PDF format.

2. *Pro se* litigants. Provided, however, that any pleading subsequent to the lead documents in a new case in excess of 10 pages and any pleading filed within seven calendar days of a prior filing shall be accompanied by a disk containing the entire pleading in PDF format.

Leave to deviate from the above requirements may be granted only by the Judge upon application with proposed order e-mailed in .wpd or .doc format to Chambers_Orders@canb.uscourts.gov. Lack of computer equipment, computer illiteracy, or lack of ECF training will generally not be valid excuses.

When an attorney or party attempts a filing in violation of the above requirements, the following procedure shall be followed:

1. The purported pleading will be scanned by the Clerk and filed unless it is so lengthy as to be burdensome, in which case the Clerk shall immediately obtain an order striking a portion of the pleading and shall scan and file the remainder.

2. The Clerk shall issue an Order to Show Cause why the pleading should not be stricken and the filer sanctioned. The hearing date shall be the next law and motion calendar which is more than five days from the issuance of the OSC. No telephonic appearances will be allowed.

3. If the court disallows the filing, an order will be issued striking the pleading from the record.

4. If the court conditions the filing on payment of a fine and the fine is not paid within three court days, the pleading will be stricken from the record.

B. Guidelines for Payment of Attorneys' Fees in Chapter 13 Cases

IN THE UNITED STATES BANKRUPTCY COURT
FOR THE NORTHERN DISTRICT OF CALIFORNIA
Santa Rosa/Eureka Division

GUIDELINES FOR PAYMENT OF ATTORNEYS' FEES IN CHAPTER 13 CASES

In this division, the court does not enforce any maximum or minimum fee structure, nor does it limit the size of counsel's pre-petition retainer. Unusually large fees will trigger scrutiny by the court as well as the trustee. No payments should be taken from the debtor after the case is filed (except through the trustee) without order of the court obtained after noticed hearing.

The court agrees with the rights and responsibilities enforced by other divisions. The court further expects that debtors with counsel of record will NEVER appear in court without representation. However, while the court expects compliance with the rights and responsibilities it does not require the filing of a formal statement.

C. Northern Counties Bankruptcy Practice

IN THE UNITED STATES BANKRUPTCY COURT
FOR THE NORTHERN DISTRICT OF CALIFORNIA
Santa Rosa/Eureka Division

NORTHERN COUNTIES BANKRUPTCY PRACTICE
Revised March 25, 2011

1. EX PARTE APPLICATIONS

Ordinarily, ex parte applications shall be submitted electronically and without oral representations by counsel. However, if a request is unusual and counsel feels the need to explain or justify it to the Court, he or she may request that it be called in open court at the conclusion of any law and motion or relief from stay calendar. If time is critical, the Court may convene specially.

Counsel are reminded that all rules concerning notice of ex parte applications (e.g., FRCP 65(b)(2), FRBP 4001(a)(3)) are strictly enforced.

2. OBTAINING CALENDAR DATES

The court issues hearing dates several months in advance. Generally, law and motion matters are heard in Santa Rosa every Friday at 9:00 and 10:00; final accounts and fee applications are heard every Friday at 10:30; relief from stay motions are heard every second and fourth Thursday at 9:00; Chapter 13 matters are heard the second and fourth Wednesdays at 1:30; and scheduling conferences are held the fourth Monday at 2:00. All Eureka matters are generally heard on the first Wednesday of each month at 9:00. Eureka matters may be heard in Santa Rosa with the consent of all parties or by order of the court.

The above are only general guidelines, and are frequently changed to accommodate holidays, unavailability of judges, etc; counsel should consult the posted calendar or contact the calendar clerk to confirm a particular date. Calendar dates are also available on the court's website at http://www.canb.uscourts.gov.

Counsel need only confirm that court will be held on a desired date. It is not necessary to reserve a date or obtain leave to have a matter placed on the calendar.

3. STAY RELIEF MOTIONS

Pursuant to Local Rule 4001-1(c), notice of 14 days is required for motions for relief from the automatic stay.

Final hearings are set by the Court if it appears that there is a disputed issue of material fact. Parties are not permitted to stipulate to a final hearing. At the final hearing, direct testimony is usually in the form of declarations filed and served at least five days before the hearing. Declarants are to be available in court for cross-examination unless the other side has waived the right to cross-examine.

4. OBJECTIONS TO CLAIMS

Unless otherwise ordered, all hearings on objections to claims are preliminary hearings, without testimony. If the objection cannot be summarily resolved, the court will order a trial at which evidence will be taken.

5. PRETRIAL and SCHEDULING CONFERENCES

Unless otherwise ordered, all pretrial and scheduling conferences are very informal proceedings and do not require written reports or briefs. However, each party not appearing pro se must be represented by counsel who knows about the case and is prepared to discuss its merits as well as appropriate dates for discovery and trial.

Telephonic appearances are not permitted at scheduling conferences. However, they may be heard by conference call if arrangements are made by calling the calendar clerk well in advance of the scheduled date. See section 7 below.

6. ORDERS AND JUDGMENTS

Except for orders submitted by pro se parties, all orders (and judgments) in this division must be submitted electronically. Registered ECF Participants may choose to upload the order via CM/ECF or submit it by email. DO NOT SUBMIT ORDERS BOTH WAYS. CHOOSE ONE OR THE OTHER. Counsel who are not Registered ECF Participants may submit only by email.

A. Orders by Email

Orders submitted by email shall be sent as an attachment to an email to Chambers_Orders@canb.uscourts.gov. The attachment must be in WordPerfect format (preferred) or MS Word format. The email must contain the following information, in the following order, in the subject line: Hearing date (mm/dd/yy), debtors' name (abbreviations OK), case number, and title of order. For example:

01/26/11 Harrington 11-12365 Order for Relief From Stay

If the order has a signature line for approval by another party, make sure that "/s/" appears on the signature line. If there is no signature line for party approval, you may certify approval in the body of your email provided that the approving counsel is copied with the email.

The court is unable to sign email orders with separate attachments. If your order requires an attachment, either incorporate it into the order as a single document or upload it via CM/ECF.

B. Orders Uploaded Via CM/ECF

The court never prints an order. Therefore, if you upload an order through CM/ECF it may contain NO BLANKS. If your order requires the Judge to add dates or anything else, submit it by email. Also, do not put the word "Proposed" in the caption.

Counsel are reminded that since uploaded orders are electronically signed in the upper right corner of the first page instead of at the end, such orders may not contain a blank signature line for the Judge or a date line. Instead, court rules applicable to all divisions require that "**END OF ORDER**" be placed at the end of all uploaded orders.

C. When in Doubt

When in doubt, submit your order by email. The Judge can make changes and corrections as necessary. He only has two choices as to uploaded orders: sign or bounce.

D. Orders After Notice Without Hearing (L.R. 9014-1(b)(4)):

First, file and docket your request electronically. Then email an order in .wpd or .doc format to Chambers_Orders@canb.uscourts.gov. Either attach a copy of the request to your email or recite in the body of the email that you have filed a request for the order.

E. Stipulations and Ex Parte Orders

Stipulations and applications for ex parte orders (including applications for the employment of professionals) should be attached to an email sent to Chambers_Orders@canb.uscourts.gov as a single document with a single caption in either .wpd or.doc format. All attorney signature lines should be dated, and signatures should be indicated either by "/s/" or an attorney's signature graphic. The other parties to a stipulation (or the U.S. Trustee, for employment and other ex parte applications) should be copied with the email.

7. TELEPHONIC CONFERENCES AND APPEARANCES

A. Definitions

A conference call is a call placed by a party using the conference call operator. The call is placed at a special time designated by the calendar clerk. Conference calls are NOT held during normal court calendars.

A telephonic appearance is an appearance by telephone during a regular court calendar.

B. Conference Calls

Because of the wide geographic area of this division, the Court encourages the use of conference calls and will usually order hearings to be held by telephone at the request of a party if counsel cannot so stipulate. Conference calls are discouraged only when one party is in pro per. In-house conferencing systems may not be used in lieu of the conference call operator. All conference calls must be arranged through Tara Arruda by telephone at 707 547-5920 or by email at Tara_Arruda@canb.uscourts.gov. It is the responsibility of the plaintiff in status conferences and the moving party in other matters to arrange the conference call.

C. Telephonic Appearances

Effective April 4, 2011, we will begin using "CourtCall" on a test basis for telephonic courtroom appearances. To request a telephonic appearance, call the CourtCall reservation line at (866) 582-6878. The request must be made at least 48 hours (exclusive of weekends and holidays) before the hearing. To learn more about the procedures go to the web site; www.courtcall.com.

Only attorneys who file electronically (ECF Registered Participants) may appear telephonically. Attorneys representing themselves may not appear telephonically. If the attorney appearing by phone does not respond immediately when the case is called, the matter will be deemed submitted.

D. Limitations

Telephonic appearances or conference calls are generally not permitted in discovery disputes, contested disclosure statement hearings, or hearings on orders to appear or orders to show cause where the order does not permit a telephonic appearance without leave of court. Exceptions can be granted only by the Judge upon ex parte application.

8. CONTINUANCES

Motions directed to specific parties may be continued as allowed by local rules or by stipulation at any time. Before the date of the hearing, the calendar clerk is to be notified; on the date of the hearing, the courtroom deputy is to be notified. The moving party is to file and serve a notice of the continued hearing; if he or she fails to do so, the motion may not be granted by default if the other side fails to appear at the continued hearing.

Motions or applications noticed to creditors generally, such as sales of assets, motions to convert, etc., may be continued only on the record at the time set for hearing in the notice. Appearance for this purpose may be by telephone in accordance with the procedure set forth above.

Trials will be continued very reluctantly, and only for the most compelling reasons, such as serious illness or death. Virtually all matters set for trial are given a date certain at a time and date when no other matters are set, so counsel should assume that the case will be called at the exact time set.

9. ELECTRONIC FILING REQUIRED

This court is entirely electronic, and does not maintain paper files. **All pleadings in this division shall be filed electronically** with ONLY the following exceptions:

1. Attorneys or law firms which did not file any pleading in this division in the previous calendar year may file ONE pleading in paper in this calendar year. If the pleading is more than 10 pages in length, it shall be accompanied by a disk containing the entire pleading in .pdf format.

2. Pro se litigants. Provided, however, that any pleading subsequent to the lead documents in a new case in excess of 10 pages and any pleading filed within seven calendar days of a prior filing shall be accompanied by a disk containing the entire pleading in .pdf format.

Leave to deviate from the above requirements may be granted only by the Judge upon application with proposed order emailed in .wpd or .doc format to Chambers_Orders@canb.uscourts.gov. Lack of computer equipment, computer illiteracy, or lack of ECF training will generally not be valid excuses.

When an attorney or party attempts a filing in violation of the above requirements, the following procedure shall be followed:

1. The purported pleading will be scanned by the Clerk and filed unless it is so lengthy as to be burdensome, in which case the Clerk shall immediately obtain an order striking a portion of the pleading and shall scan and file the remainder.

2. The Clerk shall issue an Order to Show Cause why the pleading should not be stricken and the filer sanctioned. The hearing date shall be the next law and motion calendar which is more than five days from the issuance of the OSC. No telephonic appearances will be allowed.

3. If the court disallows the filing, an order will be issued striking the pleading from the record.

4. If the court conditions the filing on payment of a fine and the fine is not paid within three court days, the pleading will be stricken from the record.

There is no requirement in this division for submission of a paper "chambers copy" of an electronically-filed pleading.

10. RULE 2002 NOTICES TO CREDITORS

Notices are governed by Local Rule 2002-1.

Litigants who for some reason cannot use the mailing labels must apply for a special order allowing them to give notice. Any motion or application noticed without using the mailing labels or obtaining special leave of court will be summarily dropped from the calendar.

Final fee applications shall be noticed by the court along with the notice of confirmation in Chapter 11 and Chapter 12 cases, and along with the notice of the trustee's account in Chapter 7 cases.

No interim fee application will be approved unless all professionals in the case were given the opportunity to seek interim compensation and all of their applications were listed in the same notice. Hearings may be set on any law and motion calendar, so long as 21 days notice was given. No application for compensation will be approved unless it was on file when the creditors received the notice.

11. SALES FREE AND CLEAR OF LIENS

The term "free and clear of liens" shall be used only in reference to specific, identified liens which are not to be paid out of escrow. No motion to sell free and clear of liens will be considered unless the liens are specifically identified, the ground for sale free and clear under section 363(f) has been identified for each such lien, and each lienholder has been given 28 days notice of the hearing (unless time has been shortened) and has been served pursuant to FRBP 7004. Local Rule 6004-1 is strictly enforced.

Even if there are no objections, an actual hearing is always required before the court will authorize a sale free and clear of liens.

12. CORRESPONDENCE WITH COURT

Correspondence with the Bankruptcy Judge is rarely appropriate and is discouraged except to the extent absolutely necessary. When in doubt, the preferred procedure for communicating with the Judge is a filed pleading showing proof of service upon all proper parties. Routine filings and inquiries should be addressed to the Clerk of the Court, not the Judge.

13. GUIDELINES FOR COMMUNICATION WITH COURT STAFF

Counsel are reminded that Rule 5-300(C) of the California Rules of Professional Conduct specifies that for disciplinary purposes a contact with the judge's research attorney, law clerk or extern is considered a contact with the judge. No attorney or litigant may initiate contact with any research attorney, law clerk, intern or extern unless such contact is clearly not a violation of Rule 5-300(C) or FRBP 9003(a). If a law clerk, extern or research attorney contacts counsel to relay a communication from the judge, counsel may not discuss the case with the caller.

If you have a question regarding the status of an order or submitted matter, you may call 707 547-5900 and your call will be routed to the appropriate deputy clerk. Alternatively, you may email Chambers_Orders@canb.uscourts.gov.

Tara Arruda, the courtroom deputy, is available to assist counsel regarding all calendar matters. She may be called at (707) 547-5920 or emailed at Tara_Arruda@canb.uscourts.gov regarding routine calendar questions, the availability of the judge for ex parte applications and emergency matters, and the continuance or settlement of calendared matters, as well as arrangement of telephonic appearances and conference calls. Counsel are reminded that copies of the court's calendar of hearing dates for the next several months are available on the court's website and that it is not necessary to reserve a spot before noticing a motion.

Counsel are reminded that the judge does not appreciate ex parte applications made by proxy through a member of the court staff. If you want an order shortening time, apply for it; don't ask the courtroom deputy if the judge is willing to shorten time.

14. SUBMITTED MATTERS

The Court almost always renders decisions on submitted matters within ten days of the hearing. Counsel are encouraged to contact the Clerk's office staff at 707 547-5900 about the status of any matter under submission for more than ten days, to make sure that it has not "slipped through the cracks." You may also email Chambers_Orders@canb.uscourts.gov.

15. CHAPTER 11 FINAL DECREES

Chapter 11 debtors in possession and trustees are expected to apply for final decrees as soon as claims disputes and any other litigation in bankruptcy court are resolved. It is not proper to wait until all payments are made before applying for a final decree. The court expects all counsel for Chapter 11 debtors to understand fully the provisions of FRBP 3022 and the Advisory Committee notes thereto.

If a final decree is sought within one year of confirmation, it may be obtained by ex parte application along with a declaration of a principal of the debtor setting forth the date that the plan was confirmed and representing that the plan payments called for by the plan have been commenced and that the debtor is substantially in compliance with the requirements of the plan.

If more than one year has passed since confirmation, a final decree must be sought by motion on at least 15 days notice to the creditors' committee and its counsel, if any, the U.S. Trustee, and any persons who filed requests for notice. If there is no committee, the 20 largest unsecured creditors must be served. The motion must contain the following statement, in capital letters:

> IF THE DEBTOR IS NOT CURRENT IN PLAN PAYMENTS, YOU MAY OBJECT TO ENTRY OF A FINAL DECREE AND ASK THE COURT TO ORDER THE LIQUIDATION OF THE DEBTOR'S ASSETS. IF THE DEBTOR FALLS BEHIND IN PLAN PAYMENTS AFTER THE ENTRY OF A FINAL DECREE, YOU MAY ASK THE COURT TO REOPEN THE CASE AND ORDER LIQUIDATION.

If a motion to reopen a case is made, the filing fee shall be paid by the debtor unless the court finds that the motion was not substantially justified.

16. EFFECT OF THESE RULES

These rules shall be considered standing orders of the court, modifiable for cause upon ex parte application.

D. Notice of Designation of CM/ECF as the Official Case Record for the Santa Rosa Division

IN THE UNITED STATES BANKRUPTCY COURT
FOR THE NORTHERN DISTRICT OF CALIFORNIA
Santa Rosa Division

Notice of Designation of CM/ECF as the Official Case Record for the Santa Rosa Division, Pursuant to the Court's Interim Operating Order Section 2.B

The undersigned, in consultation with Santa Rosa Division Manager Dennis Bilecki, hereby designates the CM/ECF system as the official case file for all pleadings/documents filed in the Santa Rosa division, effective Monday, March 1, 2004. Any document filed in paper form on or after that date shall be scanned (imaged) by Clerk's Office staff and the electronic document so created shall be the official record.

Pursuant to Section 2 of the Court's Administrative Procedures for Electronic Case Filing, all original filed paper documents which are scanned by Clerk's Office staff will be subsequently arranged by file date in a day-file bin and held for a period of five days by the Clerk's Office and then recycled. Parties and attorneys who wish to retrieve the original paper documents may visit or send a representative to this divisional office to locate the documents from the day-file bin for retrieval.

The court appreciates the efforts of staff and the bar which have made this noteworthy day possible.

Dated: February 24, 2004

ALAN JAROSLOVSKY
United States Bankruptcy Judge

E. *Notice Regarding Service of Chapter 13 Plans*

NOTICE TO COUNSEL RE SERVICE OF CHAPTER 13 PLANS

As an experiment, the Santa Rosa Clerk's office has been serving all Chapter 13 plans filed under the Bankruptcy Act. That experiment has proved unworkable. Effective immediately, the Clerk will serve the original plan ONLY, and it will be served ONLY on creditors on the original list. Responsibility for serving amended plans and the notice of any continued confirmation hearing on them will revert to the debtor, where it was under our old procedures. Debtors are also responsible for serving original plans and hearing notices on creditors added after the petition is filed.

Counsel are reminded that all creditors are entitled to be served with a copy of every plan and a notice of the confirmation hearing. At least 25 days notice must be given pursuant to FRBP 2002(b), unless the court has shortened time.

There are two recurring problems with noticing Chapter 13 plans. First, creditors are added after the original filing but are not served with the plan and notice of hearing. Second, an amended plan is filed but not served on all creditors, or it is served without notice of a hearing date, or it is served with less than 25 days notice. Counsel are reminded that a confirmed plan is not binding on anyone who did not receive proper notice.

It is fairly common for a debtor to make minor changes to meet a trustee objection or a valuation objection by secured creditor. Whether to give further notice and a copy of the amended plan to all creditors is a judgment call on your part, understanding that if a creditor is materially impacted by the amended plan and was not given proper notice then the amended plan may not bind that creditor.

Your attention is also called to case law in this circuit providing that whenever a plan contains an unusual provision, such as lien stripping or student loan modification, special notice must be given to the specially-affected creditors in the same manner as a summons and complaint. *In re Repp*, 307 B.R. 144 (9tn Cir. BAP 2004). It is ALWAYS the responsibility of the debtor to give such special notice.

Proper service of Chapter 13 plans and notices of hearing is a vital responsibility of Chapter 13 counsel which must not be taken lightly.

Dated: March 7, 2006

ALAN JAROSLOVSKY
United States Bankruptcy Judge

F. *Open Letter to Debtors and Their Counsel*

OPEN LETTER TO DEBTORS AND THEIR COUNSEL

I have noticed a disturbing trend among debtors and their counsel to treat the schedules and statement of affairs as "working papers" which can be freely amended as circumstances warrant and need not contain the exact, whole truth. Notwithstanding execution under penalty of perjury, debtors and their counsel seem to think that they are free to argue facts and values not contained in the schedules or even directly contrary to the schedules. Some debtors have felt justified signing a statement that they have only a few, or even a single creditor, in order to file an emergency petition, knowing full well that the statement is false.

Whatever your attitude is toward the schedules, you should know that as far as I am concerned they are the sacred text of any bankruptcy filing. There is no excuse for them not being 100% accurate and complete. Disclosure must be made to a fault. The filing of false schedules is a federal felony, and I do not hesitate to recommend prosecution of anyone who knowingly files a false schedule.

I have no idea where anyone got the idea that amendments can cure false schedules. The debtor has an obligation to correct schedules he or she knows are false, but amendment in no way cures a false filing. Any court may properly disregard subsequent sworn statement at odds with previous sworn statements. I give no weight at all to amendments filed after an issue has been raised.

As a practical matter, where false statements or omissions have come to light due to investigation by a creditor or trustee, it is virtually impossible for the debtor to demonstrate good faith in a Chapter 13 case or entitlement to a discharge in a Chapter 7 case. I strongly recommend that any of you harboring a cavalier attitude toward the schedules replace it with a good healthy dose of paranoia.

Dated: September 10, 1997

ALAN JAROSLOVSKY
United States Bankruptcy Judge

This page intentionally left blank.

This page intentionally left blank.

PART III

Individual Judges

Procedures and Practices
Case Management Orders and Forms
Chambers and Biographical Information

BANKRUPTCY JUDGES

Hon. Thomas E. Carlson

Bankruptcy Judge

Contact Information

U.S. Bankruptcy Court, Northern District of California
Courtroom 23
235 Pine Street, 19th Floor
San Francisco, CA 94104
Courtroom Deputy: (415) 268-2362

Biographical Information

Education:

- Beloit College, B.A. (1969)
- Brandeis University, graduate study in American History (1970-71)
- Harvard Law School, J.D. (1975)
- N.Y.U. Law School, LL.M. (Tax) (1985)

Practice:

- Law Clerk to Chief Justice Thomas Roberts, Rhode Island Supreme Court (1975-76)
- Law Clerk to Chief Justice Donald Wright, California Supreme Court (1976-77)
- Cooper, White & Cooper LLP, San Francisco, California (1977-78)
- Deputy Director of Staff Attorneys Office, Ninth Circuit Court of Appeals (1978-84)

Appointed:

- Bankruptcy Judge, Northern District of California (1985)
- Chief Bankruptcy Judge (1992-96)
- Ninth Circuit Conference of Chief Bankruptcy Judges (1992-96) Chair (1992-93)
- Executive Committee (1992-95)
- Ninth Circuit Judicial Council (1992-93)

Professional Activities:

- Principal Drafter of the "Emergency Rule" (1982)
- Consultant to House Judiciary Committee Subcommittee on Courts (1984)
- National Conference of Bankruptcy Judges (1985-present)
- Board of Governors (1991-94)
- Chair of Liaison Committee to Federal Court Study Committee (1989-90)
- Chair of Liaison Committee to National Bankruptcy Review Commission (1985-98)
- Advisor to National Bankruptcy Review Commission (1995-98)
- Federal Judicial Center, Bankruptcy Education Committee (1994-97)

Publications:

- "Are the Jurisdictional Provisions of the Bankruptcy Amendments of 1984 Constitutional?" 9 Norton Bankr. Law Adviser 1 (Sept. 1984)
- "Distinguishing Core from Noncore Proceedings," 1 Norton Bankr.Law Adviser 2 (Jan. 1985)
- "The Case for Bankruptcy Appellate Panels," 1990 B.Y.U. Law Rev.545 (1990)
- "A Primer on Jury Trials in Bankruptcy Proceedings," 1 Ass'n of Bus. Trial Lawyers Report, Northern Cal., No. 2 (March 1992)
- "What You Need to Know About the Commission's Proposal on Single-Asset Real Estate," 31 Bankr. Ct. Dec. Weekly News & Comment (LRP) A3-4 (Nov. 25, 1997)
- "The Small Business Provisions of the 2005 Bankruptcy Amendments," 79 Am. Bankr. L.J. 645 (2005)

I. Judge Carlson's Procedures and Practices

A. Trial Scheduling Order and Instructions

TRIAL SCHEDULING ORDER AND INSTRUCTIONS

Please note, you do not need to download the Trial Scheduling Order unless you have been instructed by the Court to do so.

If you are required by the Court to submit this document, you must complete all relevant sections in the order and modify the order to reflect the Court's instructions and the circumstances of your adversary proceeding. For example, if the Court has not instructed the parties to appear at a pre-trial conference or the parties have not agreed to present direct testimony by written declaration, the paragraphs in the order regarding these matters must be deleted. The Court will provide you with the discovery deadline, trial date and, if applicable, pre-trial conference date.

II. Judge Carlson's Case Management Orders

A. *Trial Scheduling Order*

IN THE UNITED STATES BANKRUPTCY COURT
FOR THE NORTHERN DISTRICT OF CALIFORNIA

In re:)	Case No. ________________
)	Chapter ___________
Debtor(s).)	Adv. No. ________________
________________________________)	
)	**SCHEDULING ORDER**
Plaintiff(s),)	B.R. 7016
v.)	Fed. R. Civ. P. 16
Defendant(s).)	
________________________________)	

A Status Conference in the above-entitled matter was held on (Date & Time). (Name of Attorney) appeared for Plaintiff. (Name of Attorney) appeared for Defendant. Upon due consideration, the court hereby establishes the following schedule:

(1) All discovery shall be completed by ______________.

(2) A Pretrial Conference shall be held on (Date) at (Time) , United States Bankruptcy Court, 235 Pine Street, Twenty-Third Floor, San Francisco, CA 94104.

The parties' counsel are directed to meet and confer in person regarding settlement and the joint pretrial conference statement before the pretrial conference. Counsel are reminded that they are required to file a joint pretrial statement seven calendar days before the pretrial conference. The pretrial conference statement shall address: (1) The substance of the action; (2) undisputed facts; (3) disputed facts; (4) disputed legal issues; (5) witnesses to be called by each party; (6) an estimate of trial time required; (7) whether separate trial of specific issues is appropriate; (8) whether it is appropriate to introduce the direct testimony of any witnesses by declaration (subject to oral cross examination).

(3) No motion for summary judgment will be heard less than thirty days before trial without permission of the court.

(4) Trial will commence on _____________ at 9:30 a.m., at the United States Bankruptcy Court, 235 Pine Street, Twenty-Third Floor, San Francisco, CA. Seven calendar days before the trial date counsel shall inform the courtroom deputy (Gordon Hom (415) 268-2362) whether the parties have settled and, if not, how much time the trial will require. During the week prior to the trial date the court may reschedule the trial to a later day during the week of the trial date. Counsel should be prepared to go to trial at any time during the week of the trial date.

(5) Seven calendar days before the scheduled trial date, counsel shall: (a) serve and file trial briefs (briefs shall not exceed twenty-five pages without prior permission of the court); (b) exchange copies of all exhibits to be offered, other than those to be used for impeachment or rebuttal; (c) serve and file statements designating excerpts from depositions, answers to interrogatories and requests for admission, other than those to be used for impeachment or rebuttal; and (d) exchange a list of expected witnesses, other than those to be

called for impeachment or rebuttal, including a brief summary of each witness' expected testimony.

(6) Counsel shall also: (a) premark all exhibits **before** trial (Plaintiff's exhibits should be marked by number, Defendant's exhibits should be marked by letter); (b) bring sufficient copies of exhibits for all counsel, the witness, and the court; (c) in any case in which the party expects to offer more than ten exhibits, place the exhibits in a three-ring binder with an appropriate tab attached to each exhibit; (d) number the pages of any exhibit that has more than one page; (e) promptly advise the opposing party of any objections to the introduction of the opposing party's proposed testimony or exhibits; and (f) meet **before** trial to attempt to reach agreement regarding the admissibility of testimony and exhibits.

(7) By agreement of the parties, all direct testimony by non-hostile witnesses regarding each party's case-in-chief shall be presented by written declaration rather than by oral question and answer. The parties shall present by oral question and answer the testimony of hostile, impeachment, and rebuttal witnesses, and shall conduct cross-examination, re-direct examination, and re-cross examination by oral question and answer. Each party shall serve and file the declarations it intends to introduce seven calendar days before trial. Each party shall notify opposing counsel in writing three calendar days before trial if it wishes to cross examine one or more of the opposing party's declarants, or if it intends to object to introduction of a declaration served by the opposing party. Failure to notify the opposing party of the intent to cross examine or object shall result in the waiver of the right to cross examine or object to the evidence. Failure to make a declarant available following timely notice form the opposing party shall result in exclusion of the testimony of that declarant.

(8) Counsel for the party who has lodged this scheduling order promptly shall serve this order on all other parties to the action, and shall file proof of such service.

The court may exclude evidence, postpone trial, or impose monetary sanctions for failure to comply with this order.

IT IS SO ORDERED.

Hon. Roger L. Efremsky

Bankruptcy Judge

Contact Information

U.S. Bankruptcy Court, Northern District of California
Courtroom 201
1300 Clay Street, Suite 300
Oakland, CA 94612
Courtroom Deputy: (510) 879-3541

Biographical Information

Education:

- Bachelor of Science, Menlo College (1978)
- Juris Doctor, Santa Clara University (1983)

Appointed:

- United States Bankruptcy Judge Northern District of California (2006)

Practice:

- Founder and partner of Efremsky & Nagel (1990-2006) specializing in representing creditors in federal bankruptcy and state court proceedings with an emphasis on the representation of secured creditors in consumer and commercial matters.

I. Judge Efremsky's Procedures and Practices

A. *Open Calendar Procedure for Judge Roger L. Efremsky*

OPEN CALENDAR PROCEDURE FOR JUDGE ROGER L. EFREMSKY

[Revised 12/2/10]

Beginning with hearings to be held after November 1, 2010, Judge Roger L. Efremsky will use an open calendar procedure for the scheduling of certain matters. This procedure will allow counsel to self-select an available date and time on the appropriate calendar and serve notice of that date and time without first having to obtain the date and time from the calendar clerk.

The court encourages all parties to set matters using the open calendar procedure whenever possible. Monica Narcisse, Judge Efremsky's courtroom deputy, will be available by telephone to schedule hearings not available for setting on the open calendar, or as needed for emergency matters. His contact information is: Monica Narcisse, 510.879-3541, or mnarcisse@canb.uscourts.gov.

1. Types of proceedings that may be set using the open calendar procedure:
    - Motions in the main case in chapter 7 and 11 cases, including motions for relief from stay: on designated Wednesdays at 2:00 p.m.
    - Motions for relief from stay in chapter 13 cases: on designated Wednesdays at 1:30 p.m.
    - Disclosure statement hearings in chapter 11 cases: on designated Tuesdays at 1:30 p.m.
    - All matters relating to chapter 13 cases requiring the presence of the chapter 13 trustee: on designated Tuesdays at 1:30 p.m. when chapter 13 confirmation hearings take place. These confirmation hearing dates will be announced in advance on a quarterly basis and posted in Judge Efremsky's calendar section on the Court's website.
    - Motions in adversary proceedings: on designated Thursdays at 11:00 a.m.

2. The open calendar procedure is not available for the following:
    - Case management conferences in adversary proceedings. The Case Administrator will select the date and time for the initial Case Management Conference before issuing the summons.
    - Plan confirmation hearings in chapter 11 cases.Following the approval of the disclosure statement, the court will schedule the date and time for the hearing on confirmation of plan.
    - Status conferences in chapter 11 cases. The court will schedule and notice a status conference on the first available status conference date after the date set for the Section 341 meeting of creditors. Status conferences are generally held on the third or fourth Tuesday of the month at 1:30 p.m.
    - Trials in adversary proceedings. All trials will be assigned a date and time and a pretrial order will be issued.
    - Any matter requiring an order shortening time. An application for an order

shortening time under B.L.R. 9006-1 is required before a hearing date will be set. Counsel should include preferred calendar dates and the notice proposed to be given to affected parties. Once the application has been reviewed, chambers will contact counsel with the date and time of the hearing as well as any special instructions regarding notice.

- Matters set by the court pursuant to an order to show cause and hearings on reaffirmation agreements.

3. Procedure:

a. In order to utilize the open calendar procedure, counsel should select an available date and time as shown on the list of dates posted in Judge Efremsky's calendar section on the court's website. The date selected must be no earlier than as required by applicable national or local rules, as nothing in this open calendar procedure alters applicable time limits.

b. After selecting an available date and time, counsel should serve proper notice of the matter in accordance with applicable rules. Note: If a hearing on a motion for relief from stay is set in accordance with this open calendar procedure more than thirty days after the date the motion is filed, the party will be deemed to have waived the thirty-day limitation of 11 U.S.C. § 362(e).

c. No later than three days after the service on other parties, counsel should provide chambers with copies of all appropriate papers in accordance with Judge Efremsky's chambers copies policy explained in his Practice and Procedures section on the court's website.

d. Once a matter is set by the open calendar procedure, with the exception of certain matters in adversary proceedings or matters noticed to all creditors, continuances may be handled through the Judge's courtroom deputy. A minimum notice of 24 hours for any continuance is encouraged. Counsel must receive e-mail or telephonic confirmation of a continuance from the courtroom deputy. Written stipulations and a proposed order are required for continuance of all case management conferences, pre-trials and scheduled trials. Matters noticed to all creditors must be continued in open court.

e. Counsel must not request that the courtroom deputy call back to confirm that the matter has been placed on the calendar. Counsel desiring confirmation that a matter has been placed on the calendar by the open calendar procedure should review the calendar on the bankruptcy court's website.

f. Failure to comply with the foregoing open calendar procedure will result in the matter not being placed on calendar. Note: Occasionally there may be a need to reschedule matters that have been placed on the calendar in accordance with this open calendar procedure. Typically this will be because of calendar congestion or unforeseen schedule changes. In those instances the courtroom deputy will contact the moving party as soon as possible so that a notice of a rescheduled hearing may be disseminated.

B. Policy and Procedures for Appearances by Telephone

POLICY AND PROCEDURES FOR APPEARANCES BY TELEPHONE
HONORABLE ROGER L. EFREMSKY
October 2010

1. Permitted Appearances.

In general, telephonic appearances are permitted except in situations where the party or counsel:

will be examining witnesses;
is the proponent of a chapter 11 disclosure statement or plan;
is counsel for a client who is present in court; or
is directed by the court to appear personally.

There are no restrictions on eligibility to appear by telephone based upon the geographic location of the counsel or the party.

2. Procedure for Arranging for Telephonic Appearances.

Telephonic appearances are arranged through Court Conference. All parties/counsel using this service must have an account or make arrangements to set one up well in advance of the hearing. If you do not have an account established with Court Conference, you must provide a credit card number at the time of making your reservation.

Appearances are arranged by reservation. To make a reservation, call **1-866-582-6878** no later than **4:00 p.m. PT the day before the appearance**.

Shortly before the Court is ready to call your matter, the Court Conference operator will contact the participant as prearranged. **All participants MUST be available when called.** If the participant is not available when called, the participant will be billed for the call and the hearing may proceed in the participant's absence. The Court may impose sanctions as set forth below.

Telephonic appearances are connected directly with the courtroom's public address system and electronic recording equipment so that a normal record is produced. To ensure a quality record, the use of car phones, cellular phones, public telephone booths, or phones in other public places is prohibited except in the most extreme emergencies. Participants should be able to hear all parties without difficulty or echo.

At the time of the hearing you may initially be in the listening mode in which case you will be able to hear the case before yours just as if you were in the courtroom. After your call is connected to the courtroom, the Courtroom Deputy will call the case. The Judge will ask for appearances and direct the manner in which the hearing proceeds. Each time a participant speaks, he or she must identify himself or herself for the record. The Court's teleconferencing system allows more than one speaker to be heard so that the Judge can interrupt a speaker to ask a question or redirect the discussion. When the Judge informs the participants that the hearing is completed, the participants may disconnect and the next case will be called.

Telephonic appearances by multiple participants are only possible where there is compliance with every procedural requirement. **Sanctions may be imposed when there is**

any deviation from the required procedures or where the court determines that a person's conduct makes telephonic appearances inappropriate. Sanctions may include dropping the matter from the calendar, continuing the hearing, proceeding in the absence of an unavailable participant, a monetary sanction of $100 or more, or a temporary or permanent prohibition against a person/firm appearing telephonically.

When the Court conducts a telephone conference on short notice and uses Court Conference, it may designate one party to bear the entire cost of the conference call. The Court may on occasion initiate calls to one or two persons directly from chambers without use of a conference operator. In those instances, the Courtroom Deputy will contact parties to inform them of the arrangements.

Because the Courtroom Deputy is usually in Court prior to the initiation of any particular call, last minute changes are generally impossible to handle and are discouraged.

Judge Efremsky's Courtroom Deputy is Monica Narcisse, 510. 879-3586. mnarcisse@canb.uscourts.gov

C. *Practices and Procedures in Judge Efremsky's Court*

PRACTICES AND PROCEDURES IN JUDGE EFREMSKY'S COURT

[revised 2/16/2012]

In addition to enforcing the Bankruptcy Local Rules for the Northern District of California ("B.L.R.") and the Federal Rules of Bankruptcy Procedure ("Rules"), Judge Efremsky has established certain practices and procedures in his court. Counsel and litigants appearing before Judge Efremsky should be aware of the following:

I. GENERAL PROCEDURES

A. Calendaring Matters

Judge Efremsky uses an "open calendar" procedure explained in the Open Calendar Procedures in Judge Efremsky's calendar section on the Court's website. Parties or counsel may also calendar matters by contacting Monica Narcisse, courtroom deputy, at 510.879-3541 or e-mail to mnarcisse@canb.uscourts.gov.

B. Telephonic Appearances

Judge Efremsky allows counsel to appear telephonically on most matters. Please review Judge Efremsky's Policy and Procedures For Appearances By Telephone in the Oakland Procedures section on the Court's website.

For relief from stay matters, chapter 13 calendar matters, adversary proceeding status conferences, and matters involving multiple telephonic appearances, parties must use Court Call for telephonic appearances (as described in more detail in the Procedures for Appearances by Telephone).

C. Communications With Chambers' Staff

Rule 9003(a) prohibits ex parte communications with the court concerning matters affecting a particular case or proceeding. Rule 5-300(C) of the California Rules of Professional Conduct specifies that for disciplinary purposes, a contact with Judge Efremsky's law clerks constitutes a contact with the judge. No attorney or party may initiate contact with the judge or his law clerks in violation of Rule 9003(a). Improper ex parte communications may include letters or e-mails to the court (especially where copies have not been provided to opposing parties and the United States Trustee) and telephone calls to the court. Individual cases may not be discussed with Judge Efremsky's law clerks except to inform the court that an ex parte request or a form of order is opposed, that an emergency pleading or request for order shortening time is being submitted, that a Chapter 11 plan proponent intends to go forward with a disclosure statement or confirmation hearing, or that a calendared matter has been settled or is being re-scheduled. In the event of a settlement or re-scheduling, counsel should also contact the judge's courtroom deputy.

To check on the status of an order, counsel should check CM/ECF or PACER. To find out how to utilize PACER, go to the Pacer Service Center website at http://pacer.psc.uscourts.gov/. If the proposed order has not been entered on the docket after seven to ten days, or if there is an urgent need for the order, counsel may contact the clerk's office.

E-mail should not be sent to Judge Efremsky, or his law clerks without prior approval.

D. Compliance With Local Rules

Counsel and parties should comply with all local rules. In particular, in order to avoid delays in the processing of orders, parties should comply with B.L.R. 9014-1(b)(4) (when requesting entry of order by default) and B.L.R. 9022-1 (when relief is sought against a particular person or entity that has not stipulated to the relief). See section II. C entitled "Submission of Orders."

E. Obtaining Continuances

Trials: Judge Efremsky will grant continuances of trials for good cause only, even when the parties stipulate to a continuance. A request for continuance must be made by noticed motion or by a written stipulation stating the reason for the requested continuance. Parties requesting a continuance of a trial should comply with B.L.R. 9006-1.

Motions: If parties agree to continue a scheduled hearing on a motion, they must contact the judge's courtroom deputy to inform her of the new date and time and file and serve a notice of continuance. No written stipulation is necessary. A party requesting a continuance that is opposed should comply with B.L.R. 9006-1.

F. Courtesy Copies for Chambers

All courtesy copies are to be submitted to the court to the attention of Judge Efremsky's courtroom deputy. A printed copy of the "Notice of Electronic Filing" shall be attached to the courtesy paper copy of the electronically filed pleading and marked "chambers's copy."

Motions for Relief From Stay: Chambers copies of the cover sheet and certificate of service are required for all motions. Chambers copies of the remaining papers are not required.

Motions to Extend the Stay or Impose the Stay: Chambers copies are required of all papers filed for such motions.

Adversary Proceedings: No chambers copies are required of the complaint, answer, counterclaim, etc., regardless of length. Chambers copies are required of all case management conference statements and all other papers regardless of length.

Fee Applications: Chambers copies are required for all fee applications.

Chapter 11 Cases: No chambers copies are required of the petition, schedules of assets and liabilities, statement of financial affairs and similar documents filed at the onset of case. Chambers copies are required of all "first day" motions and all plans and disclosure statements and all other papers regardless of length.

Chapter 7 and 13 Cases: No chambers copies are required of the petition, schedules of assets and liabilities, statement of financial affairs and similar documents filed at the onset of case. In chapter 13 cases, chambers copies of all pre-hearing conference statements and motions are required regardless of length.

G. Request To Seal Documents

A party wishing to file a document under seal should follow Civ. L.R. 79-5 (incorporated by B.L.R. 1001-2(a)). See also Rule 9018. Sealing filed documents is disfavored under the law and by this court (see 11 U.S.C. § 107); accordingly, the motion must satisfactorily explain why the court should disregard the policy of open access to public documents. Parties opposing such a request should respond as soon as possible, since the court will normally act on any such matter promptly and without a hearing.

H. Discovery Disputes

Judge Efremsky will generally hold a telephonic conference to resolve a discovery dispute in lieu of formal motions to compel or quash discovery. (See B.L.R. 1001-2(a) and Civ. L.R. 37-1(a) and (b)). Parties should comply with the procedures set forth in Civ. L.R. 37-1. To schedule a telephonic conference regarding a discovery dispute, counsel should contact the judge's courtroom deputy. Any request for sanctions relating to a discovery dispute must be made by separate noticed motion.

II. OTHER PRACTICES AND PROCEDURES

A. Obtaining an Order Shortening Time

A party seeking an order shortening time must comply with B.L.R. 9006-1. A request for an order shortening time should be made in writing. In particular, the party must submit a declaration describing the efforts made to obtain the consent of the opposing party to the order shortening time. In general, Judge Efremsky will not require the opposing party to file any written response to a motion that is scheduled on shortened time, and opposition may be presented at the hearing.

Judge Efremsky does not require an order shortening time on a motion for interim authority to use cash collateral or obtain credit (including DIP financing). See Rule 4001(b)(2) and (c)(2) (hearing may be conducted within 14 days after service of motion to avoid immediate and irreparable harm to estate pending final hearing). To obtain a date and time for the initial hearing on a motion to use cash collateral or obtain credit, counsel should contact the judge's courtroom deputy.

B. Procedures for Temporary Restraining Orders (TRO)

Judge Efremsky generally prefers at least 72 hours' notice to, and service of moving papers upon, opposing parties. Any request for a TRO (or other injunctive relief) requires an adversary proceeding. See Rule 7001(7). Accordingly, a complaint must be filed prior to the hearing. To obtain a date and time for a hearing on a request for a TRO, counsel should contact the judge's courtroom deputy.

C. Submission of Orders

Uploaded orders should be converted, not scanned.

Judge Efremsky frequently receives proposed orders from parties who have not complied with B.L.R. 9021-1 and 9022-1. The following addresses common errors, and is not a substitute for reading the rules.

A proposed order submitted after a hearing should contain the signatures of any other counsel who appeared at the hearing, approving it as to form. Otherwise, the submitting party should file a proof of service evidencing service of the proposed order on all such counsel. Orders not approved as to form will ordinarily be lodged for 7 days after service, but this is not a guarantee that they will be held for that period.

Those parties not using CM/ECF should provide copies, stamped and addressed envelopes (including a return envelope), a list of parties to be served, and a form of notice of entry of order for the clerk to use. Those parties using CM/ECF should submit orders or judgments with a service list of persons and entities to whom service is required by B.L.R. 9022-1.

Parties are frequently uncertain as to who must be served. Under Rule 9022 and B.L.R. 9022-1, notice of entry of orders or judgments must be served by the clerk on all "contesting parties" and the United States Trustee (and such other parties as the court directs). Judge Efremsky interprets "contesting parties" to mean (1) any identified, named party against whom relief is sought(including the debtor(s) and debtor(s)' counsel for all orders in response to motions for relief from the automatic stay) unless that party (a) has stipulated in writing or in open court to the relief sought (not just the more traditional "approved as to form"); or (b) was present when the order or judgment was signed in open court, and (2) to the extent relief is sought on notice to creditors generally, only those creditors who file a written objection or request for a hearing, or who appear at the hearing and object to the relief sought, unless such written or oral opposition has been expressly withdrawn. Other parties need not be served.

III. SPECIFIC MOTIONS AND ORDERS

A. Default Judgments In Adversary Proceedings

When requesting a default judgment in an adversary proceeding, the moving party must submit a proof of service showing that the request was served on the non-responding defendant. When submitting either a proposed default judgment or a proposed judgment pursuant to a stipulation that relates to the nondischargeability of a credit card debt, in addition to all other documents submitted to the court in support of the judgment, the moving party must submit copies of the credit card statements originally sent to the debtor for the time period at issue in the underlying complaint as well as one year prior to that time period. Appropriate redactions of private information must be made. These statements should be attached as an exhibit to a declaration by a party competent to testify that such statements are true and correct copies of the records in question.

In certain matters, determined on a case-by-case basis, the court may require that the plaintiff seeking a default judgment schedule a "prove-up" hearing (see Fed. R. Civ. P. 55(b)(2) and Rule 7055) and serve notice of the hearing on the defendant at least fourteen days prior to the hearing. At such hearing, any witnesses for the plaintiff must appear personally; the defaulting defendant is entitled to cross-examine the witness but is not permitted to present its own evidence or witnesses.

B. Orders Retaining Professionals

Retention orders must include all material terms of the professional's employment, including whether the employment is under 11 U.S.C. § 327 or § 1103; the date employment is effective; the basis of compensation. If the provisions of 11 U.S.C. § 328(a) limiting review of compensation are applicable, this must be clearly stated. Any proposed success fees or other back-end fees must be clearly described. Any limitation on the professionals' liability such as indemnification provisions, procedural limitations, claim limitations, damage limitations must be clearly described and, if such provisions are intended to bind successors and assigns, this must be clearly stated. Material terms of employment not set forth in the order are not included in the court's approval.

C. Motions to Avoid Judgment Liens that Impair an Exemption

In order to obtain an order avoiding a judgment lien under 11 U.S.C. § 522(f)(1)(A), the moving party must file a declaration from the debtor or some other appropriate offer of proof setting forth the grounds for avoiding the lien. In particular, the declarant(s) should provide the following information: the value of the encumbered property, the amount and nature of the debtor's exemption, the extent of the impairment, and the amount of the judgment lien and all other liens encumbering the property (see 11 U.S.C. § 522(f)(2)(A)). The moving party should also disclose any other facts supporting the contention that 11 U.S.C. §522(f)(1) is applicable.

The moving party should also ensure that service of the motion complies with Rule 7004 and Rule 9014(b). See Beneficial Cal., Inc. v. Villar (In re Villar), 317 B.R. 88 (9th Cir. BAP 2004).

D. Motions to Sell Free and Clear of Liens to Value Secured Claims, or to Assume/or Assign Executory Contracts or Leases

Parties filing motions to sell property of the estate, motions to sell free and clear of liens, motions to value secured claims, or motions to assume or assign executory contracts or leases must comply with B.L.R. 6004 1 or 6006 1 and with this court's Guidelines Re Sale Orders, available on the court's website.

Judge Efremsky expects counsel to comply with Rule 6006, dealing with omnibus motions to assume and reject executory contracts and leases.

E. Sale Motions: Section 363(m) Good Faith Determinations

Burden of Proof; Discretionary Finding: Any bidder requesting a judicial determination under 11 U.S.C. § 363(m) that its purchase of assets is in good faith (in an order authorizing a sale under § 363(b) or by separate order) has the burden to establish such good faith. This court has discretion to refuse to make such a finding, and the preclusive effect of such a finding may be limited. T.C. Investors v. Joseph (In re M Capital Corp.), 290 B.R. 743, 748-49 (9th Cir. BAP 2003).

Evidentiary Support: A bidder seeking a § 363 good faith determination must file a written declaration (or, if the bidder is not an individual, a declaration of its responsible officer or agent with personal knowledge) demonstrating the proposed bidder's good faith, including disclosure of:

1. The bidder's prepetition and postpetition relationship with other bidders, the debtor, major creditors or equity security holders in the case, or any of the debtor's officers, directors, agents, or employees;

2. The bidder's expected relationship after the sale with the debtor's present or former officers, directors, agents, or employees (including whether any offers of employment or compensation have been made or will be offered to debtor's present or former officers, directors, agents, or employees);

3. Whether any consideration is contemplated to be transferred or has been transferred by the bidder in connection with the sale to any person other than the debtor (or the trustee of the debtor's estate); and

4. The absence of fraud or collusion between the bidder and any other bidders or the debtor's officers, directors, agents or employees, or any attempt to take unfair advantage of other bidders.

For further guidance regarding good faith findings, see this court's Guidelines Re Sale Orders available in the Rules and Procedures section on the court's website.

F. Compromise/Settlement of Controversy - Rule 9019

Approval of compromises must be presented by the following: (1) a motion, and (2) a supporting declaration from someone with first hand knowledge of the reasons for, and the terms of, the settlement. The filing of a notice alone is inadequate. The motion should provide an explanation of why the compromise is "fair and equitable" and "reasonable." It should include an analysis of the four factors set out in Martin v. Kane (In re A & C Properties), 784 F.2d 1377, 1381 (9th Cir. 1986) that establishes that each of the "A & C" factors is satisfied. In routine settlements, this can be accomplished with a paragraph or two; in more complex matters a more detailed analysis is expected.

Not all documents need to be served on all parties. It is sufficient that creditors be given a notice that succinctly summarizes what has been stated in the motion and supporting declaration. See Rule 2002(a)(3).

G. First Day Motions

In the initial days of a case, Chapter 11 debtors frequently file financing motions, motions to pay prepetition wages of employees, or other motions that may have a significant effect on the future administration of the estate. Judge Efremsky requires that such motions be accompanied by declarations signed by representatives of the debtor with personal knowledge of the facts asserted and setting forth adequate financial information to put the motion(s) in context. The moving party should provide sufficient financial information to enable the court to assess the impact of the requested relief on unsecured creditors.

Specifically, the moving party should include information about the value of a debtor's assets, and the extent to which they are encumbered; the amount of current and long term liabilities, with specific mention of debts entitled to priority under 11 U.S.C. § 507; the current cash situation; the amount of prepetition wages owed and to whom (by name and position/occupation with the debtor and amount owed); the nature of the connections (if any) between the debtor and any party providing financing; and, unless unknown, the Chapter 11 exit strategy of the debtor (e.g., sale as a going concern, liquidation of assets, continuation of business with infusion of capital, etc.). See also the court's Guidelines for Cash Collateral and Financing Stipulations available in the Rules and Procedures section of the court's website.

H. Employment of Auctioneers and Brokers

Judge Efremsky will not allow auctioneers to recover labor costs or to charge a buyers' premium. Any application to employ an auctioneer should reflect the auctioneer's agreement not to charge such costs and premiums. Similarly, Judge Efremsky will not allow real estate brokers representing the estate (as seller) to represent buyers. See 11 U.S.C. § 327(a) ((trustee may employ "professional persons, that do not hold or represent an interest adverse to the estate"). Any application to employ a real estate broker should reflect the agreement of the broker that he or she will not represent the buyer.

I. Fee Applications in Chapter 13 Cases

Even though Guideline 7 of the Guidelines for Compensation and Expense Reimbursement of Professionals and Trustees for the United States Bankruptcy Court for the Northern District of California does not specifically apply to fee applications in Chapter 13 cases, Judge Efremsky does require counsel in Chapter 13 cases to provide their clients with the letter described in that Guideline.

J. Fees Generally

Travel: Judge Efremsky generally will allow up to two hours of compensation for non-working airplane travel time, to account for inevitable delays for security and administration involved in air travel. Other air travel time is not likely to be compensable, per Guideline 17 of the Guidelines for Compensation and Expense Reimbursement of Professionals and Trustees.

Conflicts Checks/Ethical Walls/Change of Firms: Judge Efremsky expects counsel to write off, and will normally disallow, time spent identifying, clearing and avoiding conflicts and complying with Rule 2014(a). Such time is not very different from a firm absorbing the time expended on its own efforts to secure a new client, for which Judge Efremsky doubts any professional would bill. For the same reasons, he expects counsel to write off, and normally will disallow, time spent by professionals who change offices or firms, and need to clear conflicts, set up new files, brief new attorneys, or perform other tasks in connection with the transition.

Retainers: Judge Efremsky does not require retainers to be held in a trust account, unless that is the agreement between the attorney and the client.

K. Disclosure Statement Hearings

B.L.R. 3017-1 will be strictly enforced. In particular, counsel for the proponent must notify chambers by telephone at least three business days prior to the hearing that the hearing will go forward and a competent witness for the plan proponent must be present at the hearing. The court will normally refuse to proceed with the hearing if this call is not made or the debtor or other plan proponent does not appear.

L. Stipulations for Relief from Stay

Generally, Judge Efremsky will not approve a stipulation for relief from stay that purports to be effective in any subsequent case filed by the debtor. Judge Efremsky will approve provisions that grant relief from the stay on ten days' notice to the debtor and debtor's counsel if the debtor defaults on agreed payments under the order before debtor becomes post-petition current. If, however, the debtor defaults after becoming post-petition current, the movant must re-set the motion on ten days' notice.

Hon. M. Elaine Hammond

Bankruptcy Judge

Contact Information

U.S. Bankruptcy Court, Northern District of California
Courtroom 215
1300 Clay Street, Suite 300
Oakland, CA 94612
Courtroom Deputy: (510) 879-3529

Biographical Information

Education:

- University of North Carolina School of Law - J.D.
- Duke University - B.A.

Appointed:

- United States Bankruptcy Judge Northern District of California (February 2012)

Practice:

- Friedman Dumas & Springwater LLP, San Francisco - Partner
- Prior to joining Friedman Dumas & Springwater LLP in 2003, was an associate with Murphy Sheneman Julian & Rogers.
- Specialized in representing debtors and creditors in commercial bankruptcy cases and out-of-court restructurings.

I. Judge Hammond's Procedures and Practices

A. *Open Calendar Procedure*

OPEN CALENDAR PROCEDURE FOR JUDGE M. ELAINE HAMMOND

Beginning with hearings to be held after March 1, 2012, Judge M. Elaine Hammond will use an open calendar procedure for the scheduling of certain matters. This procedure will allow counsel to self-select an available date and time on the appropriate calendar and serve notice of that date and time without first having to obtain the date and time from the calendar clerk.

The court encourages all parties to set matters using the open calendar procedure whenever possible. Ruby Bautista, Judge Hammond's courtroom deputy, will be available by telephone to schedule hearings not available for setting on the open calendar, or as needed for emergency matters. Her contact information is: Ruby Bautista, (510)879-3529, or ruby_bautista@canb.uscourts.gov.

1. Types of proceedings that may be set using the open calendar procedure:

- Motions in the main case in chapter 13 cases: on designated Thursdays at 9:30 a.m.
- Motions in the main case in Chapter 7 and 11 cases: on designated Thursdays at 10:30 a.m.
- Motions in adversary proceedings: on designated Mondays at 11:00 a.m.
- Motions for relief from stay: on designated Fridays at 10:00 a.m.
- All matters relating to chapter 13 cases requiring the presence of the chapter 13 trustee: on designated Tuesdays at 10:00 a.m. when chapter 13 confirmation hearings take place. These confirmation hearing dates will be announced in advance on a quarterly basis and posted in Judge Hammond's calendar section on the Court's website.

2. The open calendar procedure is not available for the following:

- **Case management conferences in adversary proceedings.**
  The Case Administrator will select the date and time for the initial Case Management Conference before issuing the summons.
- **Plan confirmation hearings in chapter 11 cases.**
  Following the approval of the disclosure statement, the court will schedule the date and time for the hearing on confirmation of plan.
- **Status conferences in chapter 11 cases.**
  The court will schedule and notice a status conference on the first available status conference date after the date set for the Section 341 meeting of creditors. Status conferences are generally held on Thursdays at 9:30 a.m.
- **Trials in adversary proceeding.**
  All trials will be assigned a date and time and a pretrial order will be issued.
- **Any matter requiring an order shortening time.**
  An application for an order shortening time under B.L.R. 9006-1 is required before a hearing date will be set. Counsel should include preferred calendar

dates and the notice proposed to be given to affected parties. Once the application has been reviewed, chambers will contact counsel with the date and time of the hearing as well as any special instructions regarding notice.

- **Matters set by the court pursuant to an order to show cause and hearings on reaffirmation agreements.**
- **Any matter in which the parties anticipate more than 30 minutes of court time will be required.**

3. <u>Procedure:</u>

a. In order to utilize the open calendar procedure, counsel should select an available date and time as shown on the list of dates posted in Judge Hammond's calendar section on the court's website. The date selected must be no earlier than as required by applicable national or local rules, as nothing in this open calendar procedure alters applicable time limits.

b. After selecting an available date and time, counsel should serve proper notice of the matter in accordance with applicable rules. **Note:** If a hearing on a motion for relief from stay is set in accordance with this open calendar procedure more than thirty days after the date the motion is filed, the party will be deemed to have waived the thirty-day limitation of 11 U.S.C. § 362(e).

c. No later than **three** days after the service on other parties, counsel should provide chambers with copies of all appropriate papers in accordance with Judge Hammond's chambers copies policy explained in her Practice and Procedures section on the court's website.

d. Once a matter is set by the open calendar procedure, with the exception of certain matters in adversary proceedings or matters noticed to all creditors, continuances may be handled through the Judge's courtroom deputy. A minimum notice of 24 hours for any continuance is encouraged. Counsel must receive e-mail or telephonic confirmation of a continuance from the courtroom deputy. Written stipulations and a proposed order are required for continuance of all case management conferences, pre-trials and scheduled trials. Matters noticed to all creditors must be continued in open court.

e. Counsel **must not** request that the courtroom deputy call back to confirm that the matter has been placed on the calendar. Counsel desiring confirmation that a matter has been placed on the calendar by the open calendar procedure should review the calendar on the bankruptcy court's website.

f. Failure to comply with the foregoing open calendar procedure will result in the matter not being placed on calendar. **Note:** Occasionally there may be a need to reschedule matters that have been placed on the calendar in accordance with this open calendar procedure. Typically this will be because of calendar congestion or unforeseen schedule changes. In those instances the courtroom deputy will contact the moving party as soon as possible so that a notice of a rescheduled hearing may be disseminated.

B. Policy and Procedures for Appearance by Telephone

POLICY AND PROCEDURES FOR APPEARANCES BY TELEPHONE

1. Permitted Appearances.

In general, telephonic appearances are permitted except in situations where the party or counsel:

will be examining witnesses;
is the proponent of a chapter 11 disclosure statement or plan;
is counsel for a client who is present in court; or
is directed by the court to appear personally.

There are no restrictions on eligibility to appear by telephone based upon the geographic location of the counsel or the party.

2. Procedure for Arranging for Telephonic Appearances.

Telephonic appearances are arranged through Court Conference. All parties/counsel using this service must have an account or make arrangements to set one up well in advance of the hearing. If you do not have an account established with Court Conference, you must provide a credit card number at the time of making your reservation.

Appearances are arranged by reservation. To make a reservation, call **1-866-582-6878** no later than **4:00 p.m. PT the day before the appearance**.

Shortly before the Court is ready to call your matter, the Court Conference operator will contact the participant as prearranged. **All participants MUST be available when called.** If the participant is not available when called, the participant will be billed for the call and the hearing may proceed in the participant's absence. The Court may impose sanctions as set forth below.

Telephonic appearances are connected directly with the courtroom's public address system and electronic recording equipment so that a normal record is produced. To ensure a quality record, the use of car phones, cellular phones, public telephone booths, or phones in other public places is prohibited except in the most extreme emergencies. Participants should be able to hear all parties without difficulty or echo.

At the time of the hearing you may initially be in the listening mode in which case you will be able to hear the case before yours just as if you were in the courtroom. After your call is connected to the courtroom, the Courtroom Deputy will call the case. The Judge will ask for appearances and direct the manner in which the hearing proceeds. Each time a participant speaks, he or she must identify himself or herself for the record. The Court's teleconferencing system allows more than one speaker to be heard so that the Judge can interrupt a speaker to ask a question or redirect the discussion. When the Judge informs the participants that the hearing is completed, the participants may disconnect and the next case will be called.

Telephonic appearances by multiple participants are only possible where there is compliance with every procedural requirement. **Sanctions may be imposed when there is any deviation from the required procedures or where the court determines that a person's conduct makes telephonic appearances inappropriate.** Sanctions may include dropping the matter from the calendar, continuing the hearing, proceeding in the absence of an unavailable participant, a monetary sanction of $100 or more, or a temporary or permanent prohibition against a person/firm appearing telephonically.

When the Court conducts a telephone conference on short notice and uses Court Conference, it may designate one party to bear the entire cost of the conference call. The Court may on occasion initiate calls to one or two persons directly from chambers without use of a conference operator. In those instances, the Courtroom Deputy will contact parties to inform them of the arrangements.

Because the Courtroom Deputy is usually in Court prior to the initiation of any particular call, last minute changes are generally impossible to handle and are discouraged.

Judge Hammond's Courtroom Deputy is Ruby Bautista, 510-879-3529. Ruby_Bautista@canb.uscourts.gov.

C. Policy for Chambers Courtesy Copies

Policy for Chambers Courtesy Copies

Following are Judge Hammond's requirements for submission of Chambers Copies of documents filed through the court's Electronic Case Filing ("ECF") system:

1. All motions for which a hearing is scheduled: Chambers copies are required where the page count of all documents, including any exhibits and proofs of service, exceeds ten (10) pages. This includes motions for relief from the automatic stay.

2. Requests for relief without hearing: Chambers copies are not required, regardless of length.

3. All Chapters: Chambers copies are not required of petitions, schedules of assets and liabilities, statements of financial affairs, and similar documents filed at the onset of the case.

4. Adversary Proceedings: Chambers copies are required of all filed documents where the page count of all documents, including any exhibits and proofs of service, exceeds ten (10) pages. This includes a complaint, answer, counterclaim, etc.

All courtesy copies are to be submitted to the court to the attention of Judge Hammond's Courtroom Deputy and marked "Chambers Copy." It is not necessary to provide a printed copy of the ECF receipt confirming the filing of the original document.

If mailing chambers copies, please address as follows:

via U.S. Postal Service:
U.S. Bankruptcy Court
Judge M. Elaine Hammond
Attention: Courtroom Deputy
P.O. Box 2070
Oakland, CA 94604-2070

via Federal Express:
Judge M. Elaine Hammond
Attention: Courtroom Deputy
U.S. Bankruptcy Court
1300 Clay St., Suite 300
Oakland, CA 94612

Hon. Alan Jaroslovsky
Chief Bankruptcy Judge

Contact Information

U.S. Bankruptcy Court, Northern District of California
99 South E. Street
Santa Rosa, CA 95404
Courtroom Deputy: (707) 547-5920

Biographical Information

Education:

- University of California Los Angeles B.A
- Golden Gate University J.D.

Appointed:

- Bankruptcy Judge Northern District of California (January 1987)

Practice:

- Solo bankruptcy practitioner in Santa Rosa prior to appointment of Bankruptcy Judge

Affiliations:

- Former professor of law and past president of the Sonoma County Bar Association
- Former Naval Officer and Vietnam veteran

Author:

- Practical Bankruptcy Procedure (Shepard's/McGraw Hill 1993)
- Published articles in the CEB Litigation Reporter, the California Real Property Law Journal and the California State Bar Journal
- Lectured and written extensively on bankruptcy law and procedure

I. Judge Jaroslovsky's Procedures and Practices

A. *ECF and Orders Procedures*

1. **Chambers Copies of Electronically Filed Pleadings**
   Chambers copies of electronically filed pleadings are not required or desired.

2. **Pleadings to be Filed in Paper**
   None. The court expects electronic filers to file all pleadings electronically.

3. **Emergency Matters**
   When an emergency motion is filed electronically, please call (707) 547-5900 and ask the Deputy Clerk to transfer you to the Order Processing Section.

4. **Orders After Hearing**
   All orders after hearing shall be sent as an attachment by email to Chambers_Orders@canb.uscourts.gov or via ECF as an Order Upload. If sent as an email attachment, it must be in WordPerfect format (preferred) or MS Word format. If there is an urgent need for an immediate order, counsel should bring it to the hearing in one of these formats on a floppy disk. The email must contain the following information, in the following order, in the subject line: Hearing date (mm/dd/yy), debtors' name (abbreviations OK), case number, and title of order. For example: 01/26/03 Harrington 02-12365 Order for Relief From Stay.

   DO NOT SUBMIT ENVELOPES unless ordered to do so.

   IF THE OPPOSING PARTY HAS APPROVED THE FORM OF ORDER, please so certify in the body of the email.

   IF YOU HAVE ONLY SERVED COPIES OF THE PROPOSED ORDER, as required by Local Rule 9021-1(c), but not sought its approval, so certify in the body of the email and state when you served it. Do not submit the order until at least five days have passed since you served it.

5. ***ExParte* Orders and Applications**
   For *ex parte* orders and applications made pursuant to FRBP 9013 (e.g., applications to employ professionals, applications to re-open cases, etc.), combine the application and order into a single document (only one caption) and submit it in WordPerfect or MS Word Format by email.

6. **Orders by Default**
   Attorneys should file their application and when you are sure that the application is on the docket, email a WordPerfect or MS Word form of order to Chambers_Orders@canb.uscourts.gov.

7. **E-Orders**
   Alternatively, attorneys may utilize the e-orders process. E-Order Procedures. (http://www.canb.uscourts.gov/files/E-Orders.pdf)

B. Notice Regarding Proposed Orders Filed with Motions

NOTICE REGARDING PROPOSED ORDERS FILED WITH MOTIONS

As I am sure you know by now, the amendments to the Federal Rules of Bankruptcy Procedure which go into effect on December 1 require the filing of proposed forms of order with certain motions. Please make sure that every proposed form of order is clearly marked as proposed, is filed only as an exhibit to a motion, and is not docketed in such a manner as to lead anyone to believe it is an order of the court.

Most importantly, note that proposed forms of order filed with motions will not actually be signed by the court. In order to have an order signed, you must either email a .wpd or .doc version to CC Chambers_Orders@canb.uscourts.gov or upload a .pdf version through CM/ECF. *DO NOT PUT "PROPOSED" ON AN ORDER WHICH IS SUBMITTED FOR SIGNATURE.*

Lastly, please do not "jump the gun" by filing under the new rules before they are in effect.

As always, thank you for your cooperation and compliance with our procedures.

Dated: November 28, 2007

ALAN JAROSLOVSKY
United States Bankruptcy Judge

C. Primer, Explanation, and Plea Regarding Uploaded Orders

PRIMER, EXPLANATION, AND PLEA REGARDING UPLOADED ORDERS

The rules for uploading orders for signature via CM/ECF require that orders submitted this way not have blank date and signature lines at the end and instead say "**END OF ORDER**." This is because this type of order is signed electronically on the upper right of the first page of the order, not at the end.

This rule is applicable to all judges in the district. However, a few of the judges still print out the orders and sign them manually. That is why some judges do not enforce the "END OF ORDER" rule. This division is the smallest, and we are very swamped. I never scan and manually sign an order. Therefore, I must ask you to comply with the "END OF ORDER" rule.

While we are on the subject, please note that documents created by Adobe software are very difficult to edit and documents created by scanning are impossible to edit. Since I can't edit them and I won't print them, if you want me to sign the order it must be submitted exactly as you want it signed. This means no "Proposed" in the caption and NO BLANKS. Submit the order exactly as you want it signed. If it needs changes, I will bounce it with the needed corrections noted.

In this division only, you have an alternative means of obtaining a signed order. You can email a wpd or doc version to chambers_orders@canb.uscourts.gov. The advantage for me is that I can edit such orders with ease before I electronically sign them. The advantages for you are that you don't have to worry about the order being bounced and you get an order which looks like a traditional court order, signed at the end. The choice is yours but please, don't submit orders both ways. Choose one or the other.

I realize these requirements place a burden on your offices. However, there is a quid pro quo: You never need to send a paper "chambers copy" of anything to me, ever. I hope that makes this all worthwhile for you.

Thank you very much for your understanding and cooperation.

Dated: August 23, 2010

____

Alan Jaroslovsky
U.S. Bankruptcy Judge

Hon. Stephen L. Johnson

Bankruptcy Judge

Contact Information

U.S. Bankruptcy Court, Northern District of California
Courtroom 3099
280 South First Street
San Jose, CA 95113
Courtroom Deputy: (408) 278-7556

Biographical Information

Education:

- Bachelor of Science, University of San Francisco
- Juris Doctor, University of California, Hastings College of Law

Appointed:

- United States Bankruptcy Judge Northern District of California, San Jose Division (October 13, 2010)

Practice:

- Assistant United States Attorney, San Francisco, California
- Trial Attorney, United States Trustee's Office
- Adjunct Professor, University of California, Hastings College of Law
- Certified Public Accountant

Extracurricular:

- Member, Editorial Board of the California Bankruptcy Journal
- Member, Insolvency Law Committee of the State Bar of California
- Member, Bench-Bar Liaison Committee for the Bankruptcy Court for the Northern District of California
- Volunteer, San Francisco Bar Association's Volunteer Legal Services Project
- Volunteer, Rebuilding Together

I. Judge Johnson's Procedures and Practices

A. Chapter 11 Status Conference Checklist

CHAPTER 11 STATUS CONFERENCE CHECKLIST

The Purpose Of The Status Conference:

- To review the reasons for the chapter 11 filing
- To understand the debtor's assets and liabilities; and
- To understand the debtors strategy for exiting chapter 11

Counsel should expect that the Court will generally set deadlines in each case, including deadlines for filing and confirming a plan of reorganization.

Chapter 11 debtors must file a Status Conference Statement at least 7 calendar days in advance of the hearing. The failure to file a timely Status Conference Statement may be cause for conversion or dismissal of a case and for sanctions against counsel.

The Status Conference Statement should discuss the following issues:

- Nature of operations and factors leading to bankruptcy filing;
- Debtor's attendance at § 341(a) Meeting of Creditors;
- Estate's need for professionals (e.g., lawyers, accountants, brokers)
- Unique issues regarding secured debt, employees, executory contracts, cash collateral, existing management and/or equity owners;
- Financial results from post-petition operations;
- Litigation status;
- Compliance with U.S. Trustee's requests (e.g., debtor-in-possession (DIP), Initial Debtor Interview);
- An outline of the proposed Chapter 11 plan; and
- A proposed deadline for the filing of a plan and disclosure statement and for confirmation.

Complying With The Requirements Of The Bankruptcy Code And Rules:

The Court expects strict compliance with the Code and Rules. Failure to comply with the following requirements often leads to an early conversion of the case:

- Attendance at § 341(a) Meeting of Creditors.
- Cash Collateral. 11 U.S.C. § 363(c)(2) prohibits the use of cash collateral unless the debtor has either the prior consent of each creditor having an interest in the collateral or an order from the Court.
- Transactions Outside the Ordinary Course of Business. 11 U.S.C. § 363(b)(1) requires prior notice and hearing.
- Post Petition Taxes. The Court expects all post petition taxes to be paid timely and all required tax returns to be timely filed.
- Monthly Operating Reports. Bankruptcy Local Rule 2015-2 requires monthly operating reports and tax reports to be filed on the 21th day of each month.
- Quarterly United States Trustee Fees. 28 U.S.C. § 1930(a)(6) requires a quarterly fee to be paid to the United States Trustee. The amount of the fee will depend

upon the amount of disbursements made by the debtor during each quarter.

- Funds of the Estate. Bankruptcy Local Rule 2015-1 requires all estate funds to be deposited and maintained in a debtor-in-possession (DIP) bank account.

B. Open Calendar Procedure

OPEN CALENDAR PROCEDURE

The San Jose Division utilizes an Open Calendar Procedure for the scheduling of certain matters. This procedure will allow counsel to self-select an available date and time on the appropriate San Jose division judge's calendar and serve notice of that date and time without first having to obtain the date and time from the calendar clerk. Procedures for each Judge is provided below.

The court encourages all parties to set matters using the Open Calendar Procedure whenever possible. The courtroom deputy for each judge will be available by telephone to schedule hearings not available for setting on the open calendar, or as needed for emergency matters.

Stephen L. Johnson, Bankruptcy Judge
Courtroom 3099
Tanya Bracegirdle, Courtroom Deputy for Judge Stephen Johnson
408-278-7556
tanya_bracegirdle@canb.uscourts.gov

1. Types of proceedings that may be set in accordance with the Open Calendar Procedure:
   - Motions for Relief from Stay for San Jose Chapter 7 and Chapter 11 cases, on designated Tuesdays at 9:30 a.m.
   - Motions for Relief from Stay for Chapter 13 cases, on designated Tuesdays at 10:00 a.m.
   - Motions in Chapter 7 and Chapter 11 main cases, on designated Wednesdays at 1:30 p.m.
   - Final Accounts, on designated Wednesdays at 1:30 p.m.
   - Fee Applications for Chapter 7 or Chapter 11 cases, on designated Wednesdays at 1:30 p.m.
   - Chapter 11 status conference hearings on designated Mondays at 1:30 p.m.
   - Chapter 11 Disclosure Statement hearings, on designated Mondays at 3:00 p.m.
   - All matters relating to the Chapter 13 main cases, on designated Thursdays at 9:30 a.m.
   - Motions in adversary cases, on designated Thursdays at 9:30 a.m.

2. The Open Calendar Procedure will not be available for the following:
   - Case Management Conferences in adversary cases
     The Case Administrator will select the date and time for the initial Case Management Conference before issuing the summons.
   - Chapter 11 hearing on confirmation of plan.
     Following the approval of the disclosure statement, the court will schedule the date and time for the hearing on confirmation of plan.
   - Chapter 11 status conferences.

The court will schedule and notice a status conference on the first available status conference date after the date set for the Section 341 meeting of creditors.

- Trials in adversary proceedings.
  All trials will be assigned a date and time by Judge Johnson.
- Any matter requiring an order shortening time.
  An application for an order shortening time under B.L.R. 9006-1 is required before a hearing date will be set. Counsel should include preferred calendar dates and the notice proposed to affected parties. Once Judge Johnson has reviewed the application, a law clerk or courtroom deputy will telephone with the date and time of the hearing as well as any special instructions regarding notice.
- Matters set by the court pursuant to an order to show cause.

3. Procedure.

a. In order to utilize the Open Calendar Procedure, counsel should select an available date and time as shown on the appropriate attached list for the judge assigned the main case. The lists will also be posted on the court's Internet website at http://www.canb.uscourts.gov. The date selected must be no earlier than as required by applicable national or local rules, as nothing in this Open Calendar Procedure alters applicable time limits.

b. After selecting an available date and time, counsel should serve proper notice of the matter in accordance with applicable rules.

Note: If a motion for relief from stay is set by a party in accordance with this Open Calendar Procedure more than thirty days after the date the motion is filed, the party will be deemed to waive the thirty-day limitation of 11 U.S.C. § 362(e).

c. No later than **three** days after the service on other parties, counsel should file all appropriate papers with the court. Counsel need not include copies of deeds of trust with motions for relief from stay or motions to avoid liens or similar motions. The court will request such copies if necessary.

d. Once a matter is set by the Open Calendar Procedure, with the exception of certain matters in adversary proceedings or matters noticed to all creditors, continuances may be handled through the assigned judge's courtroom deputy, Tanya Bracegirdle, by telephone at 408-278-7556 or by e-mail at tanya_bracegirdle@canb.uscourts.gov. A minimum notice of 24 hours for any continuance is encouraged. Counsel must receive either written confirmation of a continuance by e-mail or telephonically from the courtroom deputy. Written stipulations and a proposed order are required for all Case Management Conferences, Pre-Trials and scheduled Trials. Matters noticed to all creditors must be continued in open court.

e. Counsel **must not** request that the courtroom deputy call back to confirm that the matter has been placed on the calendar. Counsel desiring confirmation that a matter has been placed on the calendar by the Open Calendar Procedure should review the published calendars in the local legal newspapers, or its calendar on the bankruptcy court's Internet site.

f. Failure to comply with the foregoing Open Calendar Procedure will result in the matter not being placed on calendar.

Note: Occasionally there may be a need to reschedule matters that have been placed on the calendar in accordance with this Open Calendar Procedure. Typically this will be because of calendar congestion or unforeseen schedule changes. In those instances the judge's courtroom deputy will contact the moving party as soon as possible so that a notice of a rescheduled hearing may be disseminated.

C. Policy and Procedures for Appearances by Telephone

POLICY AND PROCEDURES FOR APPEARANCES BY TELEPHONE HONORABLE STEPHEN L. JOHNSON

October, 2010

1. Permitted Appearances.

In general, telephone appearances are permitted except in situations where the party or counsel:

will be examining witnesses;
is the proponent of a chapter 11 disclosure statement or plan;
is counsel for a client who is present in court; or
is directed by the court to appear personally.

There are no restrictions on eligibility to appear by telephone based upon the geographic location of the counsel or the party.

2. Procedure for Arranging for Telephonic Appearances.

Telephonic appearances are arranged through Court Conference. All parties/counsel using this service must have an account or make arrangements to set one up well in advance of the hearing. If you do not have an account established with Court Conference, you must provide a credit card number at the time of making your reservation.

Appearances are arranged by reservation. To make a reservation, call **1-866-582-6878** no later than **4:00 p.m. PT the day before the appearance**.

Shortly before the Court is ready to call your matter, the Court Conference operator will contact the participant as prearranged. **All participants <u>MUST</u> be available when called.** If the participant is not available when called, the participant will be billed for the call and the hearing may proceed in the participant's absence. The Court may impose sanctions as set forth below.

Telephonic appearances are connected directly with the courtroom's public address system and electronic recording equipment so that a normal record is produced. To ensure a quality record, the use of car phones, cellular phones, public telephone booths, or phones in other public places is <u>prohibited</u> except in the most extreme emergencies. Participants should be able to hear all parties without difficulty or echo.

At the time of the hearing you may initially be in the listening mode in which case you will be able to hear the case before yours just as if you were in the courtroom. After your call is connected to the courtroom, the Courtroom Deputy will call the case. The Judge will ask for appearances and direct the manner in which the hearing proceeds. Each time a participant speaks, he or she must identify himself or herself for the record. The Court's teleconferencing system allows more than one speaker to be heard so that the Judge can interrupt a speaker to ask a question or redirect the discussion. When the Judge informs the participants that the hearing is completed, the participants may disconnect and the next case will be called.

Telephonic appearances by multiple participants are <u>only</u> possible where there is compliance with every procedural requirement. **Sanctions may be imposed when there is**

any deviation from the required procedures or where the court determines that a person's conduct makes telephonic appearances inappropriate. Sanctions may include dropping the matter from the calendar, continuing the hearing, proceeding in the absence of an unavailable participant, a monetary sanction of **$100** or more, or a temporary or permanent prohibition against a person/firm appearing telephonically.

When the Court conducts a telephone conference on short notice and uses Court Conference, it may designate one party to bear the entire cost of the conference call. The Court may on occasion initiate calls to one or two persons directly from chambers without use of a conference operator. In those instances, the Courtroom Deputy will contact parties to inform them of the arrangements.

Because the Courtroom Deputy is usually in Court prior to the initiation of any particular call, last minute changes are generally impossible to handle and are discouraged.

Judge Johnson's Courtroom Deputy is Tanya Bracegirdle, (408) 278-7556.

D. Practices and Procedures

PRACTICES AND PROCEDURES
Honorable Stephen L. Johnson

In addition to enforcing the Bankruptcy Local Rules for the Northern District of California ("B.L.R."), the Civil Local Rules of the United States District Court ("Civil L.R.") and the Federal Rules of Bankruptcy Procedure ("Rules"), Judge Johnson's PRACTICES AND PROCEDURES are intended to assist counsel with practical procedures for litigation in his courtroom. Counsel and litigants appearing before the Court therefore should be aware of the following:

1. General Provisions

Counsel are expected to consult and comply with all provisions of the B.L.R. and Rules relating to motions, briefs, continuances, and all other matters. The failure to comply with any of the rules and orders may be deemed sufficient grounds for monetary sanctions, dismissal, entry of default, or other appropriate sanctions.

2. Communication with Court

Ex parte communication with the Court, including contact with the judge's staff or law clerk, is not permitted. See Rule 9003(a) and California Rule of Professional Conduct 5-300(C). The proper means of communicating with the Court is through Courtroom Deputy Tanya Bracegirdle. She can be reached at 408-278-7556 or tanya_bracegirdle@canb.uscourts.gov, and will respond to calendaring questions, order status, and requests for expedited hearings. When contacting Ms. Bracegirdle, parties and counsel should identify their telephone, fax, and e-mail addresses. Parties and counsel should not contact the Court or chambers staff directly. This prohibition extends to e-mail, telephone, and fax.

3. Telephonic Hearings

Counsel may appear telephonically as described in the Policy and Procedures for Appearances by Telephone.

4. Calendaring Matters

General Calendaring – The Court utilizes an Open Calendar Procedure for most regularly noticed hearings. Complete details regarding the Open Calendar Procedure for Judge Johnson are available at Judge Johnson's Open Calendar Procedure. For hearings that are not shown on the open calendar procedure contact Courtroom Deputy Tanya Bracegirdle.

Expedited Matters – To calendar a matter on shortened time, an application for an order shortening time which complies with B.L.R. 9006-1 and Rule 9006(c) must be filed together with a copy of the moving papers and a proposed order on the motion to shorten time. The application should indicate a suggested hearing schedule and the movant's proposal for providing notice to affected parties. If the motion to shorten time is merited, the Court will issue an order (a) setting the date and time of the hearing, (b) establishing requirements for notice to affected parties, and (c) indicating how opposition to the motion should be made. Written opposition to a motion made on shortened time generally is not required to be filed prior to the first hearing, and a party generally may appear at the hearing to oppose the motion orally.

TROs – Requests for temporary restraining orders will only be calendared after an adversary complaint has been filed. Counsel must include an application for an expedited hearing (see Expedited Matters above) with the request for a TRO and a copy of the complaint. Any application for an expedited hearing must comply with BLR 9006-1 and Rule 9006.

5. Continuances

Unopposed continuances – Motions directed to specific parties may be continued as allowed by the B.L.R. or by stipulation. Courtroom Deputy Tanya Bracegirdle must be notified 72 hours in advance of any scheduled hearing of such continuance. The moving party shall file and serve a notice of the continued hearing. If the moving party fails to file a notice of the continued hearing by the time of the hearing, the motion may be denied for lack of prosecution. Motions or applications noticed to creditors generally, including asset sales, motions to convert or dismiss, etc., shall be continued on the record at the time set for hearing in the notice. Courtroom Deputy Tanya Bracegirdle must be notified 72 hours in advance of such continuances.

Opposed continuances – A party requesting a continuance that is opposed must comply with B.L.R. 9006-1.

Trials – Generally speaking, trials will not be continued for anything less than a compelling reason. A request for continuance must be made by noticed motion or by a written stipulation stating the reason for the requested continuance. Parties requesting a continuance of a trial should comply with B.L.R. 9006-1. The agreement of parties to continue a trial does not bind the Court.

6. Conduct of Adversary Proceedings

Parties are advised that adversary proceedings are governed by scheduling orders entered by the Court under Rule 7016(b) (incorporating Federal Rule of Civil Procedure 16). Pursuant to the Order Setting the Telephonic Case Management Conference, case management conference statements must be filed at least 7 days before each conference and continuances must be requested in writing at least 7 days prior to the conference date.

Parties should be aware that the Court may set matters for trial at the Initial Case Management Conference or any continued conference. Short cause matters (e.g., actions for credit card abuse under 11 U.S.C. § 523(a)(2)) are likely to be set for trial immediately.

Parties may stipulate to continue the Initial Case Management Conference for up to 60 days. Any such stipulation must be filed no less than 7 days prior to the Initial Case Management Conference. Appearance at the Initial Case Management Conference is not necessary so long as a signed order continuing the matter is docketed on the Court's ECF system in advance of the hearing. If no order is docketed, the parties should appear.

In connection with trial setting, the parties are advised to review Judge Johnson's form Scheduling Order, available on the Court's website. The form order indicates the kind of matters (e.g., discovery cut-off, expert reports) for which deadlines are appropriate and will be set. Counsel should be prepared to advise the Court regarding their availability for trial.

See ¶ 5 above regarding trial continuances.

7. Discovery Disputes

The parties shall not file formal discovery motions. The Court will hold a telephonic conference to resolve a discovery dispute in lieu of formal motions to compel or quash discovery. See B.L.R. 1001-2(a)(46) and Civil L.R. 37-1(a) and (b)). Parties should comply with the procedures set forth in Civil L.R. 37-1 (particularly with respect to required conferences and meet and confer rules. See Civil L.R. 1-5(n)). To schedule a telephonic conference regarding a discovery dispute, counsel should contact Courtroom Deputy Tanya Bracegirdle. The Court may request the parties to file a joint letter brief if the matter cannot be resolved without paper.

During depositions, a party may contact the Court if another party persistently obstructs the deposition or the deponent refuses to answer a material question on the basis of any ground other than privilege or the work product doctrine. Contact should be directed through Courtroom Deputy Tanya Bracegirdle.

Any request for sanctions relating to a discovery dispute must be made by separate noticed motion. Rules 7037(a), 9014, 9020.

8. Submission of Orders After Hearings

Counsel should comply with the provisions of B.L.R. 9021-1(c) and 9022-1.

9. Objections to Claims

Unless otherwise ordered, all hearings on objections to claims are preliminary hearings, without testimony. If the objection cannot be summarily resolved, the Court will order a trial at which evidence will be taken.

10. Chapter 11 Cases

Status and Prospects – The Court calendars regular conferences on the status of each pending chapter 11 case. All chapter 11 debtors are required to file a Status Conference Statement at least 7 days prior to the conference. The status conference statement should give a brief description of the debtor's business, the events leading to the bankruptcy filing, and the debtor's prospects for exiting chapter 11 by confirmed plan, conversion, or dismissal. The Chapter 11 Status Conference Checklist, available on the Court's website, describes the Court's expectations.

Disclosure Statements – The proponent of a disclosure statement shall inform the Courtroom Deputy Tanya Bracegirdle via phone or email at least 5 days prior to the hearing to approve a disclosure statement if the party intends to go forward with the hearing. Failure to notify the Court shall result in the removal of the disclosure statement hearing from the calendar.

Asset Sales – The San Jose Division of the U.S. Bankruptcy Court for the Northern District of California has adopted Guidelines for Early Disposition of Assets in Chapter 11

Cases; Pre-Packaged Plans; and the Sale of Substantially All Assets Under § 363. Please refer to these Guidelines when preparing for a contested matter involving any of these issues.

U.S. Trustee Motions to Convert or Dismiss – Once he has filed a motion to convert or dismiss a chapter 11 case, the United States Trustee is directed not to withdraw that motion without advance approval of the Court.

11. Final Decrees in Chapter 11 Cases

Chapter 11 debtors in possession and trustees are expected to apply for final decrees as soon as claims disputes and any other litigation in Bankruptcy Court are resolved. The Court expects all counsel for Chapter 11 debtors to understand fully the provisions of Rule 3022 and the Advisory Committee notes thereto.

If a final decree is sought within one year of confirmation, it may be obtained by ex parte application along with a declaration of a principal of the debtor setting forth the date that the planwas confirmed and representing that the plan payments called for by the plan have been commenced and that the debtor is substantially in compliance with the requirements of the plan.

If more than one year has passed since confirmation, a final decree must be sought by motion on at least 15 days' notice to the creditors' committee and its counsel, if any, the U.S. Trustee, and any persons who filed requests for notice. If there is no committee, the 20 largest unsecured creditors must be served. The motion must contain the following statement, in capital letters:

> IF THE DEBTOR IS NOT CURRENT IN PLAN PAYMENTS, YOU MAY OBJECT TO ENTRY OF A FINAL DECREE AND ASK THE COURT TO ORDER THE LIQUIDATION OF THE DEBTOR'S ASSETS. IF THE DEBTOR FALLS BEHIND IN PLAN PAYMENTS AFTER THE ENTRY OF A FINAL DECREE, YOU MAY ASK THE COURT TO REOPEN THE CASE AND ORDER LIQUIDATION.

If a motion to reopen a case is made, the filing fee shall be paid by the debtor unless the Court finds that the motion was not substantially justified.

Rev. 11/01/2010

II. Judge Johnson's Case Management Orders

A. *Trial Scheduling Order*

IN THE UNITED STATES BANKRUPTCY COURT
FOR THE NORTHERN DISTRICT OF CALIFORNIA

In re:)	Case No. ________________
)	Chapter ___________
Debtor(s).)	Adv. Proc. No. ______________
________________________________)	
)	**SCHEDULING ORDER**
Plaintiff(s),)	B.R. 7016
v.)	Fed. R. Civ. P. 16
Defendant(s).)	
________________________________)	

On (Date), the court held a status conference in the above-entitled matter. Appearances were as noted on the record. Upon due consideration, the court hereby establishes the following schedule:

(1) All discovery shall be completed by ____________________.

(2) A Pretrial Conference shall be held on ______(Date)______ at __(Time)___, United States Bankruptcy Court, 280 South First Street, Courtroom 3099, San Jose, CA 95113.

(3) Experts shall be disclosed by __________________.

(4) Experts discovery shall be completed by ___________________.

The parties' counsel are directed to meet and confer in person regarding settlement and the joint pretrial conference statement before the pretrial conference. Counsel are reminded that they are required to file a joint pretrial statement seven calendar days before the pretrial conference. The pretrial conference statement shall address: (1) The substance of the action; (2) undisputed facts; (3) disputed facts; (4) disputed legal issues; (5) witnesses to be called by each party; (6) whether separate trial of specific issues is appropriate; (7) whether it is appropriate to introduce the direct testimony of any witnesses by declaration (subject to oral cross-examination); and (8) the parties shall indicate the proposed division of trial time.

(5) No motion for summary judgment will be heard less than thirty days before trial without permission of the court.

(6) Trial will commence on ________________ at 9:00 a.m., at the United States Bankruptcy Court, 280 South First Street, Courtroom 3099, San Jose, CA 95113. The trial is set for (half day (3 hours), one day (6 hours), two days (12 hours), etc). Seven calendar days before the trial date counsel shall inform the courtroom deputy (Tanya Bracegirdle (408) 278-7556) whether the parties have settled. During the week prior to the trial date the court may reschedule the trial to a later day during the week of the trial date. Counsel should be prepared to go to trial at any time during the week of the trial date.

(7) Seven calendar days before the scheduled trial date, counsel shall: (a) serve and file trial briefs (briefs shall not **exceed fifteen (15)** pages without **prior** permission of the court); (b) exchange copies of all exhibits to be offered, other than those to be used for

impeachment; (c) serve and file statements designating excerpts from depositions, answers to interrogatories and requests for admission, other than those to be used for impeachment; and (d) exchange a list of expected witnesses, other than those to be called for impeachment, including a brief summary of each witness' expected testimony.

(8) Counsel shall also: (a) premark all exhibits **before** trial (Plaintiff's exhibits should be marked by number, Defendant's exhibits should be marked by letter); (b) bring sufficient copies of exhibits for all counsel, the witness, and the court; (c) in any case in which the party expects to offer more than ten exhibits, place the exhibits in a three-ring binder with an appropriate tab attached to each exhibit; (d) number the pages of any exhibit that has more than one page; (e) promptly advise the opposing party of any objections to the introduction of the opposing party's proposed testimony or exhibits; and (f) meet **before** trial to stipulate to the introduction of evidence, including both testimony and documents.

The court may exclude evidence, postpone trial, or impose monetary sanctions for failure to comply with this order.

IT IS SO ORDERED.

****END OF ORDER****

Hon. William J. Lafferty, III

Bankruptcy Judge

Contact Information

U.S. Bankruptcy Court, Northern District of California
Courtroom 220
1300 Clay Street, Suite 300
Oakland, CA 94612
Courtroom Deputy: (510) 879-3533

Biographical Information

Education:

- University of California Hastings College of the Law - J.D.
- University of California Berkeley – B.A.

Appointed:

- United States Bankruptcy Judge Northern District of California (April 2011)

Practice:

- Joined Howard Rice Nemerovski Canady Falk & Rabkin in 1987
- Director with Howard Rice Nemerovski Canady Falk & Rabkin 1993 - 2011

Affiliations:

- Vice President, California Bankruptcy Forum
- Past President, Bay Area Bankruptcy Forum
- Past President, Bar Association of San Francisco, Commercial Law and Bankruptcy Section

Extracurricular:

- Bankruptcy & Reorganization Practice Group
- Listed in The Best Lawyers in America (Bankruptcy and Creditor-Debtor Rights Law field)
- Listed in Chambers USA's "America's Leading Lawyers for Business"
- Recognized as a Northern California Super Lawyer from 2004 through 2010
- AV rated attorney (peer awarded honor given by Martindale-Hubbell)

I. Judge Lafferty's Procedures and Practices

A. *Open Calendar Procedure*

OPEN CALENDAR PROCEDURE FOR JUDGE WILLIAM J.LAFFERTY

Beginning with hearings to be held after June 1, 2011, Judge William J. Lafferty will use an open calendar procedure for the scheduling of certain matters. This procedure will allow counsel to self-select an available date and time on the appropriate calendar and serve notice of that date and time without first having to obtain the date and time from the calendar clerk.

The court encourages all parties to set matters using the open calendar procedure whenever possible. Dianna Passadore, Judge Lafferty's courtroom deputy, will be available by telephone to schedule hearings not available for setting on the open calendar, or as needed for emergency matters. Her contact information is: Dianna Passadore, 510-879-3533.

1. Types of proceedings that may be set using the open calendar procedure:
   - Motions in Adversary Proceedings and motions in the main cases for chapter 7 and 11 cases: on designated Wednesdays at 9:30 a.m.
   - Motions for relief from stay in all chapters: on designated Wednesdays at 10:30 a.m.
   - Disclosure statement hearings in chapter 11 cases: on designated Wednesdays at 9:30 a.m.
   - All matters relating to chapter 13 cases requiring the presence of the chapter 13 trustee: on designated Thursdays at 2:00 p.m. when chapter 13 confirmation hearings take place. These confirmation hearing dates will be announced in advance and posted in Judge Lafferty's calendar section on the Court's website.
2. The open calendar procedure is not available for the following:
   - Case management conferences in adversary proceedings.
     The Calendar Clerk will select the date and time for the initial Case Management Conference before issuing the summons.
   - Plan confirmation hearings in chapter 11 cases.
     Following the approval of the disclosure statement, the court will schedule the date and time for the hearing on confirmation of plan.
   - Status conferences in chapter 11 cases.
     The court will schedule and notice a status conference.
   - Trials in adversary proceedings.
     All trials will be assigned a date and time and a pretrial order will be issued.
   - Any matter requiring an order shortening time.
     An application for an order shortening time under B.L.R. 9006-1 is required before a hearing date will be set. Once the application has been reviewed, chambers will contact counsel with the date and time of the hearing as well as any special instructions regarding notice.
   - Matters set by the court pursuant to an order to show cause and hearings on reaffirmation agreements.
3. Procedure:

a. In order to utilize the open calendar procedure, counsel should select an available date and time as shown on the list of dates posted in Judge Lafferty's calendar section on the court's website. The date selected must be no earlier than as required by applicable national or local rules, as nothing in this open calendar procedure alters applicable time limits.

b. After selecting an available date and time, counsel should serve proper notice of the matter in accordance with applicable rules. Note: If a hearing on a motion for relief from stay is set in accordance with this open calendar procedure more than thirty days after the date the motion is filed, the party will be deemed to have waived the thirty-day limitation of 11 U.S.C. § 362(e).

c. No later than three days after the service on other parties, counsel should provide chambers with copies of all appropriate papers in accordance with the court's website regarding chambers copies.

d. Once a matter is set by the open calendar procedure, with the exception of certain matters in adversary proceedings or matters noticed to all creditors, continuances may be handled through the Judge's courtroom deputy. A minimum notice of 24 hours required.

e. Counsel must not request that the courtroom deputy call back to confirm that the matter has been placed on the calendar. Counsel desiring confirmation that a matter has been placed on the calendar by the open calendar procedure should review the calendar on the bankruptcy court's website.

f. Failure to comply with the foregoing open calendar procedure will result in the matter not being placed on calendar. Note: Occasionally there may be a need to reschedule matters that have been placed on the calendar in accordance with this open calendar procedure. Typically this will be because of calendar congestion or unforeseen schedule changes. In those instances the courtroom deputy will contact the moving party as soon as possible so that a notice of a rescheduled hearing may be disseminated.

Hon. Dennis Montali

Bankruptcy Judge

Contact Information
U.S. Bankruptcy Court, Northern District of California
Courtroom 22
235 Pine Street, 19th Floor
San Francisco, CA 94104
Courtroom Deputy: (415) 268-2323

Biographical Information

Education:

- Bachelor of Arts, University of Notre Dame (June, 1961)
- Juris Doctor, University of California, Berkeley (June, 1968)

Appointed:

- United States Bankruptcy Judge Northern District of California, San Francisco Division (April 23, 1993, Reappointed April 23, 2007)
- Member, Ninth Circuit Bankruptcy Appellate Panel (May 1, 2000)
- Member, Judicial Conference of the United States, Committee on the Administration of the Bankruptcy System (October 1, 1999 - September 30, 2006)

Professional Organizations:

- Prior Secretary and Member - Business Bankruptcy Committee, Section of Corporation, Banking and Business Law, America Bar Association
- Former Member - National Bankruptcy Conference
- Fellow - American College of Bankruptcy
- Former Member - California Continuing Education of the Bar, Joint Advisory Committee, Business Law Subcommittee
- Chair, San Francisco Bar Association, Commercial Law & Bankruptcy Section(1982)
- Former Member - Debtor/Creditor and Bankruptcy Subcommittee, Business Law Section, State Bar of California
- Former Member - Bankruptcy Advisory Committee, Northern District of California

Publications:

- Former Contributing Author, Matthew Bender Company, Collier Practice Guide (three chapters on bankruptcy practice published in 1981)
- Former Contributing Author, California Continuing Education of the Bar, Course Books: Doing Business With Insolvents; The New Bankruptcy Code
- Former Contributing Author, Practising Law Institute Course Books: Bankruptcy Practice and Procedure Under the New Bankruptcy Act; Consumer Finance and Lending–Practice Under Chapters 7 and 13 of the Bankruptcy Code; Legal Assistants Course Book. 1981; Current Developments in Bankruptcy and Reorganization

I. Judge Montali's Procedures and Practices

A. *Practices and Procedures in Judge Montali's Court*

PRACTICES AND PROCEDURES IN JUDGE MONTALI'S COURT

(Revised on April 28, 2009)

In addition to enforcing the Bankruptcy Local Rules for the Northern District of California ("B.L.R.") and the Federal Rules of Bankruptcy Procedure ("Rules"), Judge Montali has established certain practices and procedures in his court. Counsel and litigants appearing before Judge Montali should be aware of the following:

I. ORDERS AND JUDGMENTS

A. Obtaining an Order Shortening Time

A party seeking an order shortening time must comply with B.L.R. 9006-1. In particular, the party must submit a declaration describing the efforts made to obtain the consent of the opposing party to the order shortening time. A request for an order shortening time should be made in writing. In general, Judge Montali will not require the opposing party to file any written response to a motion that is scheduled on shortened time, and opposition may be presented at the hearing.

Judge Montali does not require an order shortening time on a motion for interim authority to use cash collateral or obtain credit (including DIP financing). *See* Rule 4001(b)(2) and (c)(2) (hearing may be conducted within 15 days after service of motion to avoid immediate and irreparable harm to estate pending final hearing). To obtain a date and time for the initial hearing on a motion to use cash collateral or obtain credit, counsel should contact Ms. Lorena Parada, Courtroom Deputy/Calendar Clerk, at 415-268-2323 or Lorena_Parada@canb.uscourts.gov.

B. Procedures for Temporary Restraining Orders (TRO)

Judge Montali generally prefers at least 72 hours' notice to, and service of moving papers upon, opposing parties. Any request for a TRO (or other injunctive relief) requires an adversary proceeding. See Rule 7001(7). Accordingly, a complaint must be filed prior to the hearing. To obtain a date and time for a hearing on a request for a TRO, counsel should contact Ms. Lorena Parada, Courtroom Deputy/Calendar Clerk, at 415-268-2323 or Lorena_Parada@canb.uscourts.gov

C. Submission of Orders

Uploaded orders should be converted, not scanned.

Judge Montali frequently receives proposed orders from parties who have not complied with B.L.R. 9021-1 and 9022-1. The following addresses common errors, and is not a substitute for reading the rules.

A proposed order submitted after a hearing should contain the signatures of any other counsel who appeared at the hearing, approving it as to form, or otherwise the submitting party should file a proof of service evidencing service of the proposed order on all such counsel. Orders not approved as to form will ordinarily be lodged for 7 days after service, but this is not a guarantee that they will be held for that period.

Those parties not using CM/ECF should provide copies, stamped and addressed envelopes (including a return envelope), a list of parties to be served, and a form of notice of entry of order for the clerk to use. Those parties using CM/ECF should submit orders or judgments with a service list of persons and entities to whom service is required by B.L.R. 9022-1.

Parties are frequently uncertain who must be served. Under Rule 9022 and B.L.R. 9022-1, notice of entry of orders or judgments must be served by the clerk on all "contesting parties" and the United States Trustee (and such other parties as the court directs). Judge Montali interprets "contesting parties" to mean (1) any identified, named party against whom relief is sought (including the debtor(s) and debtor(s)' counsel for all orders in response to motions for relief from the automatic stay) unless that party (a) has stipulated in writing or in open court to the relief sought (not just the more traditional "approved as to form"); or (b) was present when the order or judgment was signed in open court, and (2) to the extent relief is sought on notice to creditors generally, only those creditors who file a written objection or request for a hearing, or who appear at the hearing and object to the relief sought, unless such written or oral opposition has been expressly withdrawn. Other parties need not be served.

II. SPECIFIC MOTIONS AND ORDERS

A. 522(f)(1)(A): Avoiding a Judgment Lien that Impairs an Exemption

Before he will sign an order avoiding a judgment lien under 11 U.S.C. § 522(f)(1)(A), Judge Montali requires a declaration from the debtor or some other appropriate offer of proof setting forth the grounds for avoiding the lien. In particular, the declarant(s) should provide the following information: the value of the encumbered property, the amount and nature of the debtor's exemption, the extent of the impairment, and the amount of the judgment lien and all other liens encumbering the property (*see* 11 U.S.C. § 522(f)(2)(A)). The debtor should also disclose any other facts supporting his or her contention that 11 U.S.C. § 522(f)(1) is applicable.

The movant should ensure that service of the motion complies with Fed. R. Bankr. P. 7004 and 9014(b). *See Beneficial Cal., Inc. v. Villar (In re Villar)*, 317 B.R. 88 (9th Cir. BAP 2004).

B. Default Judgments In Adversary Proceedings

When requesting a default judgment in an adversary proceeding, the moving party must submit a proof of service showing that the request was served on the non-responding defendant. Except in certain matters (e.g., trustee avoiding actions, 11 U.S.C. § 523(a)(2)(C) causes, and others as determined on a case-by-case basis), a plaintiff seeking a default judgment must schedule a "prove-up" hearing (*see* Fed. R. Civ. P. 55(b)(2) and Rule 7055) and serve notice of the hearing on the defendant at least fifteen days prior to the hearing. Any witnesses for the plaintiff must appear personally; the defaulting defendant is entitled to cross-examine the witness but is not permitted to present its own evidence or witnesses. The court will consider declarations only if the defaulted defendant agrees.

C. Motions to Sell Free and Clear of Liens to Value Secured Claims, or to Assume/or Assign Executory Contracts or Leases

Parties filing motions to sell property of the estate, motions to sell free and clear of liens, motions to value secured claims, or motions to assume or assign executory contracts or leases must comply with B.L.R. 6004-1 or 6006-1 and with this court's Guidelines Re Sale Orders, available on this court's website.

Judge Montali expects counsel to be familiar with and to comply with revisions to Fed R. Bankr. P. 6006 (effective December 1, 2007), dealing with omnibus motions to assume and reject executory contracts and leases.

D. Sale Motions: Section 363(m) Good Faith Determinations

Burden of Proof; Discretionary Finding: Any bidder requesting a judicial determination under 11 U.S.C. § 363(m) that its purchase of assets is in good faith (in an order authorizing a sale under section 363(b) or by separate order) has the burden to establish such good faith. This court has discretion to refuse to make such a finding, and the preclusive effect of such a finding may be limited. *T.C. Investors v. Joseph (In re M Capital Corp.)*, 290 B.R. 743, 748-49 (9th Cir. BAP 2003).

Evidentiary support: A bidder seeking a section 363 good faith determination must file a written declaration (or, if the bidder is not an individual, a declaration of its responsible officer or agent with personal knowledge) demonstrating the proposed bidder's good faith, including disclosure of:

1. The bidder's prepetition and postpetition relationship with other bidders, the debtor, major creditors or equity security holders in the case, or any of the debtor's officers, directors, agents, or employees;

2. The bidder's expected relationship after the sale with the debtor's present or former officers, directors, agents, or employees (including whether any offers of employment or compensation have been made or will be offered to debtor's present or former officers, directors, agents, or employees);

3. Whether any consideration is contemplated to be transferred or has been transferred by bidder in connection with the sale to any person other than the debtor (or the trustee of the debtor's estate); and

4. The absence of fraud or collusion between the bidder and any other bidders or the debtor's officers, directors, agents or employees, or any attempt to take unfair advantage of other bidders.

For further guidance regarding Judge Montali's policies regarding good faith findings, *see M Capital Corp.*, 290 B.R. at 748-49. See also this court's Guidelines Re Sale Orders (available on the court's website).

E. Compromise/Settlement of Controversy – Federal Bankruptcy Rule of Procedure 9019

Judge Montali requires that approval of compromises be presented by the following: 1) a motion, and 2) a supporting declaration from someone with first-hand knowledge of the reasons for, and the terms of, the settlement. The filing of a notice alone is inadequate. The motion should provide an explanation of why the compromise is "fair and equitable" and "reasonable." It should include an analysis of the four factors set out in *Martin v. Kane (In re A & C Properties)*, 784 F.2d 1377, 1381 (9th Cir. 1986) that establishes to the court each of the "A & C" factors have been satisfied. In routine settlements, the factors can be accomplished with a paragraph or two; in more complex matters Judge Montali expects a more detailed analysis.

Not all documents need to be served on all parties. It is sufficient that creditors be given a notice that succinctly summarizes what has been stated in the motion and supporting declaration. *See* Fed. R. Bankr. P. 2002(a)(3).

F. First Day Motions

In the initial days of a case, Chapter 11 debtors frequently file financing motions, motions to pay prepetition wages of employees, or other motions that may have a significant effect on the future administration of the estate. Judge Montali requires that such motions be accompanied by declarations signed by representatives of the debtor with personal knowledge of the facts asserted and setting forth adequate financial information to put the motion(s) in context. The moving party should provide sufficient financial information to enable Judge Montali to assess the impact of the requested relief on unsecured creditors.

Specifically, Judge Montali requires information about the value of a debtor's assets, and the extent to which they are encumbered; the amount of current and long term liabilities, with specific mention of debts entitled to priority under 11 U.S.C. § 507; the current cash situation; the amount of prepetition wages owed and to whom (by name and position/occupation with the debtor and amount owed); the nature of the connections (if any) between the debtor and any party providing financing; and, unless unknown, the Chapter 11 exit strategy of the debtor (e.g., sale as a going concern, liquidation of assets, continuation of business with infusion of capital, etc.). *See also* the court's Guidelines for Cash Collateral and Financing Stipulations.

Judge Montali expects counsel to be familiar with and to comply with revisions to Fed R. Bankr. P 4001(b), (c) & (d)(effective December 1, 2007), dealing with motions to use cash collateral, to obtain credit, and for approval of certain stipulations.

III. OTHER PRACTICES AND PROCEDURES

A. Adversary Proceeding Status Conference Reports

Judge Montali does not normally require status conference reports in adversary proceedings.

B. Calendaring Matters

Judge Montali utilizes "open calendar" procedures. Go to http://www.canb.uscourts.gov and click on the "Division Procedures" button and then the "San Francisco Open Calendar Procedure" link. Parties or counsel may also calendar matters by contacting Ms. Lorena Parada, Courtroom Deputy/Calendar Clerk via telephone at 415-268-2323 or e-mail at Lorena_Parada@canb.uscourts.gov.

C. Telephonic Appearances

Judge Montali allows counsel to appear telephonically on most matters. Go to http://www.canb.uscourts.gov and click on the "Judges' Procedures" button, then select "Procedures For Appearances By Telephone" under "San Francisco Division." Those procedures identify the exceptions to Judge Montali's general acceptance of telephonic appearances. For relief from stay matters, chapter 13 calendar matters, adversary proceeding status conferences, and matters involving multiple telephonic appearances, parties must use CourtCall for telephonic appearances (as described in more detail in the Procedures for Appearances by Telephone). On other matters, the court may initiate the phone call, and the party wishing to appear telephonically should contact Ms. Lorena Parada (415-268-2323) no less than 72 hours prior to the hearing.

D. Communications With Chambers' Staff

Rule 9003(a) prohibits *ex parte* communications with the court concerning matters affecting a particular case or proceeding. Rule 5-300(C) of the California Rules of Professional Conduct specifies that for disciplinary purposes, a contact with Judge Montali's law clerk constitutes a contact with the judge. No attorney or party may initiate contact with the judge or his law clerk in violation of Rule 9003(a). Improper *ex parte* communications may include letters or e-mails to the court (especially where copies have not been provided to opposing parties and the United States Trustee) and telephone calls to the court. Individual cases may not be discussed with Judge Montali's law clerk or judicial assistant except to inform the court that an *ex parte* request or a form of order is opposed, that an emergency pleading or request for order shortening time is being submitted, that a Chapter 11 plan proponent intends to go forward with a disclosure statement or confirmation hearing, or that a calendared matter has been settled or is being re-scheduled. (In the event of a settlement or re-scheduling, counsel should also contact Ms. Lorena Parada, Courtroom Deputy/Calendar Clerk, at 415-268-2323 or Lorena_Parada@canb.uscourts.gov.)

To check on the status of an order, counsel should check CM/ECF or PACER. To find out how to utilize PACER, go to the Pacer Service Center website at http://pacer.psc.uscourts.gov/. If the proposed order has not been entered on the docket after seven to ten days, or if there is an urgent need for the order, counsel may contact the clerk's office at 415-268-2300.

E-mail should not be sent to Judge Montali, his law clerks, or his judicial assistant without prior approval.

E. Obtaining Continuances

Trials: Judge Montali will grant continuances of trials for good cause only, even when the parties stipulate to a continuance. A request for continuance must be made by noticed motion or by a written stipulation stating the reason for the requested continuance. Parties requesting a continuance of a trial should comply with B.L.R. 9006-1.

Motions: If parties agree to continue a scheduled hearing on a motion, they merely need to contact Ms. Lorena Parada (415-268-2323 or Lorena_Parada@canb.uscourts.gov) to inform her of the new date and time. No written stipulation is necessary. A party requesting a continuance that is opposed should comply with B.L.R. 9006-1.

F. Discovery Disputes

Judge Montali will generally hold a telephonic conference to resolve a discovery dispute in lieu of formal motions to compel or quash discovery. (See B.L.R. 1001-2(a)(46) and Civil L.R. 37-1(a) and (b)). Parties should comply with the procedures set forth in Civ. L.R. 37-1. To schedule a telephonic conference regarding a discovery dispute, counsel should contact Ms. Lorena Parada, Courtroom Deputy/Calendar Clerk, at 415-268-2323 or Lorena_Parada@canb.uscourts.gov.

Any request for sanctions relating to a discovery dispute must be made by separate noticed motion.

G. Request To Seal Documents

A party wishing to file a document under seal should follow Civ. L.R. 79-9 (incorporated by B.L.R. 1001-2(a)(63). *See also* Fed. R. Bankr. P. 9018. Sealing filed documents is disfavored under the law and by this court (*see* 11 U.S.C. § 107); accordingly, the motion must satisfactorily explain why the court should disregard the policy of open access to public documents. Parties opposing such a request should respond as soon as possible, since the court will normally act on any such matter promptly and without a hearing.

H. Employment of Auctioneers and Brokers

Judge Montali will not allow auctioneers to recover labor costs or to charge a buyers' premium. Any application to employ an auctioneer should reflect the auctioneer's agreement not to charge such costs and premiums. Similarly, Judge Montali will not allow real estate brokers representing the estate (as seller) to represent buyers. *See* 11 U.S.C. § 327(a) (trustee may employ "professional persons, that do not hold or represent an interest adverse to the estate"). Any application to employ a real estate broker should reflect the agreement of the broker that he or she will not represent the buyer.

I. Fee Applications in Chapter 13 Cases

Even though Guideline #7 of the Guidelines for Compensation and Expense Reimbursement of Professionals and Trustees for the United States Bankruptcy Court for the Northern District of California (go to http://www.canb.uscourts.gov and click on the "Guidelines" button, then select "Guidelines for Compensation and Expense Reimbursement of Professional and Trustees"), does not specifically apply to fee applications in Chapter 13 cases, Judge Montali does require counsel in Chapter 13 cases to provide their clients with the letter described in that Guideline.

J. Fees Generally

Travel: Judge Montali generally will allow up to two hours of compensation for non-working airplane travel time, to account for inevitable delays for security and administration involved in air travel. Other air travel time is not likely to be compensable, per Guideline 17 of the Guidelines for Compensation and Expense Reimbursement of Professionals and Trustees.

Conflicts Checks / Ethical Walls / Change of Firms: Judge Montali expects counsel to write off, and will normally disallow, time spent identifying, clearing and avoiding conflicts and complying with Bankruptcy Rule 2014(a). Such time is not very different from a firm absorbing the time expended on its own efforts to secure a new client, for which Judge Montali doubts any professional would bill. For the same reasons, he expects counsel to write off, and normally will disallow, time spent by professionals who change offices or firms, and need to clear conflicts, set up new files, brief new attorneys, or perform other tasks in connection with the transition.

Retainers: Judge Montali does not require retainers to be held in a trust account, unless that is the agreement between the attorney and the client.

K. Disclosure Statement Hearings

Judge Montali strictly enforces B.L.R. 3017-1. In particular, a competent witness for the plan proponent must be present at the hearing and counsel for the proponent must notify Chambers by telephone at least three business days prior to the hearing that the hearing will go forward. The court will normally refuse to proceed with the hearing if this call is not made or the debtor or other plan proponent does not appear.

L. Stipulations for Relief from Stay

Generally, Judge Montali will not approve a stipulation for relief from stay that purports to be effective in any subsequent case filed by the debtor. Judge Montali will approve provisions that grant relief from the stay on ten days' notice to debtor and debtor's counsel if the debtor defaults on agreed payments under the order before debtor becomes post-petition current. If, however, the debtor defaults after becoming post-petition current, the movant must re-set the motion on ten days' notice.

M. Compliance With Local Rules

Counsel and parties should comply with all local rules. In particular, in order to avoid delays in the processing of orders, parties should comply with B.L.R. 9014-1(b)(4) (when requesting entry of order by default) and B.L.R. 9022-1 (when relief is sought against a particular person or entity that has not stipulated to the relief – see section I(D) above entitled "Submission of Orders After Hearing").

N. Conflicts checks

Judge Montali does not expect counsel to run every creditor and party in interest through a conflicts check. He does expect counsel to use professional judgment in determining the scope of an appropriate conflicts check. At a minimum Judge Montali believes that counsel should include in their conflicts check any party who has a major interest in the case (e.g., major unsecured creditors, secured creditors, major equity security holders / owners, officers and directors, landlords / lessors, and other professionals retained in the case). Counsel should disclose potential conflicts with any such party, including anticipated future conflicts.

O. Temporary attorneys, paralegals and other personnel

Judge Montali permits the engagement of temporary attorneys, paralegals and other personnel, including both short term employees and independent contractors. This is a common and accepted practice, and therefore any firm whose employment is authorized may retain temporary personnel without the need for a separate employment application. Each order authorizing employment will be deemed to include a "further order," within the meaning of the applicable rules, authorizing the retention of temporary personnel. *See* Fed. R. Bankr. P. 2014(b) (if firm is employed, "regular associate" may act as attorney without "further order" of court), 9001(9) (definition of "regular associate").

Nevertheless, the authorization to retain temporary personnel does not alter the requirement to adhere to the applicable ethical rules, including the rules governing conflicts of interest. Unless otherwise noted in the employment application papers, Judge Montali will presume that any temporary personnel will be subject to at least the same safeguards as those used for other lateral personnel to determine whether their past engagements at other firms (a) may have exposed such individuals to confidences or secrets of an adverse party, (b) might have created a duty of loyalty to an adverse party, or (c) raise any other conflicts issue.

In addition, Judge Montali is aware that temporary personnel may work for more than one firm concurrently, or may have an ongoing relationship with more than one firm. These arrangements may increase the potential for conflicts of interest arising from present or future engagements. On the other hand, temporary personnel may have a restricted involvement in the day to day operations of each firm, and therefore they may be screened somewhat from exposure to confidential or secret information. *See County of Los Angeles v. District Court (In re County of Los Angeles)*, 223 F.3d 990 (9th Cir. 2000). Judge Montali will expect any firm retaining temporary personnel to bear these factors in mind when establishing conflicts procedures, ethical screens, or other safeguards.

II. Judge Montali's Case Management Orders

A. *Trial Scheduling Order*

IN THE UNITED STATES BANKRUPTCY COURT
FOR THE NORTHERN DISTRICT OF CALIFORNIA

In re:	)	Bankruptcy Case No. ____________
	)	Chapter _____
Debtor(s).	)	Adversary Proceeding No. __________
________________________________	)	
Plaintiff,	)	
v.	)	
Defendant.	)	
________________________________	)	

SCHEDULING ORDER FOR:

[ ] TRIAL IN ADVERSARY PROCEEDING

[ ] FINAL HEARING ON MOTION FOR RELIEF FROM STAY

[ ] TRIAL ON OBJECTIONS TO CLAIM

[ ] HEARING ON OBJECTIONS TO CONFIRMATION OF CHAPTER PLAN

[ ] OTHER:

[ ] A Status Conference in this adversary proceeding
[ ] A preliminary hearing on this motion for relief from stay
[ ] A hearing regarding objections to claim
[ ] A prehearing conference regarding objections to confirmation of plan
[ ] Other: __________________________ was held on ____________.

Appearances were as follows:

[ ] For plaintiff __________________ ("Plaintiff"), _________________ ;
[ ] For defendant __________________ ("Defendant"), _________________;
[ ] For Debtor(s): __________________;
[ ] For Moving Party: ______________; ____________________________;
[ ] For Trustee: __________________;
[ ] For Creditor: __________________ ("Creditor"), _________________;
[ ] For United States Trustee: ______________;
[ ] Other(s): ____.

Upon due consideration, the court hereby enters the following scheduling order.

TRIAL. The trial or hearing ("Trial") on the above matter(s) will commence on the

Date and Time of Trial, set forth below, at the United States Bankruptcy Court, 235 Pine Street, Twenty-Second Floor, San Francisco, CA 94104. The Time Reserved for Trial is also shown below. During the week prior to the Trial, the court may move the starting time or day. The court's Calendar Clerk/Courtroom Deputy will advise the parties of any such change by telephone. **All parties are cautioned to be prepared to adjust their schedules accordingly.**

MOTIONS. Unless otherwise ordered, (a) motions to join other parties and to amend the pleadings must be filed not later than 30 days after entry of this scheduling order and (b) motions for summary judgment must be heard no later than **30** calendar days before the Date and Time of Trial.

DISCOVERY. Discovery shall be completed by the Discovery Deadline shown below. Completion means that depositions must be concluded, although not necessarily transcribed. As to written and production discovery, responses must be due before the Discovery Deadline. The court will attempt to resolve all discovery disputes on an expedited basis via telephonic conference, which any party may initiate by request to the court's Calendar Clerk/Courtroom Deputy and notice to the other party after they have met and conferred and made a good faith effort to resolve the dispute. The party requesting the conference should submit a brief letter explaining the issues to be presented.

The Discovery Deadline may be extended by the parties by agreement, without an order of the court.

EVIDENCE. On motions for relief from stay, evidence at the Trial must be in written form, unless the court by order allows oral testimony. B.L.R. 4001-1(e). Any motion for permission to introduce any oral testimony shall be filed and served (with chambers copies provided) no later than **14** calendar days before the Date and Time of Trial and shall include the names of the witnesses, the subject of their expected testimony, and a statement of the reasons why the testimony cannot properly be introduced by declaration. Any opposition shall be filed and served (with chambers copies provided) no later than **10** calendar days before the Date and Time of Trial. The court will rule on the motion without a hearing. No such motion is required for cross-examination or redirect examination of expert witnesses.

Except on motions for relief from stay, declarations of nonexpert witnesses will not be considered except by stipulation of the parties.

PRE-TRIAL SUBMISSIONS. Not later than **7** calendar days before the Date and Time of Trial, each party shall:

(a) File and serve a trial brief, which shall include a summary of the facts to be proven and the legal theories on which the party relies. Briefs shall not exceed **15** pages without prior permission of the court. The court will not normally request or permit post-trial briefs.

(b) Except for motions for relief from stay, file and serve a witness list, including a brief summary of the anticipated testimony from each witness. If a party to the matter will be called as a witness (even as an adverse witness) that party's name must be included on the witness list. The presence of a witness' name on the witness list is to alert the court and the other side that the witness may be called. It does not mean that that person will be called. Accordingly, each party is responsible for ensuring the attendance of every witness the party intends to call, whether or not named by the other side. Except in exceptional circumstances, and absent consent by the other side, a party will not be allowed to call a witness not named on that party's witness list. This subparagraph shall not apply to expert witnesses or their testimony.

(c) On motions for relief from stay, file and serve (i) a notice identifying any declarations or memoranda previously filed in connection with the preliminary hearing and (ii) any additional declarations the party wishes the court to consider.

(d) File and serve a list of exhibits (other than those to be used for impeachment or rebuttal) and exchange, but not file, copies of all exhibits the party intends to introduce into evidence. Any paper(s) in the court's file of which a party intends the court to take judicial notice must be copied and included as an exhibit(s). Copies of the declarations filed and served in accordance with this order shall be marked as exhibits in the manner described herein. All exhibits are to be premarked for identification.

In adversary proceedings, Plaintiff's exhibits should be marked by number and defendant's exhibits should be marked by letter. On motions for relief from stay and other contested matters initiated by motion, Moving Party's exhibits should be marked by number and Respondent's, Debtor's or Trustee's exhibits should be marked by letter. On objections to claim(s) and objections to confirmation of plans, Creditor's exhibits should be marked by number and Debtor's or Trustee's exhibits should be marked by letter.

Each page of any exhibit that has more than one page is to be numbered consecutively. The parties shall bring to Trial copies of all exhibits for opposing counsel, the witnesses and the court, together with an exhibit list. If a party has more that **10** exhibits, the exhibits should be placed in a three-ring binder with a tab for each exhibit and the exhibit list placed at the front of the binder.

EXPERTS. The presentation of expert testimony at Trial shall be governed by the following:

(a) Direct evidence shall be presented by a declaration that authenticates the report of the expert. See FRCP 26(a)(2)(B), incorporated via Fed. R. Bankr. P. 7026. Each party shall file and serve declarations of experts and other documentary evidence related thereto no later than **30** calendar days prior to the Discovery Deadline; provided, however, on motions for relief from stay, such declarations shall be filed and served no later than **14** calendar days prior to the Date and Time of Trial.

(b) To cross-examine an opposing party's expert declarant, a party shall notify the opposing party in writing or by e-mail at least **3 court** days before the Date and Time of Trial, in which case the declarant will be required to attend the Trial. Any party who fails to notify the opposing party will not be permitted to cross-examine the opposing party's expert. Any party who requests the right to cross-examine an expert and then does not do so will be expected to reimburse the opposing party no less than the expenses incurred in producing the expert at the Trial.

PRE-TRIAL OBJECTIONS. Promptly after receipt of the items mentioned in **PRE-TRIAL SUBMISSIONS**, above, each party must advise the opposing party of any objections to the introduction of testimony or exhibits. Parties must meet and confer before Trial to attempt to reach agreement regarding admissibility. The court expects the parties to make good faith efforts to resolve all evidentiary issues.

MOTIONS IN LIMINE. If efforts to resolve disputes regarding the introduction of testimony or exhibits are unsuccessful, motions in limine should be filed and served no later than **4 court** days before the Date and Time of Trial. Such motions should include a certification that the moving party has complied in good faith with the meet and confer requirements of the preceding paragraph. Opposition should be filed and served no later than **1 court** day before the Date and Time of Trial.

Copies of motions and oppositions should be delivered or faxed directly to Chambers. Motions in limine will be heard at the commencement of Trial.

STIPULATIONS. At the commencement of Trial, the parties must be prepared to stipulate into evidence all exhibits that are admissible for at least one purpose. Bona-fide objections may be reserved, with the issue of admissibility deferred until the exhibit is offered into evidence.

ORDER OF PRESENTATION AT TIRAL. Unless otherwise agreed by the parties or ordered by the court, Plaintiffs in adversary proceedings, moving parties on motions for relief from stay, and claimants on objections to claims will present their cases-in-chief first. On objections to confirmation of plans, debtors or other plan proponents will present their cases-in-chief first.

IMPEACHMENT AND REBUTTAL WITNESSES. The requirement of advance identification of witnesses and production of exhibits does not apply to witnesses and exhibits presented for purposes of impeachment or rebuttal.[1] This paragraph supercedes the expert disclosure procedure of FRCP 26(a)(2)(D)(ii), incorporated via Fed. R. Bankr. P. 7026.

NOTICE TO COURT. No later than the Monday of the week prior to the Date and Time of Trial, counsel for: Plaintiff (in an adversary proceeding); Moving Party (on a motion for relief from stay); and the Debtor or Trustee (on objections to claim or objection to plan confirmation) **must** telephone or e-mail the court's Calendar Clerk/Courtroom Deputy, Ms. Lorena Parada (415-268-2323; Lorena_Parada@canb.uscourts.gov) and report: whether the parties intend to go forward with the Trial as scheduled; if settlement is likely; whether the time reserved for the Trial is realistic; and any other relevant information.

---

[1] The proper function of rebuttal evidence is to contradict, impeach or defuse the impact of the evidence offered by an adverse party. Testimony offered only as additional support to an argument made in a case in chief is improper on rebuttal. Peals v. Terre Haute Police Dept., 535 F.3d 621, 630 (7th Cir. 2008); see also Daly v. Far Eastern Shipping Co., 238 F.Supp.2d 1231, 1238 (W.D. Wash. 2003), aff'd 108 Fed. Appx. 476 (9th Cir. 2004).

NON-COMPLAINCE. Any failure of a party to comply timely with this scheduling order may result in judgment against such party, removal of the Trial from calendar, exclusion of evidence or imposition of monetary or non-monetary sanctions. See FRCP 16(f)(1)(C), incorporated via Fed. R. Bankr. P. 7016.

DATE AND TIME OF TRIAL:

TIME RESERVED FOR TRIAL:

DISCOVERY DEADLINE:

OTHER PROVISIONS:

END OF ORDER

Hon. Charles Novack

Bankruptcy Judge

Contact Information

U.S. Bankruptcy Court, Northern District of California

Courtroom 3070
280 South First Street
San Jose, CA 95113
Courtroom Deputy: (408) 278-7578
(for San Jose hearings)

Salinas Quadrangle
1000 South Main Street, Suite 214
Salinas, CA 93901
(for Salinas hearings)

Biographical Information

[Not available]

I. Judge Novack's Procedures and Practices

A. *Chapter 11 Status Conference Checklist*

CHAPTER 11 STATUS CONFERENCE CHECKLIST

The Purpose Of The Status Conference

- To review the court's expectations regarding management of the case.
- To begin developing a schedule for the case

Complying With The Requirements Of The Bankruptcy Code And Rules

The court expects strict compliance with the Code and Rules. Failure to comply with the following requirements often leads to an early conversion of the case:

- Monthly Operating Reports. Bankruptcy Local Rule 2015-2 requires monthly operating reports and tax reports to be filed on the 20th day of each month.
- Quarterly United States Trustee Fees. 28 U.S.C. § 1930(a)(6) requires a quarterly fee to be paid to the United States Trustee. The amount of the fee will depend upon the amount of disbursements made by the debtor during each quarter.
- Cash Collateral. 11 U.S.C. § 363(c)(2) prohibits the use of cash collateral unless the debtor has either the consent of each creditor having an interest in the collateral or an order from the court.
- Ordinary Course of Business. 11 U.S.C. § 363(c)(1) authorizes the debtor to enter into transactions in the ordinary course of business without notice and a hearing. If not in the ordinary course of business, notice and a hearing is required.
- Post Petition Taxes. The court expects all post petition taxes to be paid timely and all required tax returns to be timely filed.
- Funds of the Estate. Bankruptcy Local Rule 2015-1 requires all estate funds to be deposited and maintained in a debtor-in-possession (DIP) bank account.

Developing A Schedule For The Case

How much time will the court give the debtor to reorganize?

The debtor will be given a reasonable time to reorganize. How much time is reasonable depends on the circumstances of the case, the debtor's compliance with the Bankruptcy Code and Rules and the debtor's progress toward a successful reorganization.

What is the reorganization goal?

- Generating cash for creditors by the sale of some or all of the debtor's assets.
- Raising cash through borrowing or an infusion of capital such as a sale of stock.
- Becoming profitable and paying creditors through future profits.

When is a reorganization plan and disclosure statement likely to be filed?

The reorganization case will normally be terminated by a dismissal or conversion of the case to Chapter 7 and the liquidation of assets by a trustee. Dismissal or conversion normally occurs as a result of a motion brought by one of the creditors or the Unites States Trustee.

B. Courtroom Procedures for Trial

COURTROOM PROCEDURES FOR TRIAL

Trial Exhibits. The following provisions govern all exhibits except those used for purposes of impeachment.

(a) All copies of exhibits shall be pre-marked. Plaintiff's exhibits shall be identified numerically commencing with "Exhibit No.1." Defendant's exhibits shall be marked alphabetically commencing with "Exhibit No. A" through "Z," "AA" through "AZ," "BA" through "BZ," etc.

(b) If a party has ten (10) exhibits or less, the exhibits shall be marked with the party's number or letter in the lower right hand corner in ink. If a party has in excess of ten (10) exhibits, then the party's exhibits shall be assembled in three ring binders. No binder may exceed three inches in thickness. The exhibits shall be divided by tabs extending beyond the page on the right hand side and the tab shall bear the number or letter of the exhibit.

(c) If a party has in excess of 25 exhibits, the party shall contact the Courtroom Deputy and obtain exhibit markers which shall be completed prior to submission of the party's exhibits. Exhibit markers are to be affixed to the lower right hand corner of the exhibit provided, if the marker would cover any information on the exhibit, then the marker is to be affixed to the reverse side of the exhibit.

(d) Each party shall prepare an Exhibit List in the attached form. All items shall be completed with the exception of the date boxes pertaining to identification and admittance which are to be left blank.

(e) The parties shall exchange exhibits, together with a copy of the Exhibit List, seven days prior to trial.

(f) Not later than noon the day preceding the commencement of trial each party shall deliver to the Courtroom Deputy the original and two copies of the party's exhibits, together with the original and two copies of the party's Exhibit List.

(g) There shall be sufficient copies of exhibits for all counsel participating in the trial.

(h) The Court expects the parties to stipulate into evidence all exhibits to which there is no objection.

(i) The Courtroom Deputy will maintain all exhibits whether marked for identification or admitted in evidence. When counsel wants a witness to examine an exhibit, counsel should ask the Courtroom Deputy to provide the particular exhibit to the witness.

Trial Briefs. Each party shall serve and file a trial brief seven days prior to trial which shall briefly state the party's contentions, the relevant facts expected to be proved at trial, and the law on the issues material to the decision.

Findings of Fact and Conclusions of Law. Each party shall serve and lodge with the Court seven days prior to trial proposed findings of fact and conclusions of law on all material issues.

Demonstrative Evidence. The use of sketches, models, diagrams, pictures, summaries, charts, and other demonstrative evidence is encouraged. Summaries may be required by the Court in actions on account, preferences, or other issues involving voluminous documentation of financial transactions. The courtrooms are equipped with a chalkboard, a white board, a video player, and a projection screen that are available for use either during presentation of the case or during argument. However, before electronic equipment can be brought into the Courtroom, prior permission of the Court is required so that the U.S. Marshall's Office can arrange for clearance through the first floor security station.

Electronic Recording Equipment. The proceedings are recorded by electronic recording equipment. Counsel are reminded that only one person may speak at a time to avoid overlapping tracks on the tape. The system is quite sensitive but it is helpful if counsel remains in the general vicinity of one of the four microphones located on the counsel tables, the podium, and the witness stand.

There is a counter located on the top of the podium which indexes the recording tape and corresponds to the notes taken by the system operator. By noting the counter reading it is possible to order a portion of a transcript rather than an entire transcript. The system is also capable of repeating a question directed to a witness such as where an objection has been interposed.

Counsel Tables. Plaintiff or moving party should utilize the counsel table in the front of, and closest to, the witness stand. The defendant or responding party should utilize the counsel table furthest from the witness stand.

Witnesses. Any request to exclude witnesses from the courtroom prior to testimony should be made before opening statements. Witnesses may be called out of order to accommodate subpoenaed witnesses or experts.

A witness may not bring notes, documents, or other papers to the witness stand without permission of the Court. A witness may not be shown such writings during his or her testimony without permission of the Court unless the writings have been marked for identification or admitted in evidence.

Examination of Witnesses. Counsel may examine witnesses from the podium, from counsel table, either seated or standing, or may move generally about the courtroom keeping in mind the electronic recording system. Counsel may approach a witness without obtaining prior permission of the Court.

Objections and Argument. Counsel should stand when making evidentiary objections. Closing argument may be made from the podium or counsel may move about the courtroom keeping in mind the electronic recording system.

Recesses. Generally there will be a mid-morning and a mid-afternoon recess. In lengthy matters, there will be a ten minute recess after the parties have rested and before commencement of closing argument.

Attorney Conference Rooms. Conference rooms are available for use between 8:00 a.m. and

4:30 p.m. As the conference rooms are normally locked for security reasons, please check with the Courtroom Deputy to insure availability. It a conference room is locked upon your arrival at the Courthouse, use the telephone in the Clerk's Office to contact the Courtroom Deputy. Counsel's trial materials may be left in the courtroom during the noon recess provided counsel notifies the Courtroom Deputy at the conclusion of the session so the courtroom may be properly secured.

C. *Guidelines for Motions for Relief from Stay*

GUIDELINES FOR MOTIONS FOR RELIEF FROM STAY

Decisions in the relief from stay context are equitable decisions. I take into consideration the numbers involved, which include the value of the property, the amount of debt against the property, the amount of the pre-petition default and the post-petition default, whether property values are appreciating or depreciating, realistic prospects for sale or refinance, and the amount of the equity cushion. However, a multitude of other factors are also significant, such as the length of time the case has been pending, the debtor's efforts to reorganize, the debtor's employability and stability in the job, whether other family members are contributing to the debtor's efforts or are dependent upon the debtor, what caused a post-petition default and whether the situation is on-going or resolved, and so on. As a result, it is difficult to generalize about results in the relief from stay context.

Nonetheless, I try to provide consistency and predictability in hopes that lawyers may better advise their clients and negotiate consensual resolutions. I expect all counsel to come to the podium fully informed about their cases, having communicated both with their clients and with opposing counsel. I expect to rule at the first hearing unless there is a material fact in dispute.

To assist counsel, I am providing the following guidelines indicating how I am likely to rule in most situations.

RESIDENTIAL REAL ESTATE

CHAPTER 7

1. If the property is the debtor's residence and there is significant equity, relief is granted effective the day after the last day for filing complaints objecting to discharge. The stay is modified to allow scheduling the sale in accordance with the relief granted.

2. In other situations, unless the trustee opposes the motion, it will generally be granted.

CHAPTER 13

3. If there was no post-petition default when the motion was filed, it will be denied.

4. If Notice of Default is not yet filed, relief is granted to post a Notice of Default only (even if the default was cured before the hearing and assuming there is a pre-petition default). If the post-petition default is not cured within the 90 day notice period, the moving party may restore the motion to calendar on 10 days' notice to the debtor and the debtor's counsel. A new motion and filing fee are not required.

5. Curing Post-Petition Defaults: I expect counsel for the debtor to present a proposal for curing defaults. In considering a proposal, the most important factors to me are the amount and reason for the defaults, the equity cushion, the debtor's pre-petition conduct, the length of time the case has been pending and the length of time proposed for the cure.

6. If there is a large equity cushion, generally the adequate protection order will

not be self-executing and requests for further relief in the future require the motion being restored to calendar on 10 days notice to the debtor and debtor's counsel. This is because there may be other creditor interests to protect and to assure that the debtor has an opportunity to sell or refinance if current payments cannot be made.

7. If the equity cushion is small, generally the order is self-executing, shifting the risk of non-performance to the debtor.

8. Accounting Disputes: I expect counsel to work together in good faith to resolve accounting questions. A continuance will be granted for this purpose.

9. If there is no insurance, the debtor must provide proof of homeowner's insurance within 10 days of the preliminary hearing or relief is granted. This becomes a permanent order for the remainder of the case. In the event of a future lapse, a 10 day notice by letter is given to the debtor and the debtor's attorney and, if not cured, relief is granted.

10. Property Taxes: The debtor must pay post-petition property taxes timely.

11. Attorneys' Fees are generally paid through the plan by amendment to the proof of claim. However, payment of moving party's attorneys' fees may be required as part of the cure in order to impress upon the debtor that delayed payment becomes expensive.

12. Civil Code § 2924g(d): Where I establish a future date for the termination of the automatic stay, a "drop dead" date, the seven day waiting period provided for in California Civil Code § 2924g(d) will be considered waived provided that the original written order on the motion contains a specific reference to the waiver of the section.

13. If Notice of Trustee's Sale has already been published, moving party should come to court prepared to indicate the new sale date. The order should specify the new sale date.

14. Ex Parte Orders Following Default: Where an adequate protection order provides for a future order terminating the automatic stay to be obtained on an ex parte basis upon the default, or uncured default, of the debtor, a request for the future order will only be granted when the request is accompanied by a proof of service reflecting service of the request, the declaration setting forth the default and the proposed order on the debtor and the debtor's counsel. A file stamped copy of the adequate protection order providing for the ex parte request must be attached to the declaration setting forth the default. If unaccompanied by a proof of service, the proposed order will not be signed.

15. Relief Granted to Senior Secured Creditor: Where a senior secured creditor is given relief to actually conduct a foreclosure sale, relief will also be granted to a junior secured creditor. Noticed hearing or restoration to the calendar is still required, however.

16. If more than one property is collateralized by the same loan, generally the order will allow relief for only one property at a time.

17. Repeat Filings do not automatically trigger a different result. The most important factors considered are the number of filings, the length of time between the dismissal of a previous case and the filing of a new case, the reason for the subsequent filing and whether stay relief was sought or granted in the previous case. When it appears the system is being abused, relief will be granted.

18. If there is little or no equity cushion, but the moving party's position is

improving, generally complete relief will not be granted. In case of a future default, the order will be self-executing to shift the risk of loss to the debtor.

VEHICLES

CHAPTER 7

19. Unless the trustee opposes the motion, relief is generally granted.

CHAPTER 13

20. If there is no insurance, generally relief is granted if a binder is not provided to the moving party within 48 hours of the hearing. This becomes a permanent order for the remainder of the case. In the event of a future lapse, a 10 day notice by letter is given to the debtor and the debtor's attorney and, if not cured, relief is granted.

21. If payments are not made as provided by the plan, generally relief depends upon whether adequate protection payments are made (determined by depreciation of the vehicle as shown in the Kelly Blue Book).

UNLAWFUL DETAINER ACTIONS

22. Notice will be shortened to three days (excluding Sundays and holidays) by first class mail. (E.g., mail Friday for hearing on Wednesday; mail Monday for hearing on Thursday; mail Thursday for hearing on Tuesday [assumes no holiday]). The motion can be placed on any available calendar.

23. If involving a month-to-month tenancy on an apartment or single family residence: the motion will be granted.

PROCEEDING AGAINST INSURANCE COVERAGE

24. If relief is requested to pursue insurance coverage, the stay is modified to liquidate the claim or pursue insurance coverage, but remains in effect to prohibit execution upon the debtor or property of the estate without further order of the court. The stay does not prohibit the obtaining of the judgment in excess of insurance coverage or the filing of a proof of claim.

ASSUMPTIONS MADE BY THE COURT

Unless parties indicate to the contrary, the court makes the following assumptions:

25. Continued Hearings - Stay Remains in Effect. Where the preliminary hearing is continued for either a further preliminary hearing or a final hearing, the automatic stay remains in effect.

26. Time to Cure Default. Where an adequate protection order establishes a procedure for the curing of a future default after notice to the debtor and the debtor's counsel, the time to cure (for example, ten days) is calculated pursuant to Fed.R.Bankr.P. 9006. The first day for counting purposes shall be the day following the day when the notice is mailed.

27. Partial Cure of Default. Where the adequate protection order establishes a

procedure for the curing of a future default after notice to the debtor and the debtor's counsel, and the creditor accepts partial payment after issuing the notice, the creditor must issue a new notice in order to proceed.

28. Payment Accepted After Order Granting Relief Obtained. When a creditor accepts payment after obtaining an order granting complete relief to foreclose, the creditor is presumed to have agreed not to enforce that order at any time. The creditor should request that I vacate the order and proceed in accordance with the original adequate protection order in the event of a future default.

29. Attorneys' Fees. Unless a specific ruling is made at the time of a hearing, attorneys' fees which may be claimed under 11 U.S.C. § 506 are subject to subsequent objection as to reasonableness.

30. Trustees. Any order for relief will only be effective against parties who were served with the original motion. If a trustee was not served with a motion, the trustee will not be bound by the terms of the order for relief.

31. Real Property - Continuing Trustee's Sales. Where a trustee's sale has been noticed prior to the filing of a bankruptcy petition, the sale may be continued under California law or the laws of the state where the real property is located.

32. Real Property - Noticing Trustee's Sales. Where I modify the automatic stay to allow a creditor secured by real property to record and publish a notice of default, and the stay remains in effect to prohibit a trustee's sale without further order of the court, the recording and publishing of a notice of trustee's sale is also prohibited without further order.

33. Real Property - Adequate Protection Payments. Where adequate protection payments are made to a creditor secured by real property, and the secured creditor has previously recorded and published a notice of default or notice of trustee's sale, the secured creditor may accept the adequate protection payments. Receipt of payments shall not invalidate the notice of default or notice of trustee's sale previously recorded assuming it is otherwise valid.

SIGNING OF ORDERS

Proposed orders must be submitted in accordance with Bankruptcy Local Rules 9021-1 and 9022-1 and the division procedures for the submission of e-orders. Orders lodged in court at the conclusion of the hearing are normally processed and returned within three business days following submission. Orders submitted subsequent to the hearing will generally be lodged for 7 days after service unless approved as to form by the opposing party. While it is not required unless specifically ordered, I appreciate orders being approved as to form. Approval by opposing counsel can be by a facsimile signature page.

D. Open Calendar Procedure

OPEN CALENDAR PROCEDURE

The San Jose Division utilizes an Open Calendar Procedure for the scheduling of certain matters. This procedure will allow counsel to self-select an available date and time on the appropriate San Jose division judge's calendar and serve notice of that date and time without first having to obtain the date and time from the calendar clerk. Procedures for each judge is provided below.

The court encourages all parties to set matters using the Open Calendar Procedure whenever possible. The courtroom deputy for each judge will be available by telephone to schedule hearings not available for setting on the open calendar, or as needed for emergency matters.

Open Calendar Procedure for Judge Novack

Note: Unless otherwise noted, all hearings should be noticed for Courtroom 3070 in San Jose

Charles Novack, Bankruptcy Judge

Courtroom 3070
280 South First Street
San Jose, CA
(for San Jose hearings)

Salinas Quadrangle
1000 South Main Street, Suite 214
(for Salinas hearings)

Millie McGowan
Courtroom Deputy for Judge Charles Novack
(408) 278-7578
millie_mcgowan@canb.uscourts.gov

1. Types of proceedings that may be set in accordance with the Open Calendar Procedure:
   - Motions for Relief from Stay for San Jose Chapter 7 and Chapter 11 cases, which are heard on designated Wednesdays at 2:00 p.m. in Courtroom 3070.
   - Motions for Relief from Stay for Chapter 13 cases, which are heard on designated Wednesdays at 3:00 p.m. in Courtroom 3070. These hearings are all conducted telephonically in San Jose.
     Note: All motions for relief from stay are to be served with a copy of Judge Novack's Order Setting Telephonic Hearing for Relief from Automatic Stay which is available on the court's Internet website under <u>Division</u> and <u>Judges' Procedures</u>. Please note that this order is to be submitted for the Salinas Chapter 13 cases only. All relief from stay motions are to be accompanied by a <u>Relief from Stay coversheet</u>.
   - Motions in Chapter 7, Chapter 11 and Chapter 13 main cases, final accounts, fee applications for Chapter 7 or Chapter 11 cases, and Chapter 11 Disclosure Statement and Confirmation of Plan hearings, which are heard on the Law &

Motion calendar on designated Thursdays at 2:00 p.m. in Courtroom 3070.

- Motions in adversary cases which are heard on designated Tuesdays or Thursdays at 2:00 p.m. in Courtroom 3070.
- All matters relating to the Chapter 13 main cases, except for Motions for Relief from Stay, which are heard on one designated Friday per month at 10:00 a.m. in Salinas. Location: The Quadrangle, 1000 S. Main St., # 214, Salinas, CA.

Note: The court's form <u>Order re Prehearing Conference on Objection to Claim</u> is required to be served with all noticed hearings on objections to claims.

2. The Open Calendar Procedure will not be available for the following:
   - Case Management Conferences in adversary cases
     The Case Administrator will select the date and time for the initial Case Management Conference before issuing the summons.
   - Chapter 11 status conferences.
   - Trials in adversary proceedings.Counsel will be contacted by telephone by the courtroom deputy Millie McGowan and advised of the exact date and time for trial.
   - Any matter requiring an order shortening time.
     An application for an order shortening time under B.L.R. 9006-1 is required before a hearing date will be set. Counsel should include preferred calendar dates, the notice proposed to affected parties, and a proposed order. Once Judge Novack has reviewed the application, she will issue the order setting the date and time of the hearing and specifying any special instructions regarding notice, as appropriate.
   - Matters set by the court pursuant to an order to show cause.

3. Procedure for scheduling a hearing:

   a. In order to utilize the Open Calendar Procedure, counsel should select an available date and time from the appropriate calendar dates listed for the judge assigned to the main case. The list of available dates will be posted on the court's Internet website at http://www.canb.uscourts.gov under Calendars. Available dates for each calendar year will be updated regularly and are subject to change. The lists of available dates will also be placed on bulletin boards in the clerk's office and outside of each judge's courtroom. The date selected must be no earlier than as required by applicable national or local rules, as nothing in this Open Calendar Procedure alters applicable time limits.

   b. After selecting an available date and time, counsel should serve proper notice of the matter in accordance with applicable rules.

   Note: If a motion for relief from stay is set by a party in accordance with this Open Calendar Procedure more than thirty days after the date the motion is filed, the party will be deemed to waive the thirty-day limitation of 11 U.S.C. § 362(e).

   c. No later than three days after the service on other parties, counsel should file all appropriate papers with the court, including one copy marked "Judge's Copy" and one copy marked "Clerk's Copy."

d. Once a matter is set by the Open Calendar Procedure, with the exception of certain matters in adversary proceedings or matters noticed to all creditors, continuances may be handled through the assigned judge's courtroom deputy, Millie McGowan, by telephone at (408) 278-7578 or by e-mail at millie_mcgowan@canb.uscourts.gov. A minimum of three days' written notice of any continuance is required. Counsel must receive either written confirmation of a continuance by e-mail or telephonically from the courtroom deputy. Written stipulations and a proposed order are required for all Case Management Conferences, Pre-Trials and scheduled Trials. Matters noticed to all creditors must be continued on seven days' written notice or in open court.

e. Counsel must not request that the courtroom deputy call back to confirm that the matter has been placed on the calendar. Counsel desiring confirmation that a matter has been placed on the calendar by the Open Calendar Procedure should review the published calendars in the local legal newspapers, posted outside the division's courtrooms or its calendar on the bankruptcy court's Internet site.

f. Failure to comply with the foregoing Open Calendar Procedure will result in the matter not being placed on calendar.

Note: Occasionally there may be a need to reschedule matters that have been placed on the calendar in accordance with this Open Calendar Procedure. Typically this will be because of calendar congestion or unforeseen schedule changes. In those instances the judge's courtroom deputy will contact the moving party as soon as possible so that a notice of a rescheduled hearing may be disseminated.

E. Policy for Courtesy Copies

JUDGE NOVACK'S POLICY FOR COURTESY COPIES

Courtesy copies shall be provided to the chambers of the assigned judge in a case pursuant to the procedures set forth below by each judge. A printed copy of the "Notice of Electronic Filing" shall be attached to the courtesy paper copy of the electronically filed pleading and marked "Judge's copy." All courtesy copies are to be submitted to the court to the attention of the Courtroom Deputy of the judge assigned to the case.

For Judge Novack's cases, submit copies to the attention of Millie McGowan.

1. Motions for Relief From Stay:

   A. Chambers copies of a cover sheet and certificate of service in all cases.

   B. No chambers copy of the remaining papers are required regardless of length.

2. In Adversary Proceedings:

   A. No chambers copies are required of the complaint, answer, counterclaim, etc., regardless of length.

   B. Chambers copies are required of all Case Management Conference Statements.

   C. Chambers copies of other papers are not required unless page count of all related documents, e.g., notice, motion/application, declaration, and points and authorities – exceeds 25 pages. Page count includes exhibits but not proofs of service.

3. In All Chapters:

   A. Chambers copies are required of fee applications with time records.

4. In Chapter 11 Cases:

   A. Chambers copies are required of all "first day" motions and all plans and disclosure statements.

   B. Chambers copies of other papers are not required unless page count of all related documents, e.g., notice, motion/application, declaration, and points and authorities – exceeds 25 pages. Page count includes exhibits but not proofs of service.

   C. No chambers copies are required of the petition, schedules of assets and liabilities, statement of financial affairs and similar documents filed at the onset of case.

5. In Chapter 7 and 13 Cases:

   A. Chambers copies are required of all motions to extend or impose the automatic stay and supporting documents.

   B. Chambers copies of papers are not required unless page count of all related documents, e.g., notice, motion/application, declaration, and points and authorities - exceeds 25 pages. Page count includes exhibits but not proofs of service.

   C. No chambers copies are required of the petition, schedules of assets and liabilities, statement of financial affairs and similar documents filed at the onset of case.

F. Practices and Procedures

Practices and Procedures
Honorable Charles Novack

Judge Novack's **PRACTICES AND PROCEDURES** are presented as a tool in providing efficient and effective services by counsel. The hope is that this information will provide you and your client with an accurate expectation of the processes used in this court. Emphasizing the importance of expectations: *"Disappointment is a sort of bankruptcy – the bankruptcy of a soul that expends too much in hope and expectation"* (American philosopher Eric Hoffer).

1. Calendaring Matters. Judge Novack has separate calendars for relief from stay, adversary motions, case motions, chapter 11 disclosure statements and plan confirmations, chapter 13 confirmations, final accounts and fee applications, chapter 11 status conferences, adversary case management conferences, and trial setting conferences.

The San Jose Division uses an Open Calendar that allows counsel to self-select an available hearing date. Complete details regarding the Open Calendar procedure for the division and for Judge Novack are available at Calendar Procedures for San Jose Division.

To calendar an emergency matter to be heard on shortened time, an application for an order shortening time that complies with Bankruptcy Local Rule 9006-1 is required before a hearing date will be set. Counsel should include preferred calendar dates and the proposed notice to affected parties as part of their application and a proposed order. Requests for temporary restraining orders will only be calendared after an adversary complaint has been filed. You should include an application for an expedited hearing with the request for TRO and complaint. Generally, Judge Novack requires a minimum of four hours notice to affected parties prior to conducting a hearing on a TRO.

Once Judge Novack has reviewed an application for shortened time, he will issue an order setting the date and time of the hearing and specifying any special instructions regarding notice, as appropriate. Written opposition is generally not required to be filed prior to a hearing set on shortened time, and a party may appear at the hearing to oppose the motion orally.

If you need to contact Judge Novack's courtroom deputy to schedule a hearing not subject to the open calendar procedure, you may call Millie McGowan at (408) 278-7578. Her email address is millie_mcgowan@canb.uscourts.gov.

2. Continuing or Withdrawing Calendared Matters. We receive many inquiries about how to continue or remove a matter on the court calendar. As a matter of courtesy to the court and opposing counsel, we suggest the following procedures.

To remove a new matter from the calendar, you may submit a written withdrawal to the court no later than 3 days prior to the hearing. If you wish to continue a new matter, the timing depends upon who has received notice. If the matter has been noticed to all creditors, please submit a notice of continued hearing and serve it on all creditors at least 7 days prior to the hearing. If the matter concerns only specific parties in interest, such as a motion for relief from stay, contact the court and counsel 24 hours in advance to advise of the continuance.

If you wish to continue a hearing on a matter that has already been before the court, you have two options. You may submit a stipulation and order (if the parties agree) or application and order at least 3 days prior to the hearing. If the hearing is in less than 3 days, please contact chambers to advise the court that you will request a continuance at the hearing. Generally, Judge Novack prefers that appearances to request a continuance be made telephonically.

3. Calling Chambers. You may call Judge Novack's law clerks at (408) 278-7538 if you have questions regarding procedural matters. Please keep in mind that Federal Rule of Bankruptcy Procedure 9003 prohibits ex parte contacts with the court and is applicable to law clerks as well as judges. Additionally, you may contact chambers to check on the status of an order or to inform the court of the following matters:

- an objection to a proposed form of order;
- a settlement of a matter calendared for hearing; or
- that the parties will go forward with a chapter 11 disclosure statement or plan confirmation hearing.

Finally, you may contact chambers to obtain assistance with a discovery dispute. When appropriate under Civil Local Rule 37-1(b), Judge Novack will attempt to resolve discovery disputes through a telephonic conference with all parties.

4. Submission of Orders After Hearings. Please observe the provisions of Bankruptcy Local Rule 9021-1(c) and 9022-1.

5. Telephonic Hearings. Counsel may appear telephonically as described in Telephonic Appearance Policy. Judge Novack encourages counsel to appear telephonically when appropriate because of the savings in time and cost. Generally, Judge Novack has three procedures for telephonic appearances.

The first involves case management conferences in adversary proceedings. This is an "optout" system; that is, Court Conference will arrange a telephonic appearance unless you advise them you are going to appear personally. On this calendar, nearly all appearances are telephonic. Instructions for this telephonic appearance are attached to the order setting telephonic case management conference. Because the court coordinates a large number of telephonic conferences, continuances are allowed only with leave of court and must be sought in writing at least fourteen days before the hearing date. Forms of Application/Stipulation to Continue Telephonic Case Management Conference and Order Continuing Telephonic Case Management Conference are posted on this site.

The second involves chapter 13 relief from stay hearings from the Salinas venue. This is a "mandatory" system. Both the moving party and debtor's counsel appear telephonically from their offices. At the time a hearing is calendared, the moving party should download the Order Setting Telephonic Hearing For Relief From Stay, insert the pertinent information regarding the date, time and location of the hearing and serve a copy with the motion. Please note that the Order has been pre-signed by Judge Novack and is effective as soon as the movant self-selects a hearing date from the list of available dates listed in the Open Calendar, fills in the blanks and serves the Order upon the debtor. Do not prepare a new Order on your word processor or submit the Order (or any order setting the preliminary hearing) for signature by the court. Costs for this appearance are paid by the moving party. If a party is appearing in pro per, the motion is generally heard on the 2:00 p.m. calendar where personal appearances are allowed.

Finally, with respect to most other matters, Judge Novack has an "opt-in" system. If you want to appear telephonically on a matter, please contact Court Conference at 1-866-582-6878 at least 24 hours in advance of a hearing to insure that arrangements are completed in time for the hearing.

6. Relief From Stay. The Guidelines for Motions for Relief from Stay explain the factors Judge Novack considers in ruling on a relief from stay motion. Most stay motions are resolved at the preliminary hearing. If a final hearing is set, it is generally an evidentiary hearing.

All relief from stay motions are to be accompanied by a relief from stay coversheet, which is available on-line or at the clerk's office. The coversheet is Judge Novack's most important preparation tool for the relief from stay calendar. If the relief from stay coversheet is not accurate and complete, the motion may be denied without prejudice.

Unless an order specifically provides to the contrary, Judge Novack makes certain assumptions regarding every order submitted following a motion for relief from stay. These assumptions should be taken into account when submitting or reviewing proposed orders.

Please refer to paragraph 5 above regarding the special procedures for relief from stay hearings in chapter 13 cases from the Salinas venue.

7. Adversary Proceedings. Adversary proceedings progress on written orders issued by the court. Each confirms dates, times and procedures. The first is the order setting the telephonic case management conference which is served with the summons and complaint. Pursuant to these orders, case management conference statements are generally required at least 7 days before each conference and continuances must be requested in writing at least 14 days prior to the conference date.

Short cause matters are generally set for trial after the first status conference. In more complex cases, Judge Novack issues a trial setting order requiring counsel to prepare a joint pre-trial order. The pre-trial order supersedes all pleadings in the case. The trial setting orders contain the protocol for courtroom procedures for trial or evidentiary hearing. Once a matter has been set for trial, Judge Novack will continue the trial to document a settlement but not because of ongoing negotiations. Where the settlement documentation (Judgment, Stipulation For Judgment or Dismissal) has been filed with the court prior to the trial date no appearance by counsel is necessary. Otherwise, counsel must appear at the calling of the calendar to put the settlement on the record. With prior approval, counsel may appear by telephone for this purpose.

The Bankruptcy Dispute Resolution Program (BDRP) established by the district provides opportunities for mediation, arbitration and settlement. A request for referral may be made at any time through procedures outlined in the Local Bankruptcy Rules. B.L.R. 9040 et. seq.

8. Chapter 11 cases. Judge Novack calendars regular conferences on the status of each pending chapter 11 case. Chapter 11 Status Conference Checklist describes Judge Novack's expectations for both the conferences and the case.

The San Jose Division of the U.S. Bankruptcy Court for the Northern District of California has adopted Guidelines for Early Disposition of Assets in Chapter 11 Cases; Pre-Packaged Plans; and the Sale of Substantially All Assets Under § 363. Please refer to these Guidelines when preparing for a contested matter involving any of these issues.

9. Forms. Both Northern District and official bankruptcy forms are available on this website. The San Jose Division has its own forms for scheduling orders in adversary proceedings and Chapter 13 forms that counsel are encouraged to use.

10. Judge Novack observes the following guidelines:

- Bankruptcy Petition Preparer Guidelines
- Guidelines for Cash Collateral and Financing Motions and Stipulations
- Guidelines for Compensation and Expense Reimbursement of Professionals and Trustees
- Guidelines for Early Disposition of Assets in Chapter 11 Cases, Pre-Packaged Plan, the Sale of Substantially All Assets Under § 363(b)
- Guidelines for Legal Services to be Provided by Debtor's Attorney in Chapter 7 Cases
- Guidelines re: Sale Orders
- Rights and Responsibilities of Chapter 13 Debtors and Their Attorneys (San Jose Division)

G. *Preparation of Orders Retaining Professionals*

PREPARATION OF ORDERS RETAINING PROFESSIONALS

The Court has discontinued its prior practice of signing retention orders that incorporate either the supporting application or any attachments.

Retention orders must now include all material terms of the professional's employment. Such terms include:

1. Whether the employment is under § 327 or § 1103.

2. The date employment is effective.

3. The basis of compensation such as hourly, contingency or some other basis.

4. If the provisions of § 328(a) limiting review of compensation are applicable, such must be clearly stated.

5. Any proposed success fees or other back-end fees must be clearly described.

6. Any limitation on the professionals liability such as indemnification provisions, procedural limitations, claim limitations, damage limitations must be clearly described as well as whether such provisions are intended to bind successors and assigns.

7. Other material terms.

Material terms of employment not set forth in the order are not included in the court's approval.

H. Procedures for Reaffirmation Hearings

PROCEDURES FOR REAFFIRMATION HEARINGS

The following guidelines are promulgated to provide flexibility for debtors and creditors seeking a reaffirmation hearing pursuant to § 524(c) or (d) of the Bankruptcy Code.

1. **Regular Hearings**-A courtroom reaffirmation hearing may be added to any existing calendar. Arrangements are made by calling the Courtroom Deputy, Millie McGowan, at least 7 days before the requested hearing date. Ms. McGowan can be reached at (408) 278-7578. Telephonic appearances are available using the Court's normal procedure.

2. **Special Settings**-The Court will attempt to accommodate debtors who need a courtroom hearing at a particular time. Requests for such special settings should be made to Ms. McGowan at (408) 278-7578. Telephonic appearances are available using the Court's normal procedure.

3. **Telephonic Reaffirmations**-Where circumstances warrant, the Court will conduct a reaffirmation with all parties appearing by telephone. Requests for such telephonic hearings should be made to Ms. McGowan at (408) 278-7578.

II. Judge Novack's Case Management Orders

A. Order Continuing Telephonic Case Management Conference

IN THE UNITED STATES BANKRUPTCY COURT
FOR THE NORTHERN DISTRICT OF CALIFORNIA

In re:	)	Case No. ________________
[Debtor's Name]	)	Chapter ___________
	)	Adversary No. ______________
Debtor(s).	)	
________________________________	)	**ORDER CONTINUING TELEPHONIC**
[Plaintiff's Name]	)	**CASE MANAGEMENT CONFERENCE**
	)	
Plaintiff(s),	)	**[Date]**
v.	)	**[Time]**
	)	**Telephonic**
[Defendant's Name]	)	
	)	
Defendant(s).	)	
________________________________	)	

The court having considered the **[Stipulation/Application]** to Continue Telephonic Case Management Conference filed herein, and good cause appearing, IT IS ORDERED that:

1. The Telephonic Case Management Conference scheduled for **[CMC Date]** at **[CMC Time]** is hereby continued to **[CMC Date]** at **[CMC Time]**.

2. Each party shall file, jointly or separately, and serve on all other parties an updated case management conference statement at least _7_ days before the continued Telephonic Case Management Conference.

*** * * END OF ORDER * * ***

B. Order Regarding Prehearing Conference on Objection to Claim

**ORDER RE PREHEARING CONFERENCE
ON OBJECTION TO CLAIM**

It is ordered that a PREHEARING CONFERENCE be held on at the United States Bankruptcy Court, Rm ______.

THE CLAIMANT AND THE OBJECTOR ARE O RDE RED to confer by telephone at least fourteen days prior to the PREHEARING CONFERENCE to discuss resolution of the objection. At least seven days prior to the PREHEARING CONFERENCE the parties shall file and serve a PREHEARING STATEMENT with the court not to exceed two pages in length, addressing the following:

1) A statement of the date and time of the telephone conference required by this order.

2) The estimated time for hearing and desired hearing date.

3) A precise and separate statement of each factual and legal issue which must be

determined to resolve the objection and a brief statement of the facts in support thereof.

COUNSEL FOR THE OBJECTOR (OR THE OBJECTOR, IF UNREPRESENTED BY COUNSEL) is ordered to serve this **PREHEARING CONFERENCE ORDER** on the Claimant within seven calendar days from the date of this Order.

Ordered this day of ____________________.

____
CHARLES NOVACK
United States Bankruptcy Judge

C. *Order Setting Telephonic Hearing for Relief from Stay (Chapter 13 - Salinas cases only)*

IN THE UNITED STATES BANKRUPTCY COURT
FOR THE NORTHERN DISTRICT OF CALIFORNIA

In re:	)	Case No. ____________
[Debtor's Name]	)	R.S. No. ____________
	)	
Debtor(s).	)	**CHAPTER 13**
	)	
	)	**ORDER SETTING TELEPHONIC**
______________________________	)	**HEARING FOR RELIEF FROM STAY**

IT IS HEREBY ORDERED that a preliminary hearing will be held telephonically on ____________________ at _____ _.m., or as soon thereafter as the matter may be heard, to consider the attached motion for relief from stay. This Order modifies Bankruptcy Local Rule 4001-1 by requiring telephonic, rather than personal appearances, by the parties on a motion for relief from stay. The moving party shall complete the information in this Order, serve a copy of this Order with the moving papers and file all pleadings as well as proof of service at least fourteen days before the noticed hearing date.

All telephonic appearances shall be through Court Conference. Any questions regarding procedures for the telephonic hearing may be directed to Court Conference at 1-866-582-6878.

The parties shall, in good faith, confer before the hearing regarding the issues raised by the motion and resolution of the motion. If debtor's counsel or the debtor does not appear telephonically, the Court may presume there is no opposition to the motion. If either counsel or the parties abuse the process for telephonic hearings, the Court may order sanctions as appropriate, which may include removing the matter from the calendar, granting relief from the automatic stay, or awarding monetary sanctions.

____
CHARLES NOVACK
United States Bankruptcy Judge

III. Judge Novack's Forms

A. *Application/Stipulation to Continue Telephone Case Management Conference*

**IN THE UNITED STATES BANKRUPTCY COURT
FOR THE NORTHERN DISTRICT OF CALIFORNIA**

In re: [Debtor's Name] Debtor(s). _______________________	Case No. ______________ Chapter __________ Adversary No. ______________
[Plaintiff's Name] Plaintiff(s), v. [Defendant's Name] Defendant(s). _______________________	**[APPL./STIP.] TO CONTINUE TELEPHONIC CASE MANAGEMENT CONFERENCE** **[Date]** **[Time]** **Telephonic**

[Plaintiff/Defendant] respectfully request(s) that the telephonic case management conference currently scheduled for [Date] at [Time] be continued for the following reason(s):

[reason]

[Plaintiff/Defendant] request that the telephonic case management conference be continued for approximately [#] days to [Date] at [Time].

DATED: ________________ ________________________

[Attorney Name]

Hon. Arthur S. Weissbrodt

Bankruptcy Judge

Contact Information

U.S. Bankruptcy Court, Northern District of California
Courtroom 3020
280 South First Street
San Jose, CA 95113
Courtroom Deputy: (408) 278-7564

Biographical Information

[Not available]

I. Judge Weissbrodt's Procedures and Practices

A. *Open Calendar Procedure*

OPEN CALENDAR PROCEDURE

The San Jose Division utilizes an Open Calendar Procedure for the scheduling of certain matters. This procedure will allow counsel to self-select an available date and time on the appropriate San Jose division judge's calendar and serve notice of that date and time without first having to obtain the date and time from the calendar clerk. Procedures for each judge is provided below.

The court encourages all parties to set matters using the Open Calendar Procedure whenever possible. The courtroom deputy for each judge will be available by telephone to schedule hearings not available for setting on the open calendar, or as needed for emergency matters.

Open Calendar Procedure for Judge Weissbrodt

Arthur Weissbrodt, Bankruptcy Judge
Courtroom 3020, San Jose
Brook Esparza, Courtroom Deputy for Judge Arthur Weissbrodt.
408-278-7564
brook_esparza@canb.uscourts.gov

1. Types of proceedings that may be set in accordance with the Open Calendar Procedure:
   - Motions for Relief from Stay for San Jose Chapter 7, Chapter 11 or Chapter 13 cases.
   - Motions in San Jose Chapter 7 and Chapter 11 main cases
   - Final Accounts
   - Fee Applications for Chapter 7 or Chapter 11 cases
   - Motions in adversary cases
   - Chapter 11 Disclosure Statement hearings
   - All matters relating to the Chapter 13 main cases

2. The Open Calendar Procedure will not be available for the following:
   - Case Management Conferences in adversary cases
     The Case Administrator will select the date and time for the initial Case Management Conference before issuing the summons.
   - Chapter 11 hearing on confirmation of plan.
     Following the approval of the disclosure statement, the court will set the date and time for the hearing on confirmation of plan.
   - Chapter 11 status conferences.
     The court will schedule and notice a status conference on the first available status conference date after the date set for the Section 341 meeting of creditors.
   - Trials in adversary proceedings.
     Counsel will be contacted by telephone by the courtroom deputy Brook Esparza and

advised of the exact date and time for trial.

- Evidentiary hearings of any type for a main case or adversary case will be scheduled by the court.
- Any matter requiring an order shortening time.
  An application for an order shortening time under B.L.R. 9006-1 is required before a hearing date will be set. Counsel should include preferred calendar dates and the notice proposed to affected parties. Once Judge Weissbrodt has reviewed the application, a law clerk or courtroom deputy will telephone with the date and time of the hearing as well as any special instructions regarding notice.
- Matters set by the court pursuant to an order to show cause.

3. Procedure

a. In order to utilize the Open Calendar Procedure, counsel should select an available date and time as shown on the appropriate attached list for the judge assigned the main case. The lists of available dates will be updated regularly and will be placed on bulletin boards in the clerk's office and outside of each judge's courtroom. The lists will also be posted on the court's Internet website at http://www.canb.uscourts.gov. The date selected must be no earlier than as required by applicable national or local rules, as nothing in this Open Calendar Procedure alters applicable time limits.

b. After selecting an available date and time, counsel should serve proper notice of the matter in accordance with applicable rules.

Note: If a motion for relief from stay is set by a party in accordance with this Open Calendar Procedure more than thirty days after the date the motion is filed, the party will be deemed to waive the thirty-day limitation of 11 U.S.C. § 362(e).

c. No later than **three** days after the service on other parties, counsel should file all appropriate papers with the court, including **one copy marked "Clerk's Copy."**

d. Once a matter is set by the Open Calendar Procedure, with the exception of certain matters in adversary proceedings or matters noticed to all creditors, continuances may be handled through the assigned judge's courtroom deputy, Brook Esparza, by telephone at 408-278-7564 or by e-mail at brook_esparza@canb.uscourts.gov . A minimum notice of 24 hours for any continuance is encouraged. Counsel must receive either written confirmation of a continuance by e-mail or telephonically from the courtroom deputy. Written stipulations and a proposed order are required for all Case Management Conferences, Pre-Trials and scheduled Trials. Matters noticed to all creditors must be continued in open court.

e. Counsel **must not** request that the courtroom deputy call back to confirm that the matter has been placed on the calendar. Counsel desiring confirmation that a matter has been placed on the calendar by the Open Calendar Procedure should review the published calendars in the local legal newspapers, posted outside the division's courtrooms or its calendar on the bankruptcy court's Internet site.

f. Failure to comply with the foregoing Open Calendar Procedure will result in the matter not being placed on calendar.

Note: Occasionally there may be a need to reschedule matters that have been placed on the calendar in accordance with this Open Calendar Procedure. Typically this will be because of calendar congestion or unforeseen schedule changes. In those instances the judge's courtroom deputy will contact the moving party as soon as possible so that a notice of a rescheduled hearing may be disseminated.

B. Policy and Procedures for Appearances by Telephone

POLICY AND PROCEDURES FOR APPEARANCES BY TELEPHONE

1. **Permitted Appearances**
Telephonic appearances can save the parties substantial time and expense. For that reason, parties are encouraged to appear telephonically when appropriate. Telephonic appearances are not permitted where either the party appearing *in propria persona* or counsel:

    will be examining witnesses;
    is the proponent of a chapter 11 disclosure statement or plan being considered by the court;
    is a creditor seeking relief from stay as to real property or the debtor's residence (except to request a continuance, enter a stipulation on the record or note that the debtor has stated in writing that the debtor surrenders the property at issue);
    is counsel for a client who is present in court; or
    is directed by the court to appear personally.

    There are no restrictions on eligibility to appear by telephone based upon the geographic location of the counsel or the party.

    Telephonic appearances are a privilege for the convenience of the parties. Abuses of these procedures will result in cancellation of these privileges of the offending party.

2. **Procedure for Arranging for Telephonic Appearances**
Telephonic appearances are arranged through Court Conference. All parties and counsel using this service must have an account or make arrangements to set one up well in advance of the hearing. If you do not have an account established with Court Conference, you must provide a credit card number at the time of making your reservation. Appearances are arranged by reservation. To make a reservation, call **1-866-582-6878** at least 24 hours in advance of the hearing.

    Shortly before the Court is ready to call your matter, the Court Conference operator will contact the participant as prearranged. **All participants <u>MUST</u> be available when called.** If the participant is not available when called, the participant will be billed for the call and the hearing may proceed in the participant's absence. The Court may impose sanctions as set forth below.

    If a Debtor is unable to establish an account with Court Conference, a Debtor may appear by telephone at no charge by contacting the Court's Courtroom Deputy, Ms. Brook Esparza, by telephone at (408) 278-7564 at least three (3) business days prior to the scheduled hearing.

    Telephonic appearances are connected directly with the courtroom's public address system and electronic recording equipment so that a normal record is produced. To ensure a quality record, all parties should use a land line. The use of car phones, mobile phones, public telephone booths, phones in other public places or headsets is prohibited except in the most extreme emergencies. Participants should be able to hear all parties without difficulty or echo. The use of speaker phones, headsets or other remote listening devices is not permitted (even before their particular case is called).

At the time of the hearing you may initially be in the listening mode in which case you will be able to hear the case before yours just as if you were in the courtroom. After your call is connected to the courtroom, the Judge or Courtroom Deputy will call the case. The Judge will ask for appearances and direct the manner in which the hearing proceeds. Each time a participant speaks, he or she must identify himself or herself for the record. The Court's teleconferencing system allows more than one speaker to be heard so that the Judge can interrupt a speaker to ask a question or redirect the discussion. When the Judge informs the participants that the hearing is completed, the participants may disconnect and the next case will be called.

Telephonic appearances by multiple participants are <u>only</u> possible where there is compliance with every procedural requirement. **Sanctions may be imposed when there is any deviation from the required procedures or where the court determines that a person's conduct makes telephonic appearances inappropriate.** Sanctions may include dropping the matter from the calendar, continuing the hearing, proceeding in the absence of an unavailable participant, a monetary sanction of **$100** or more, or a temporary or permanent prohibition against a person/firm appearing telephonically.

When the Court conducts a telephone conference on short notice and uses Court Conference, it may designate one party to bear the entire cost of the conference call. The Court may on occasion initiate calls to one or two persons directly from the Courtroom without use of a conference operator. In those instances, the Courtroom Deputy will contact parties to inform them of the arrangements.

Because the Courtroom Deputy is usually in Court prior to the initiation of any particular call, last minute changes are generally impossible to handle and are discouraged.

C. *Practice Tip – Service by Mail on Corporations, Partnerships, and Financial Institutions*

PRACTICE TIP: SERVICE BY MAIL ON CORPORATIONS, PARTNERSHIPS AND FINANCIAL INSTITUTIONS

On several occasions, matters before the Court have been continued due to improper service under Rules 7004 and 9014 of the Federal Rules of Bankruptcy Procedure ("FRBP"). The majority of these service problems relate to service by mail on corporate entities and financial institutions in contested matters. To help the parties avoid these errors in future, the applicable provisions are outlined below.

FRBP 9014(b) provides that a motion in a contested matter must be served in accordance with the manner of service provided for service of a summons and complaint under FRCP 7004. See also, In re Villar, 317 B.R. 88 (9th Cir. BAP 2004). FRBP 7004 provides, in pertinent part, as follows:

Rule 7004. Process; Service of Summons, Complaint

. . .

(b) Service by first class mail.
Except as provided in subdivision (h), in addition to the methods of service authorized by Rule 4(e) -(j) F.R.Civ.P., service may be made within the United States by first class mail postage prepaid as follows:

. . .

(3) Upon a domestic or foreign corporation or upon a partnership or other unincorporated association, by mailing a copy of the summons and complaint to the attention of an officer, a managing or general agent, or to any other agent authorized by appointment or by law to receive service of process and, if the agent is one authorized by statute to receive service and the statute so requires, by also mailing a copy to the defendant.

. . .

(g) Service on the debtor's attorney.
If the debtor is represented by an attorney, whenever service is made upon the debtor under this Rule, service shall also be made upon the debtor's attorney by any means authorized under Rule 5(b) F. R. Civ. P.
(h) Service of process on an insured depository institution.
Service on an insured depository institution (as defined in section 3 of the Federal Deposit Insurance Act) in a contested matter or adversary proceeding shall be made by certified mail addressed to an officer of the institution unless—

(1) the institution has appeared by its attorney, in which case the attorney shall be served by first class mail;
(2) the court orders otherwise after service upon the institution by certified mail of notice of an application to permit service on the institution by first class mail sent to an officer of the institution designated by the institution; or

> *(3) the institution has waived in writing its entitlement to service by certified mail by designating an officer to receive service.*

Please Note:

1. The Guidelines for Valuing and Avoiding Liens in Individual Chapter 11 Cases and Chapter 13 Cases for the United States Bankruptcy Court for the Northern District of California ("Guidelines for Valuing and Avoiding Liens") specifically provide:

   Because a motion to strip lien seeks relief against a specific, identifiable party, debtor must comply with B.L.R. 9014-1(b) & (c). Debtor should take care to serve the affected lienholder in the manner required by the FRBP, and in particular FRBP 7004(b) and 7004(h) as to certain lenders.

   Guidelines for Valuing and Avoiding Liens, ¶ 2.

2. When a corporation is served to the attention of an agent for service of process, a copy of the motion must also be served on the corporation. Service on the registered agent alone is insufficient. FRBP 7004(b)(3).

3. Service to the "attention of an officer, a managing or general agent" under FRBP 7004(b)(3) requires that the movant "determine the name of the president or other officer and make sure the envelope is addressed to him or her, by name." In re Schoon, 153 B.R. 48, 49 (Bankr. N.D. Cal. 1993). Accord Villar, 317 B.R. at 93; In re Pittman Mechanical Contractors, Inc., 180 B.R. 453, 457 (Bankr. E.D. Va. 1995). Service to "Attn: Officer" is insufficient.

4. The official website of the Federal Deposit Insurance Corporation has a "Bank Find" search feature, which allows the searcher to determine if a financial institution is an "insured depository." If an institution is an "insured depository" then the institution must be served in accordance with the provisions of FRBP 7004(h). This "Bank Find" search can be found at http://www2.fdic.gov/idasp/main_bankfind.asp.

5. If the party being served has failed to properly update his or her address, service on the old address of record is proper. In re Cossio, 163 B.R. 150 (9th Cir. BAP 1994), aff'd 56 F.3d 70 (9th Cir. 1995). The burden is the party who has changed his or her address to ensure that his or her address is properly updated in the official records.

6. If relief is sought against any entity that has filed a claim, all papers shall be mailed to the address shown on the proof of claim. B.L.R. 9014-1(b)(4)(A).

7. Service of an objection to a proof of claim is governed by FRBP 3007, not 7004. Therefore, service of an objection on the person designated on the proof of claim as the notice recipient is sufficient. In re State Line Hotel, Inc., 323 B.R. 703 (9th Cir. BAP 2005), vacated and remanded as moot, 242 Fed. Appx. 460 (9th Cir. 2007).

D. *Practice Tip – Service upon the United States and Federal Agencies*

PRACTICE TIP – SERVICE UPON THE UNITED STATES AND FEDERAL AGENCIES

Rule 9014 of the Federal Rules of Bankruptcy Procedure ("FRBP") provides that FRBP 7004(b)(4) applies to Adversary Proceedings and contested matters. FRBP 7004(b)(4) provides that service by mail upon the United States must be addressed "to the civil process clerk at the office of the United States Attorney for the district in which the action is brought and . . . to the Attorney General of the United States at Washington, District of Columbia, and in any action attacking the validity of an order of an officer or an agency of the United States not made a party, by also mailing a copy of the summons and complaint to that officer or agency." In re Morrell, 69 B.R. 147 (N.D. Cal. 1986) holds that an objection to a claim by the Internal Revenue Service must be served in accordance with FRBP 7004(b)(4).

If there is a different name or address on the proof of claim filed by the United States or an agency thereof, I suggest you serve the United States both as per the above requirements and at the address provided on the proof of claim.

E. *Procedures for Orders Modifying Chapter 13 Plans After Confirmation*

PROCEDURES FOR ORDERS MODIFYING CHAPTER 13 PLANS AFTER CONFIRMATION

If a proposed form of order approving the modification of a confirmed Chapter 13 plan, pursuant to 11 U.S.C. § 1329, is submitted by a party other than the Chapter 13 Trustee, the Chapter 13 Trustee must approve the proposed form of order as to form. If the proposed form of order does not bear the Chapter 13 Trustee's signature, it will normally not be signed by Judge Weissbrodt. A declaration indicating the Chapter 13 Trustee has not opposed the motion to modify, or has approved the modification, is insufficient. If the Chapter 13 Trustee and the moving party cannot agree on a proposed form of order, the moving party or the Chapter 13 Trustee may set the matter for hearing on 7-days notice to the other party.

F. Procedures for Proposed Judgments Relating to Credit Card Debts

JUDGE WEISSBRODT'S PROCEDURES FOR PROPOSED JUDGMENTS RELATING TO CREDIT CARD DEBTS

When submitting either a proposed default judgment or a proposed judgment pursuant to a stipulation that relates to the non-dischargeability of a credit card debt, in addition to all other documents submitted to the Court in support of the judgment, the parties must submit copies of the credit card statements for the time period at issue in the underlying complaint as well as one year prior to that time period. These statements should be attached as an exhibit by a party competent to testify that such statements are true and correct copies of the records in question.

II. Judge Weissbrodt's Case Management Orders

A. Order Regarding Prehearing Conference on Objection to Claim

IN THE UNITED STATES BANKRUPTCY COURT
FOR THE NORTHERN DISTRICT OF CALIFORNIA

In re:	)	Case No. ________________
	)	
Claim:	)	**ORDER RE PREHEARING**
	)	**CONFERENCE ON OBJECTION TO**
________________________________	)	**CLAIM**

It is ordered that a PREHEARING CONFERENCE be held on ____________ at __________________ at the United States Bankruptcy Court, Rm ______.

THE CLAIMANT AND THE OBJECTOR ARE ORDERED to confer by telephone at least fourteen days prior to the PREHEARING CONFERENCE to discuss resolution of the objection. At least seven days prior to the PREHEARING CONFERENCE the parties shall file and serve a PREHEARING STATEMENT with the court not to exceed two pages in length, addressing the following:

1) A statement of the date and time of the telephone conference required by this order.

2) The estimated time for hearing and desired hearing date.

3) A precise and separate statement of each factual and legal issue which must be determined to resolve the objection and a brief statement of the facts in support thereof.

COUNSEL FOR THE OBJECTOR (OR THE OBJECTOR, IF UNREPRESENTED BY COUNSEL) is ordered to serve this **PREHEARING CONFERENCE ORDER** on the Claimant within seven calendar days from the date of this Order.

Ordered this ________ day of _________.

____
ARTHUR S. WEISSBRODT
United States Bankruptcy Judge

www.ingramcontent.com/pod-product-compliance
Lightning Source LLC
LaVergne TN
LVHW080042210926
848481LV00011B/3260
* 9 7 8 0 9 8 3 8 3 0 2 4 5 *